With My Best Wishes,

John e Christine Nowell

# A Day Above
# Yorkshire

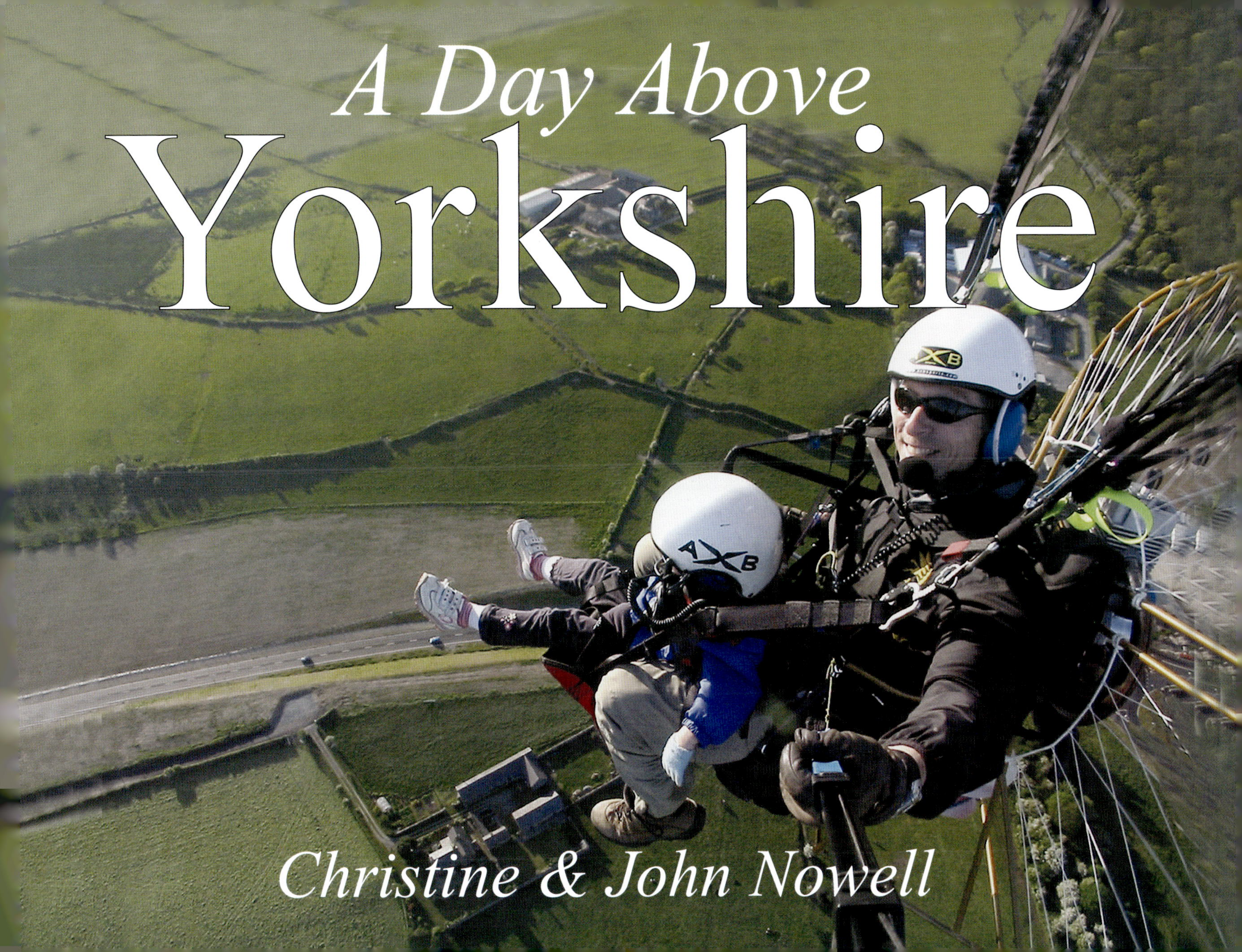


Christine & John Nowell

Foreword

I am not an airman; I am a man of the land. Of Yorkshire. I grew up in Ilkley on the banks of the River Wharfe and those are my roots. But I remember vividly, a dawn take-off from London Heathrow bound for New York and flying north towards Manchester and being able to look out of the starboard window down across the Pennines, the Vale of York, the North York Moors and the Vale of Pickering and, with my face pressed against the window, being moved by the sheer grandeur of the view. From 35,000 feet, I could see the entire traditional county of Yorkshire; from the River Tees and Middlesbrough to the north, the eastern coastline running down past Whitby, Scarborough and Bridlington to Spurn Head, Hull and the Humber and, sparkling against the early morning sunlight, all the silver tributaries that feed into that great Estuary, and following these rivers back, I could see Ilkley, well almost, in Wharfedale. More than anything else, I was struck by the vast expanse of the green landscape – and the brown of the Pennines and Moors. I knew that down there were vast cities – Sheffield, Leeds, Bradford, Hull, Doncaster et al, yet, despite all that industrial and housing development, the green landscape predominates overwhelmingly and the grey sprawl of the cites fades into the surrounding landscape. Mine was a fleeting, high level glimpse of Yorkshire but now, here in this fascinating book - by a Yorkshireman, the first of several volumes I suspect, is the chance to take a lingering look at just some of the sights of Yorkshire from a third dimensional viewpoint, a chance to spend time to enjoy all that is so glorious about our county of Yorkshire.

Alan Titchmarsh.

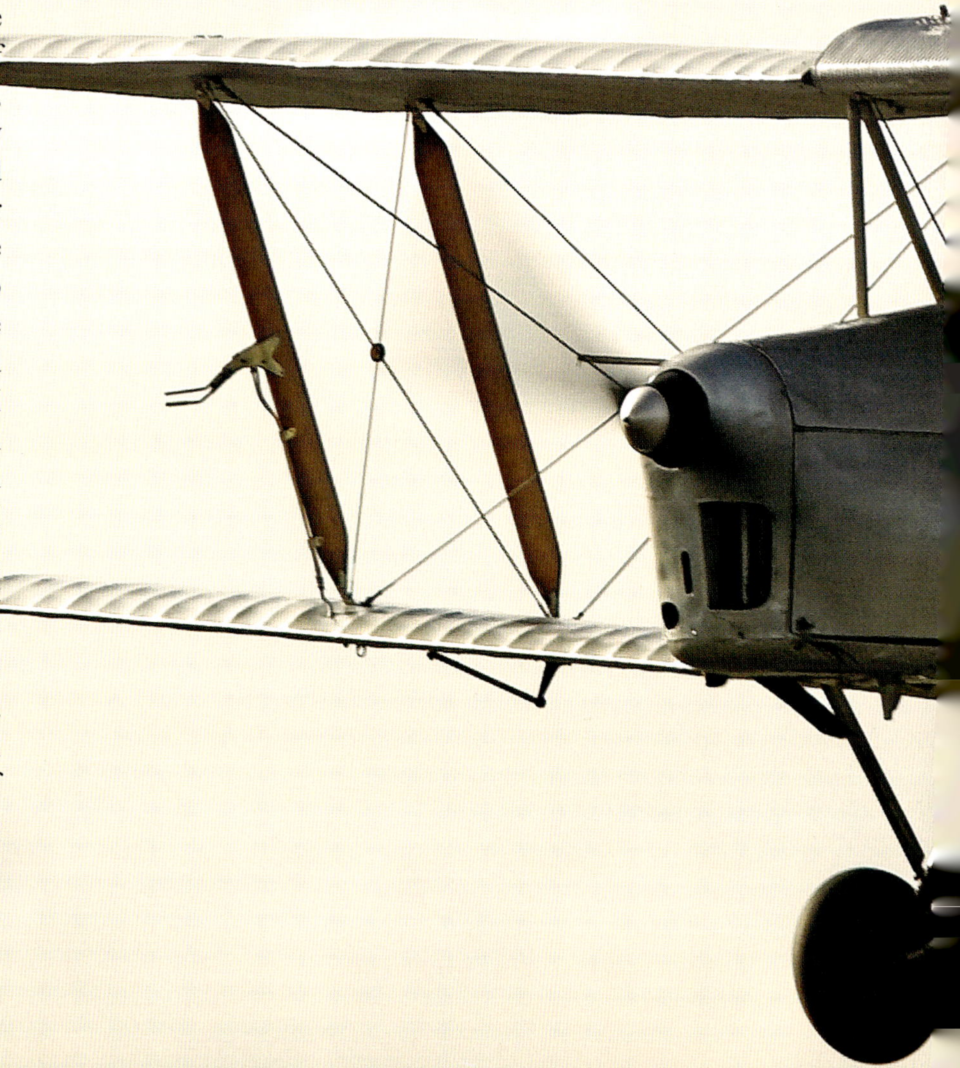

# A Day Above Yorkshire

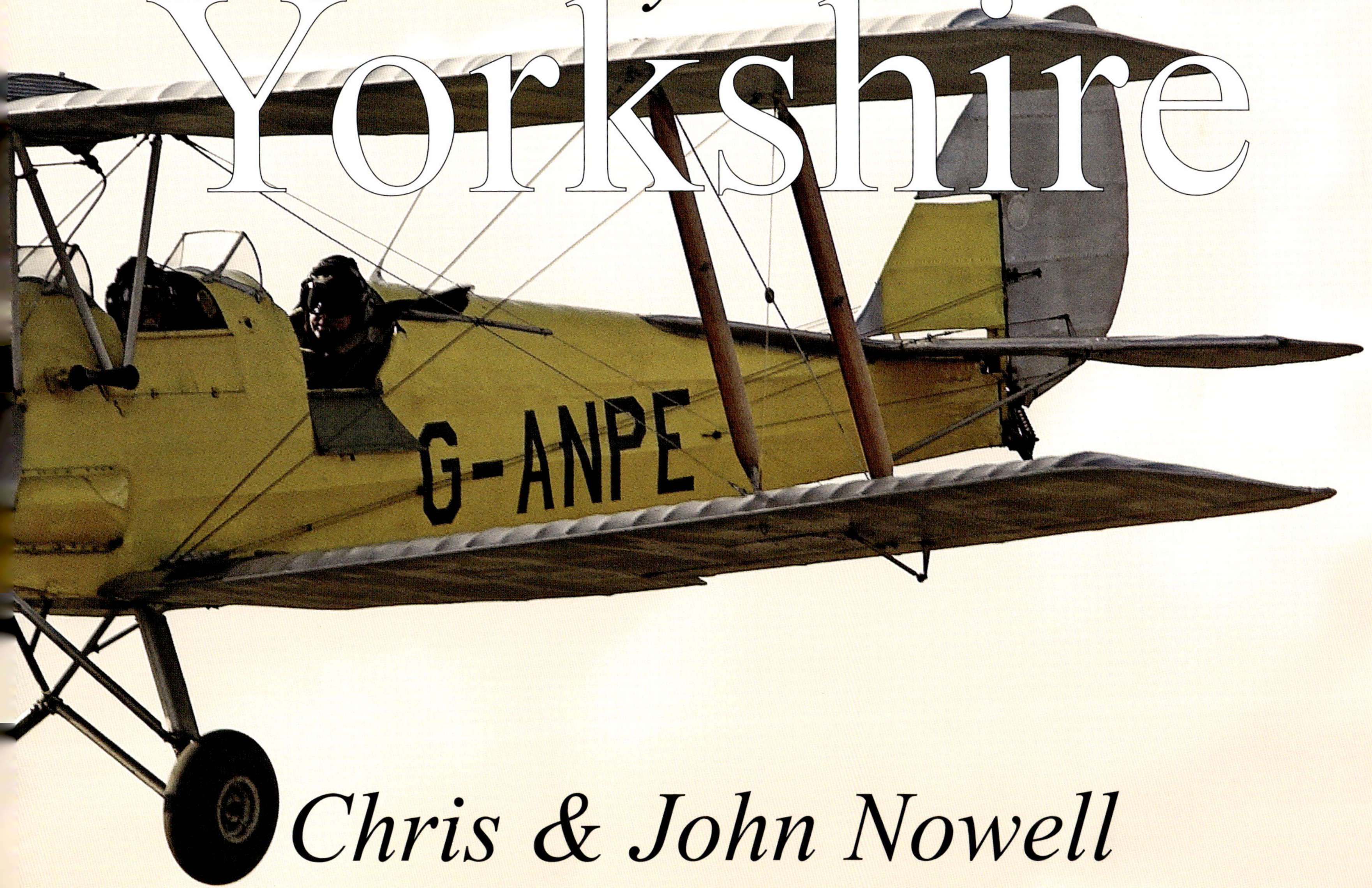


*Chris & John Nowell*

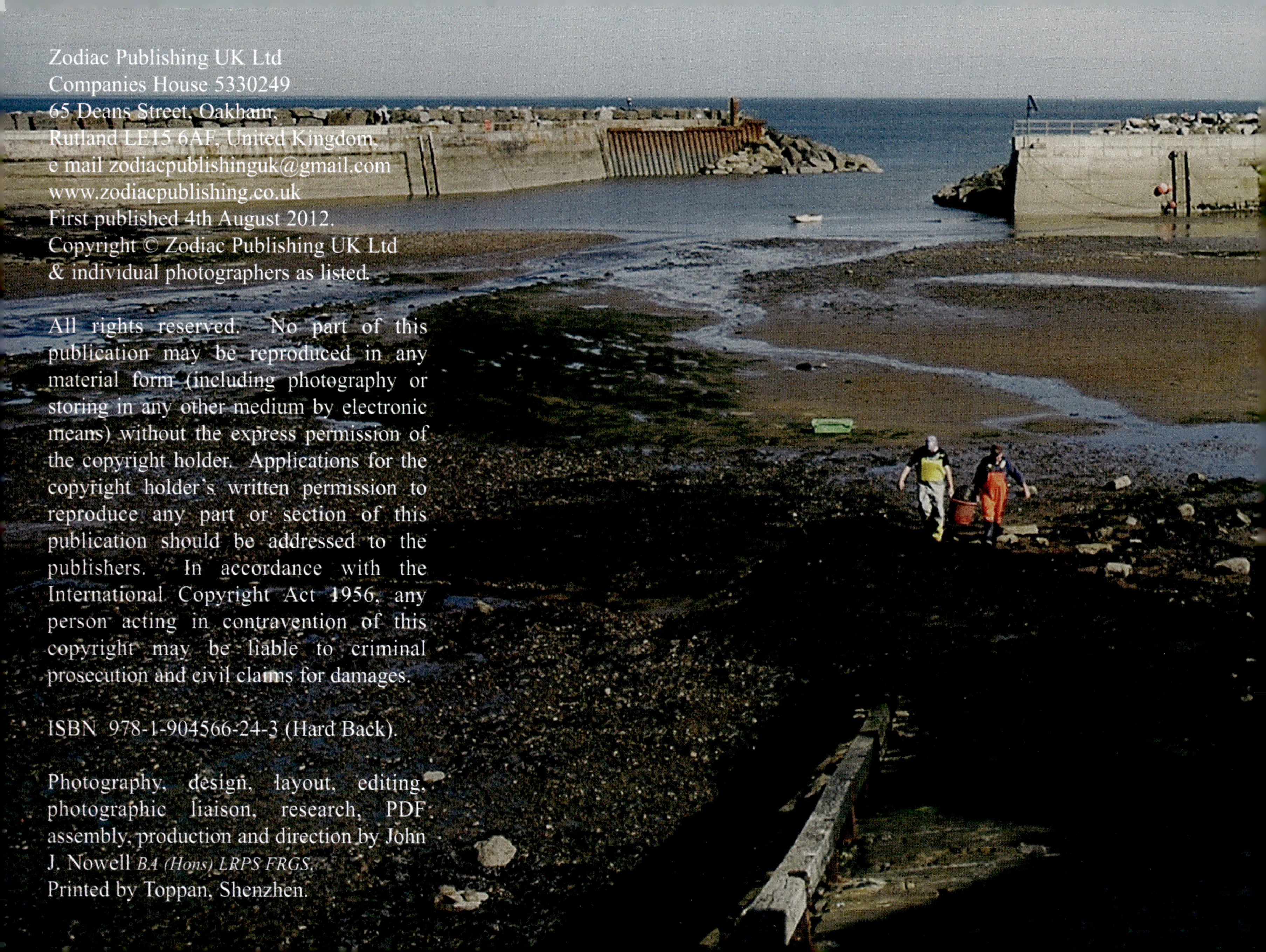

Zodiac Publishing UK Ltd
Companies House 5330249
65 Deans Street, Oakham,
Rutland LE15 6AF, United Kingdom,
e mail zodiacpublishinguk@gmail.com
www.zodiacpublishing.co.uk
First published 4th August 2012.


ISBN 978-1-904566-24-3 (Hard Back).

Photography, design, layout, editing, photographic liaison, research, PDF assembly, production and direction by John J. Nowell *BA (Hons) LRPS FRGS.*
Printed by Toppan, Shenzhen.

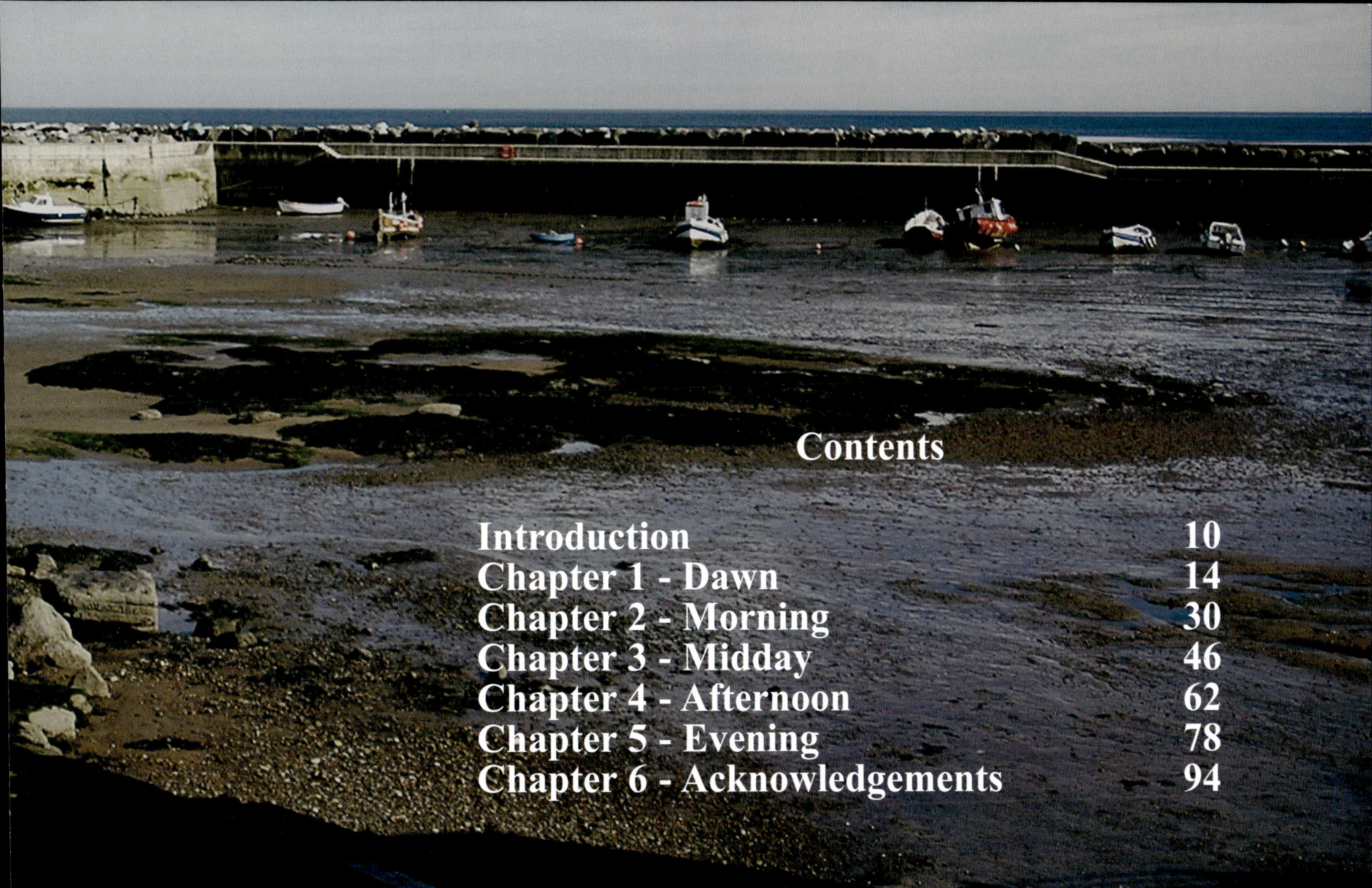

# Contents

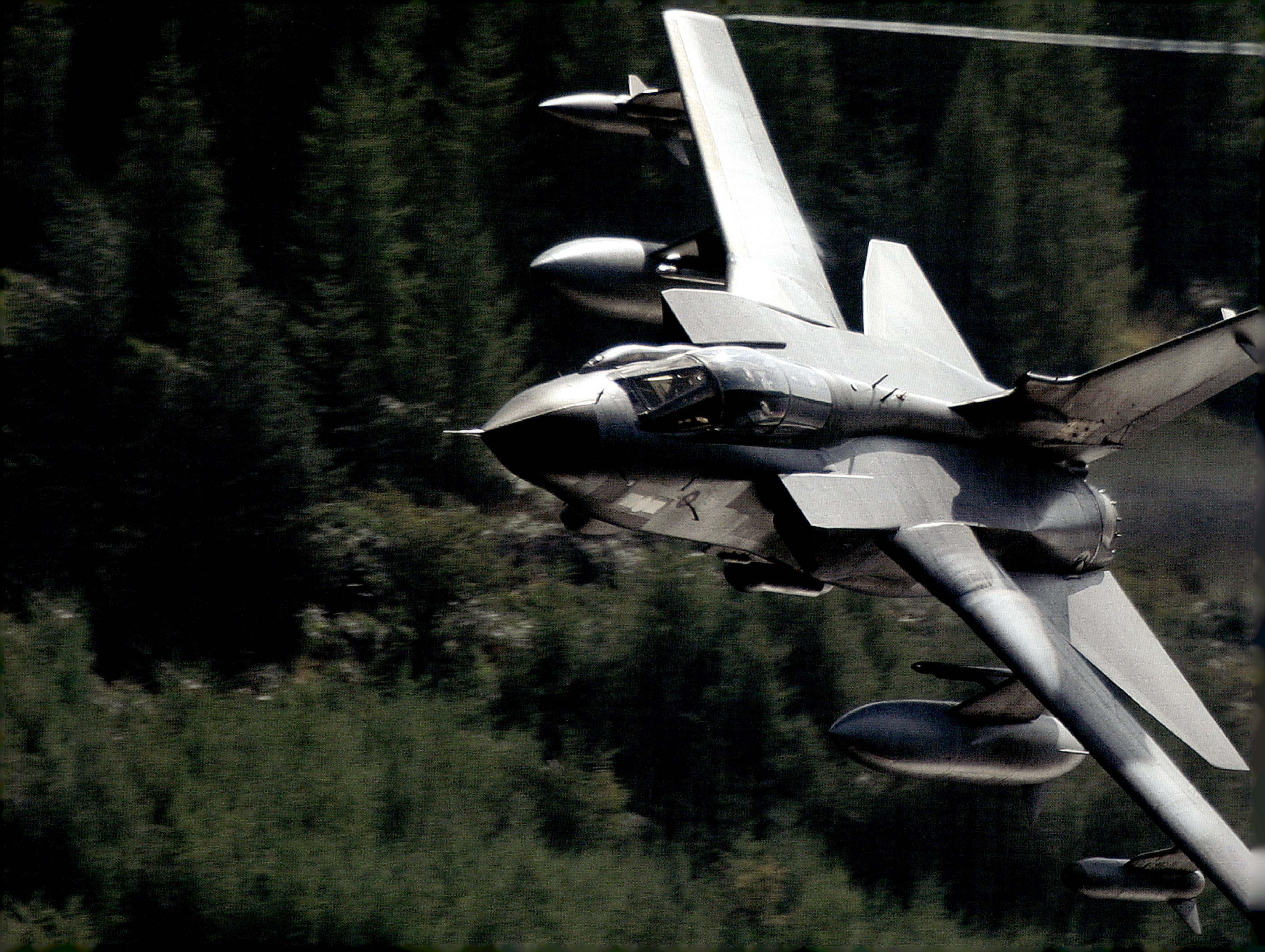

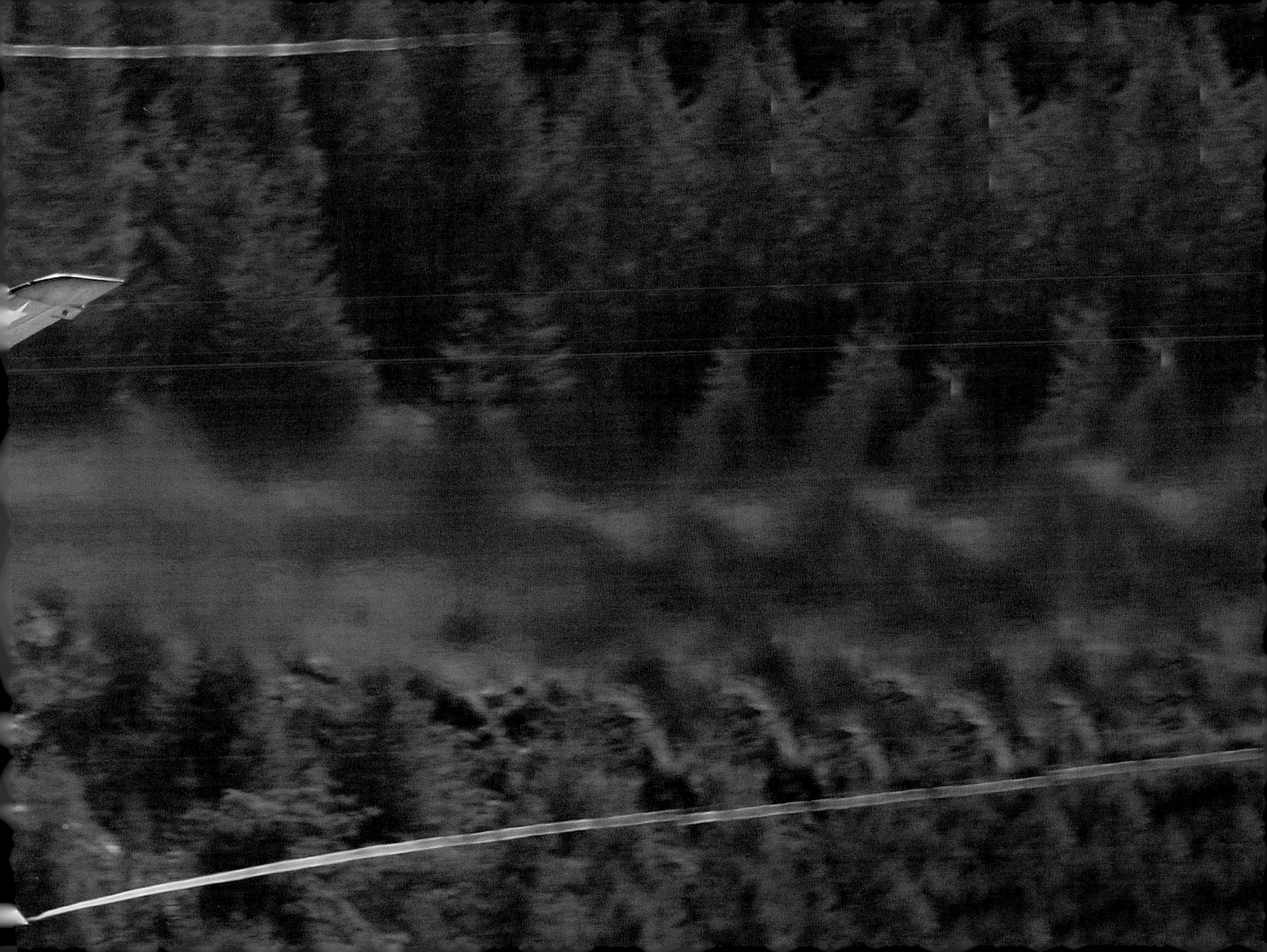

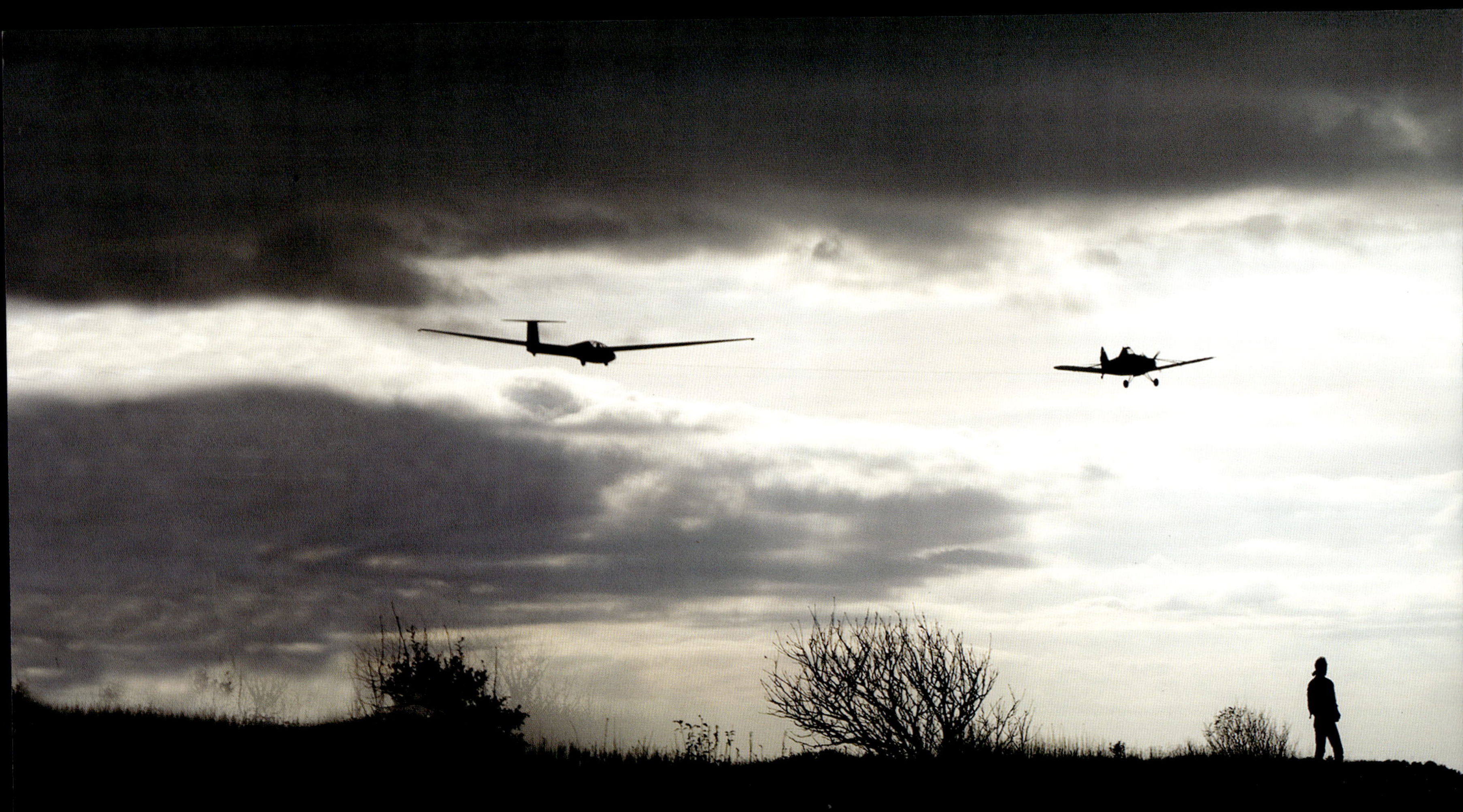

Front cover: The Display Hawk built at Brough, near Hull,
over the North Yorkshire moors.
Page 1: Father and daughter, Amelia, over South Yorkshire.
Page 2/3: Tiger Moth descending to Sherburn-in-Elmet airfield.
Page 4/5: Two fishermen at Staithes, East Yorkshire.
Page 6/7: Pulling a few 'G's over Ribblesdale.
Page 8/9: Going for a glide off Sutton Bank.
Back cover: Three DH Chipmunks of the Leeds University Air Squadron.

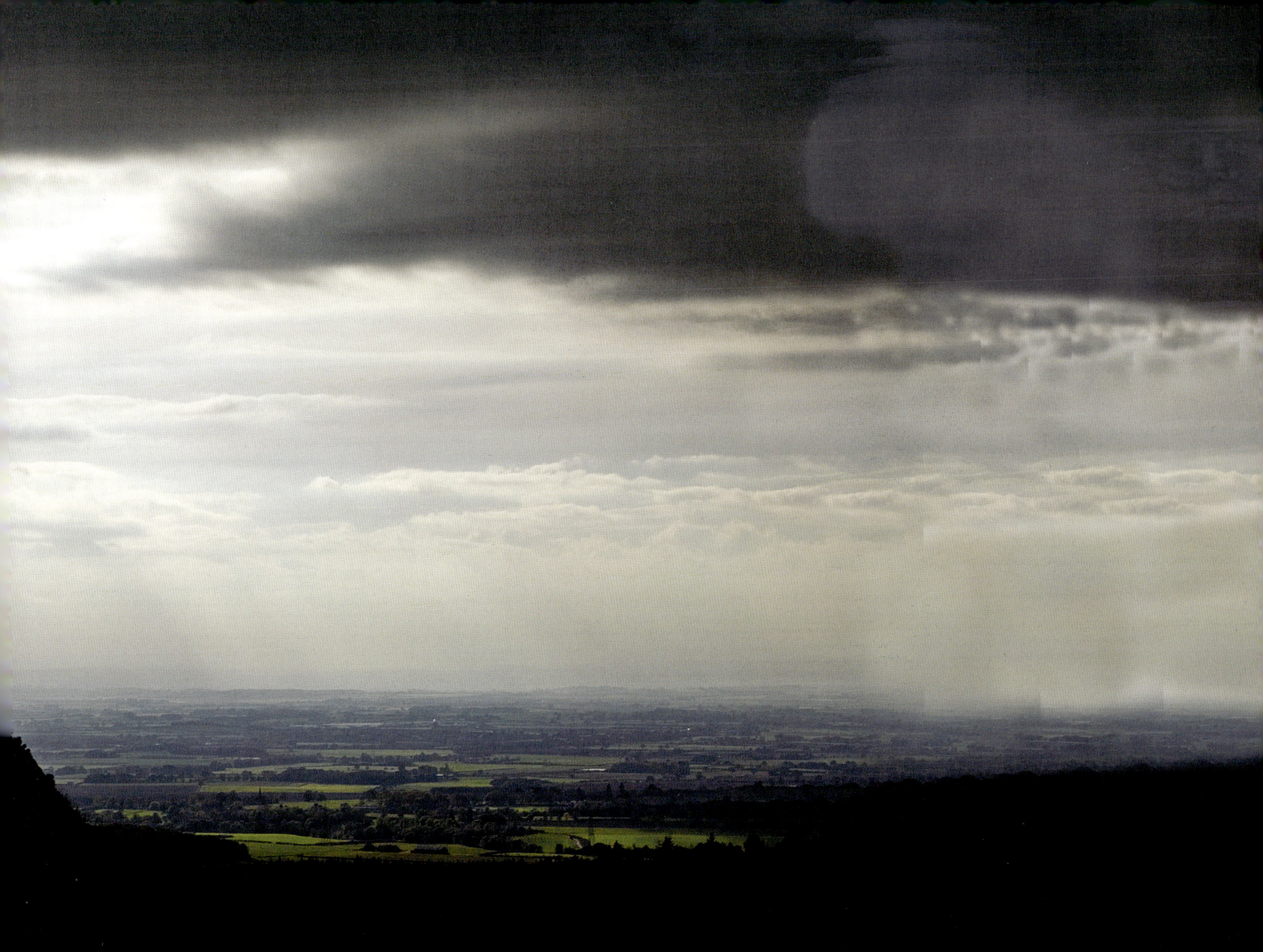

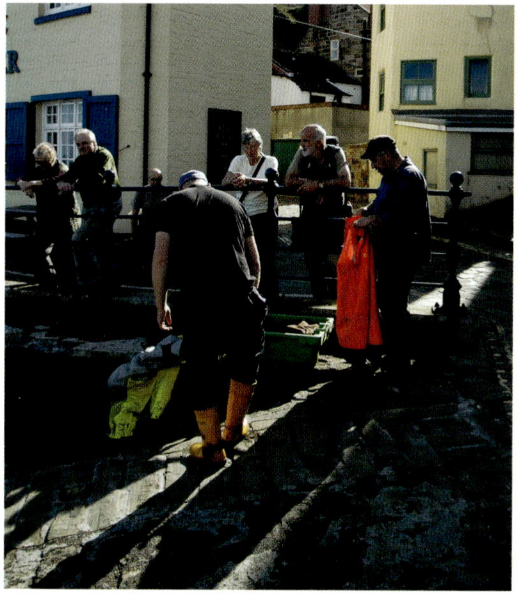

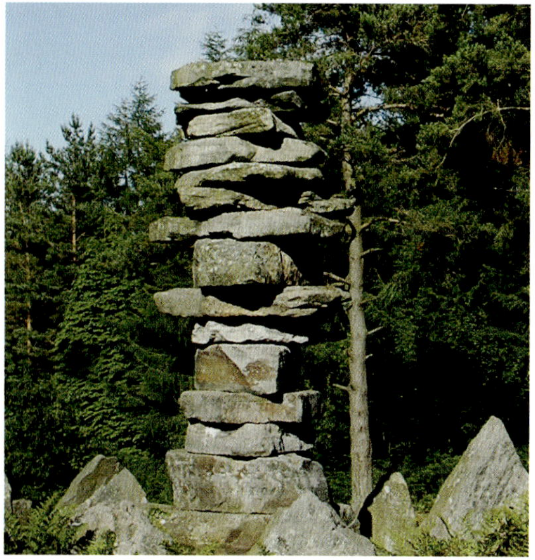

Introduction.

This book is not meant to be a history book; it is quite simply, a photographic book with brief, but informative captions and text. However, the scenes and the subjects shown in these photographs are all the product of history. Only 10,000 years ago Yorkshire was largely covered by an ice cap but there were no North Sea barriers. Our hardy Stone Age ancestors were the most powerful people in northern Europe and during the last ice age, made their way across the frozen glaciers of what is now the North Sea. They were in pursuit of the abundant game and sheltered in isolated caves. One such cave is at Kirkdale near Kirbymoorside, which was discovered in 1821 by limestone quarry workers. Within the cave were bones of lions, tigers, elephants, ox, bear and wolves and is the most northerly location where the bones of hippopotamus were found. As the North Sea was formed by the receding ice, the Celts, as they were later termed, became isolated and began to migrate southward. These people were the origins of the Celtic tribes known as the Brigantes and the Parisii. By the 1st century AD, the Brigantes, Parisii, Trinovantes, Iceni and Catuvellauni Celtic tribes had established themselves across Britain. After the Roman invasion in 43 AD, the tribes swore allegiance to Rome but in 60 AD, Prasutagas, Chieftain of the Iceni died and local centurions flogged his widow, Boudicca, and raped her daughters. The response was a bloody revolt with Boudicca leading the tribes in pursuit of the Roman 9th Legion across the Welland near Stamford to annihilate the entire Legion and going on to destroy Camulodunum, Verulamium and Londinium. 70,000 people died before the revolt was put down at Mancetter in modern Warwickshire.

As peace reigned, the Romans commenced building their arrow straight roads, draining low-lying land and constructing their fortified cities such as Eboracum, which became York. In this process, the landscape of Yorkshire began to change forever. Eboracum was named as capital of Britannia Inferior and joint capital of all Roman Britain. Emperor Septimus Severus visited Eboracum in 211 AD and made his base for the planned invasion of Scotland. Emperor Constantius Chlorus died in Yorkshire during a visit in 306 AD and his son, Constantine the Great, was proclaimed Emperor in the city. Constantine was renowned for his Christian faith and his regal statue resides in the grounds of York Minster today. But by 410 AD, the Roman Empire was declining rapidly and Roman rule ceased in the Yorkshire area with the withdrawal of the last active Roman troops.

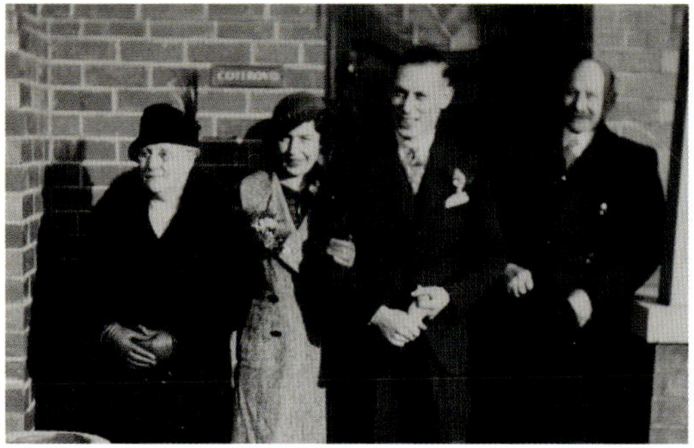

Small Celtic kingdoms then developed as the Northumbrian Angles gradually took over the entire area until Northumbria under King Edwin stretched east-west from the Irish Sea to the North Sea and north-south from present day Edinburgh to South Yorkshire. Then, an army of Danish Vikings invaded in 866 AD, established the Kingdom of Jorvik, which prospered with trade to north-west Europe, thc Mediterranean and the Middle East. By the end of the first millennium, the English were unified under one King. The development that became the ‘Ridings’ that formed the county of Yorkshire began with the Vikings who used the term ‘Threthingr’ meaning a ‘Third Part’, which defined the three historic Yorkshire Ridings - East, West and North. Around 1000 AD all England began to be divided into shires until there were forty shires. This division occurred after the re-conquest of the Danelaw by King Alfred the Great, who also established the navy and the first standard of English prose in the form of the Anglo-Saxon Chronicle – King Alfred’s copy of the Chronicle is now in the library of Corpus Christi College, Cambridge. The first capital of England was Winchester and it is here that the modern-day statue of King Alfred stands. Some historic shires were former independent kingdoms such as Sussex or Cornwall but Yorkshire was formed based on the ‘Ridings’ centered on the principal town of York which gave its name to the county.

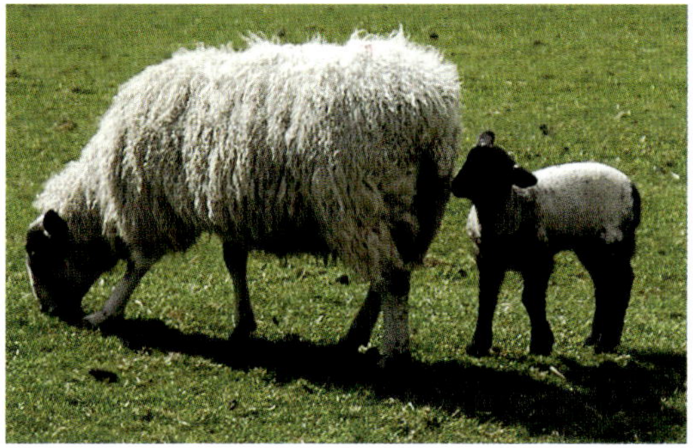

The Normans invaded in 1066 and took stock of their newly conquered but rebellious country. To exercise control, the Normans built a series of wood, later stone castles such as Richmond, which still dominates the town to this day. Others, such as Helmsley, which, although ‘slighted’ during the Civil War, still demonstrate the power of Norman rule by the sheer size of the earthworks on which the castle was built. With such control came organisation and the Domesday Book was initiated. With the establishment of Norman power, great religious construction commenced with the great abbeys such as Fountains and Rievaulx being built and the building of York Minister was started. By 1603, when Queen Elizabeth I died, the population of England was a mere five million but by 1750, the population had expanded dramatically to six and a half million and England was ready for the Industrial Revolution. During this period between the Norman invasion and the Tudors, the woollen industry developed

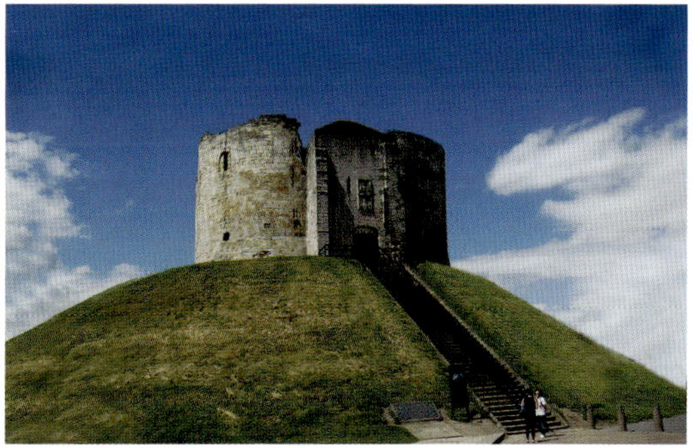

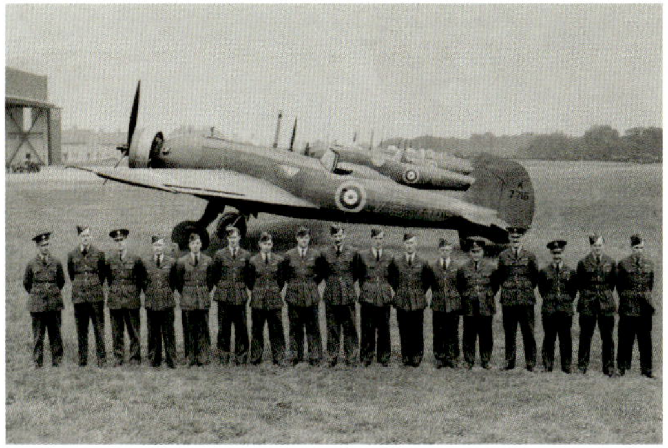

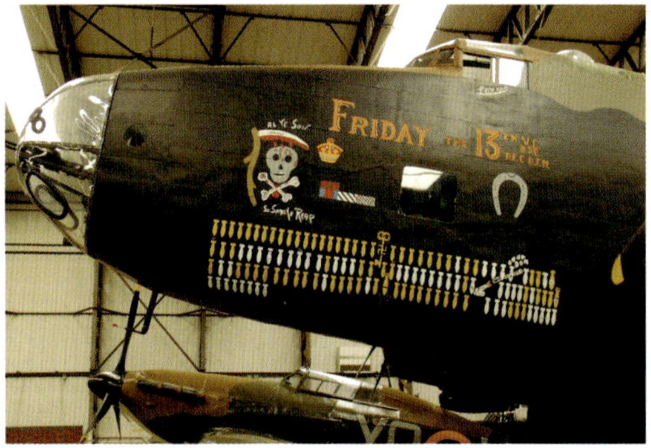


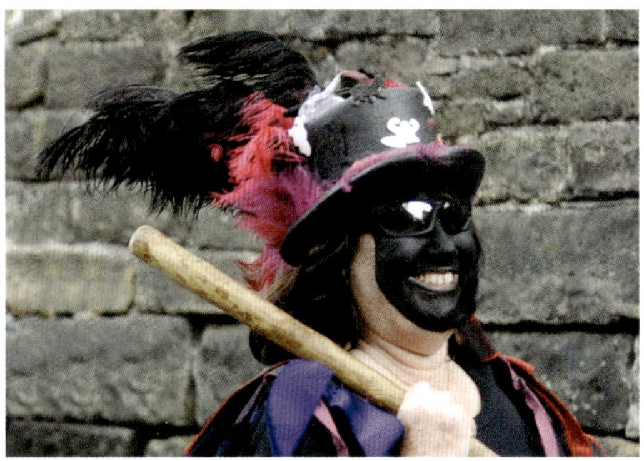

remarkably in Yorkshire to be the raw material that fuelled the industrial revolution. The Yorkshire that we can take stock of today is a land full of superlatives and firsts. Geologically and ceremonially, Yorkshire is the largest county in England. It has the highest waterfall above ground - Hawdraw Falls with a 100 foot drop located behind the Green Dragon Inn in Wenslydale. The deepest underground waterfall with a 360 foot unbroken fall, is within the Gaping Gill Cavern which is also the largest cave chamber in England. Religiously, Yorkshire has the largest medieval cathedral, the largest Abbey ruins, the largest stained glass window in the world occupying 1330 square feet - the so-called 'five sisters' window in York Minster, immortalised by Charles Dickens in his novel ' Nicholas Nickleby'. Between 1923 and 1925, the great window was re-leaded and by an amazing find, the correctly 'dated' lead was found and used. The lead had been stripped from the roof of Rievaulx Abbey and melted down but before it could be transported away, the nave of the Abbey, now stripped of its protective lead, collapsed onto the stacks of lead bars. Surely a classic case of 'being hoist by one's own petard'. The lead remained buried until discovered and used in the great window. Ripon is the oldest city in the UK, the longest city walls surround York, and with York Minster being the largest gothic cathedral in Europe. Yorkshire also has the oldest guildhall, the oldest living convent and the largest monastic ruins. Castle Howard has the longest drive of lime trees and Richmond Castle, built by the Normans over 1,000 years ago, has the oldest original castle walls in UK.

Industrially, the legacy of Yorkshire stretches world-wide. Middlesbrough may still only be a town and not yet a city but it is most certainly the largest industrial spread in Yorkshire once containing the largest petro-chemical centre in Europe and became the world leader in steel production. Bridges, manufactured in Middlesbrough, were assembled across Sydney Harbour, over Wembley Stadium and the world's largest transporter bridge spanned the River Tees in the heart of Middlesbrough. Yorkshire has the steepest canal locks at Bingley on the Leeds - Liverpool canal; the tallest lock gates in UK are at the bottom of the Bingley Five-Rise locks. The largest silk mill in the world was in Bradford and even the UK's highest public house at Tan Hill was actually built for an industrial purpose - to give sustenance to local coal miners. Mother Shipton's Well is the oldest tourist attraction in the UK, Leeds Bridge was the focal point of the world's first film and England's tallest free-standing structure - the Emley Moor mast, is 1084 feet (330m) tall. Yorkshire's great cities are, of course, full of records and of record-breaking people. Captain Cook is probably the greatest explorer/navigator of all time making three circum-navigations of the world but in complete contrast, Yorkshire once hosted the world's longest running situation comedy - '*Last of the Summer Wine*'. The largest fish and chip shop is still in Guiseley. Britain's tallest man, William Bradley, 7 feet 9 inches tall, was born in Market Weighton in 1787 though Prime Minister Harold Wilson, who won four general elections, said that Freddie Trueman was the greatest Yorkshireman. In 1805, York hosted the first race where a female jockey won the race against male jockeys - the first all-female horse race had taken place at Ripon in 1723. Redcar has the oldest lifeboat in the UK called the 'Zetland' and the largest loss of life took place at the Battle of Towton in 1461 when 28,000 soldiers died in one day!

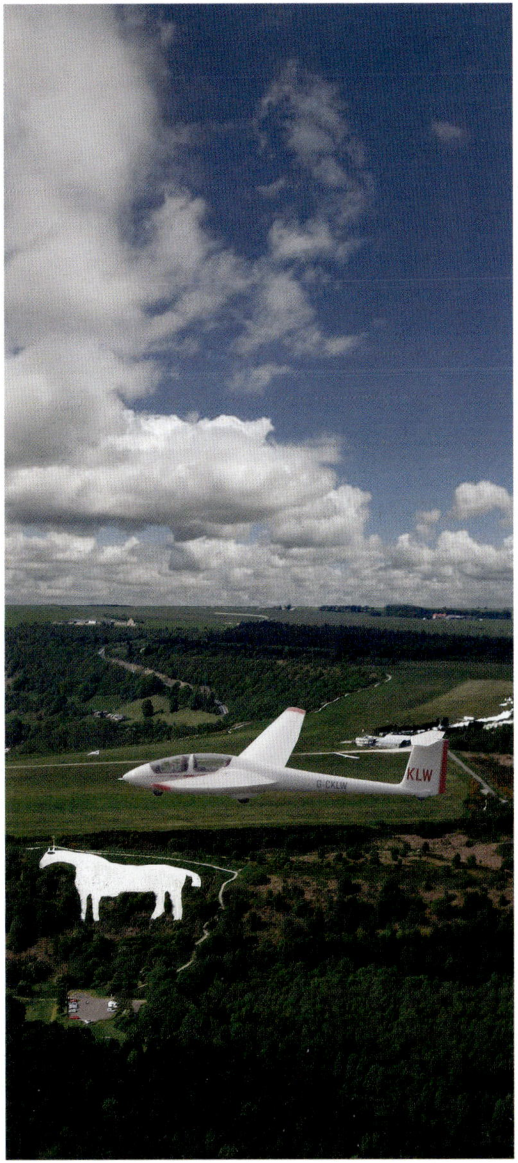


But this book is primarily aimed at aviation in Yorkshire, which probably started at Bempton Cliffs, the largest breeding cliffs for birds in England. For it may have been here that the young George Cayley observed the flight of birds and eventually deduced the classic equations of flights - that in stable flight, Thrust = Drag and Lift = Weight. This led to his experiments with flying machines and his coachman became the first man to fly when he flew a short distance down a slope in 1853. It took another fifty years before the Wright Brothers claimed the honour of the first powered flight in 1903. Aviation in England was still in its infancy and much of the enabling technology for successful powered flight was emerging through developments that started with Sir George Cayley's theories. But aviation literally took off and the world has never been the same since. Though the first passenger to die in a flying machine took place on Filey Sands in 1911, today we all can enjoy the benefits of Cayley's amazing deductions and millions worldwide now enjoy the freedom of world-wide jet travel. It also seems appropriate that the first UK astronaut in space was a Yorkshirewoman and now Alistair Brownlee, Luke Campbell, Ed Clancy, Katherine Copeland, Jessica Ennis, Andrew Hodge and the remarkable Nicola Adams are all world-class-Gold Yorkshire athletes. Read on.

John J. Nowell.

# Chapter 1

# Dawn

# 6 am

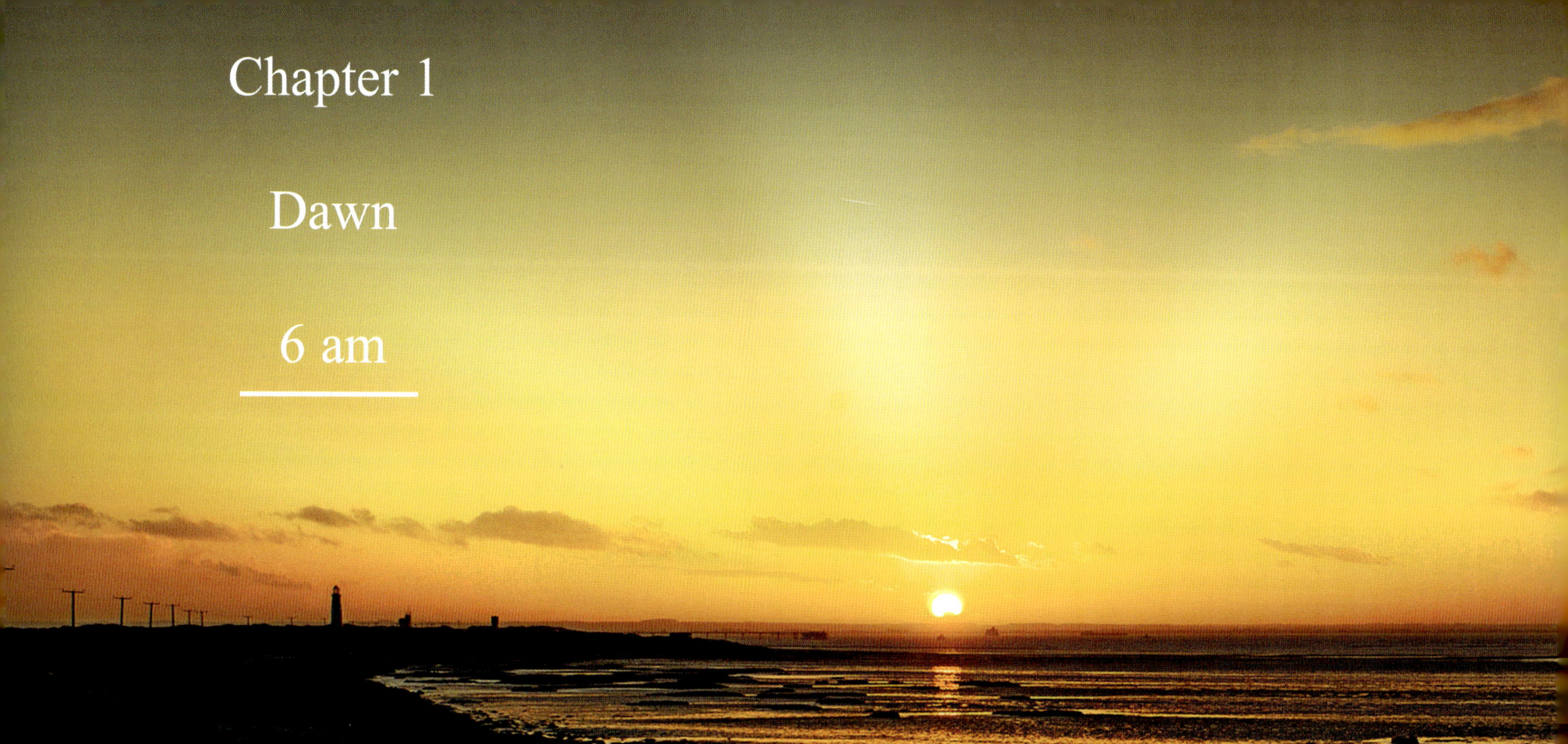

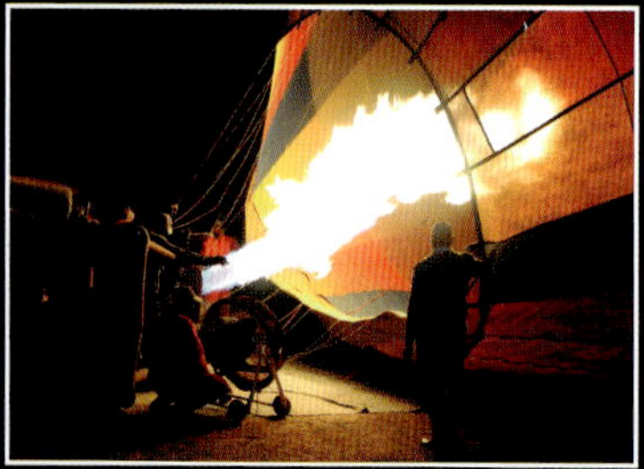

Dawn at Spurn Head where the lighthouses are silhouetted by the rising sun. The Royal National Lifeboat Institute lifeboat, 'Pride of the Humber' is stationed here, manned by seven, full-time crewmembers. The lifeboat was bought by the people of Humberside and the Northeast who raised £1,400,000 - the largest single amount raised in one appeal for the RNLI. Opposite, the first departure of the new day from Leeds-Bradford International Airport while, above left, flames roar into a hot-air balloon in the pre-dawn darkness.

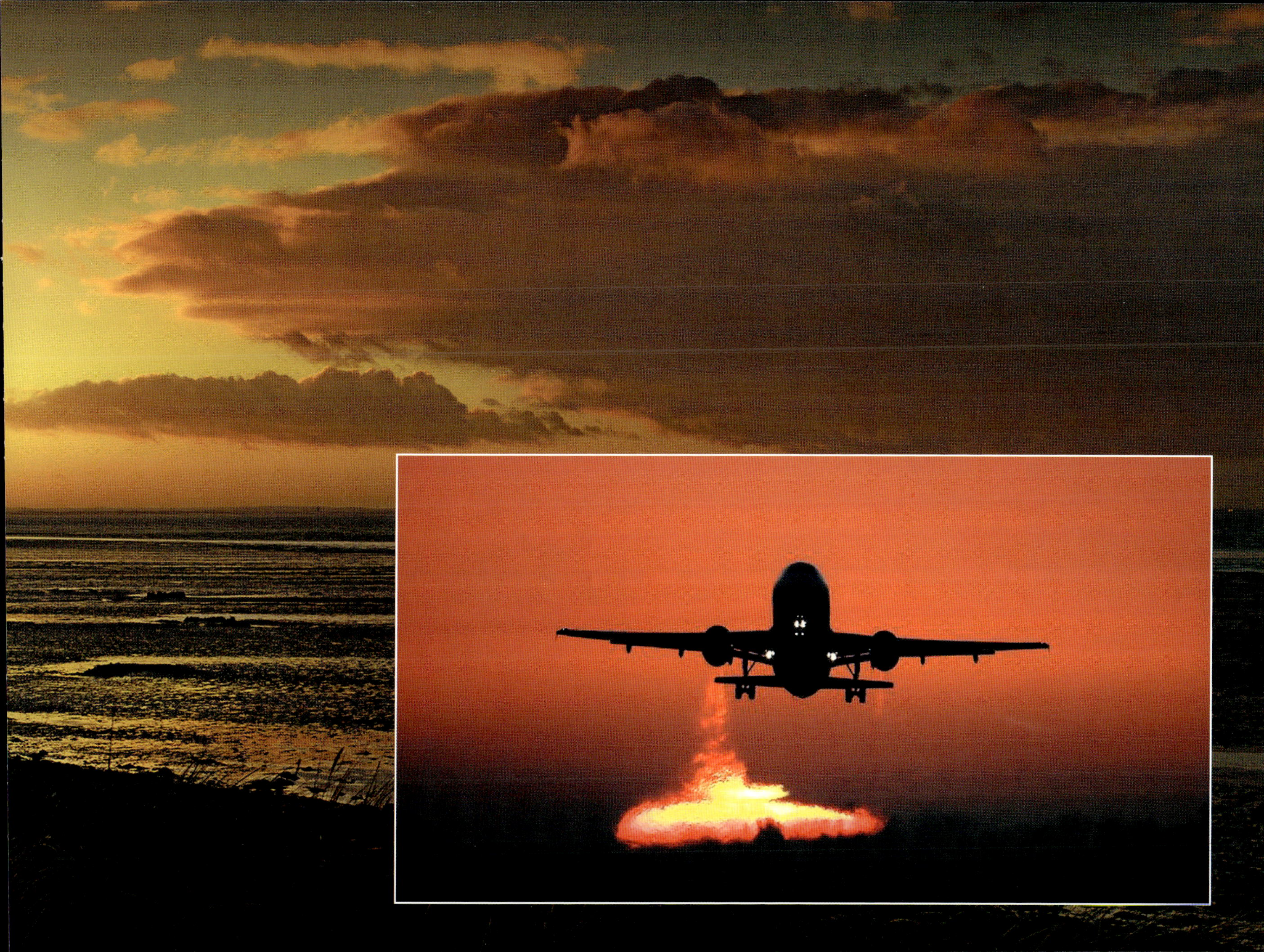

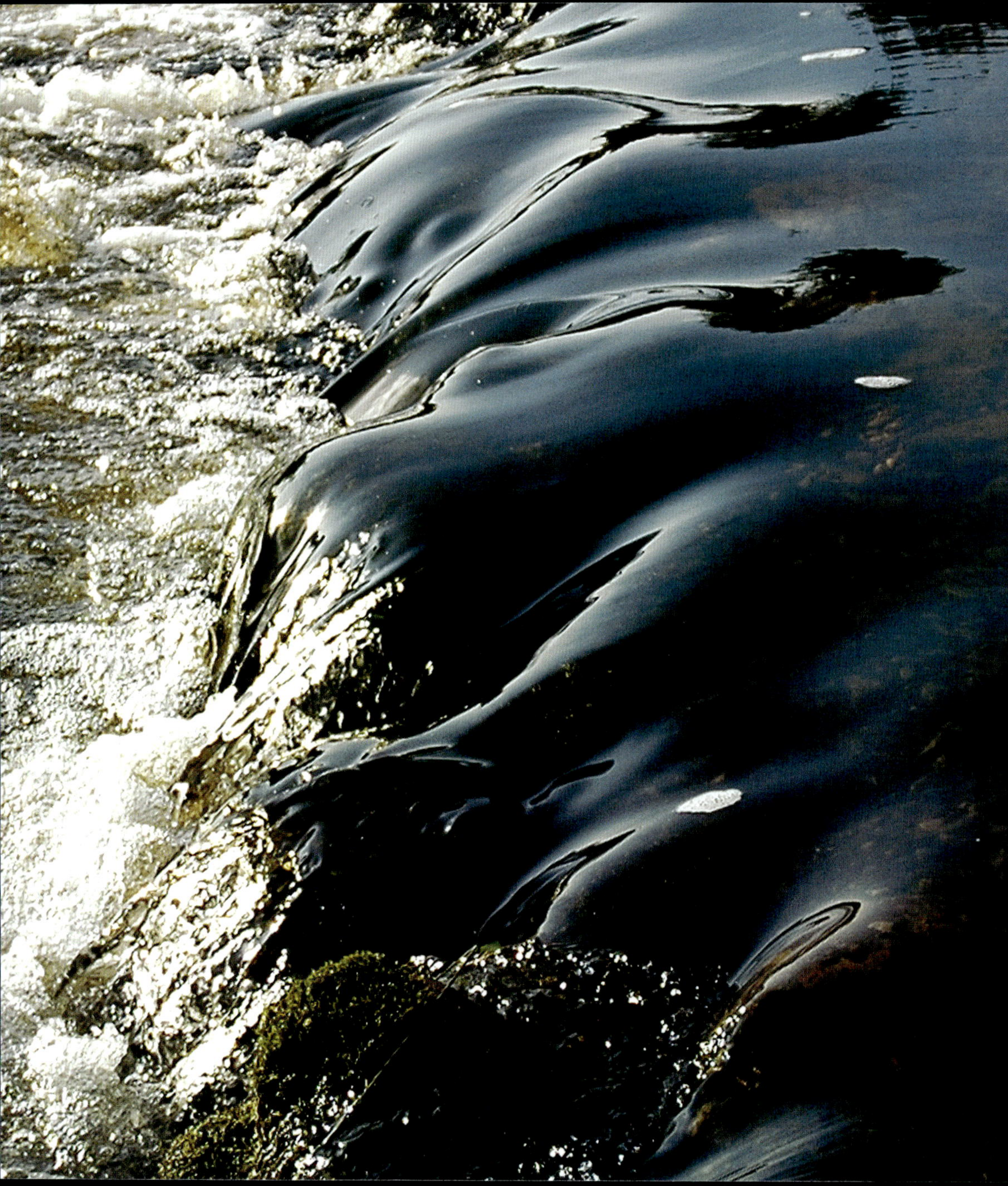

6.15 am

Water was one of the key issues when siting Rievaulx Abbey. The photograph opposite shows Rievaulx as the sun rises above Mossy Bank Wood with only a solitary horse in view. This Abbey was founded in 1135AD, the first Cistercian abbey to be built in the north of England. It was founded by twelve monks from the Cistercian motherhouse at Clairvaux at Ville-sous-la-Ferte in northern France and became the second greatest abbey of the north, second only to Fountains Abbey. The first church at the site was built between 1135-1142AD, and, as clearly shown in the photograph, the steeply sloping nature of the land meant that the monks had to align the abbey along a north-west/south-east axis instead of the more usual east/west axis. Today, the ruins of Rievaulx appear to be remarkably complete, against the slope of a mature wooded valley. However, only around half of the original 72 buildings have survived, giving some idea of the destruction on the orders of Henry VIII. The elegant skeleton of the abbey church is one of the most distinguished examples of its kind in England. Its graceful arches still evoke its original splendour, helping the visitor to contemplate the majesty and magnificence of the ruins and the sheer beauty of the protective valley. This site is now maintained by the National Trust.

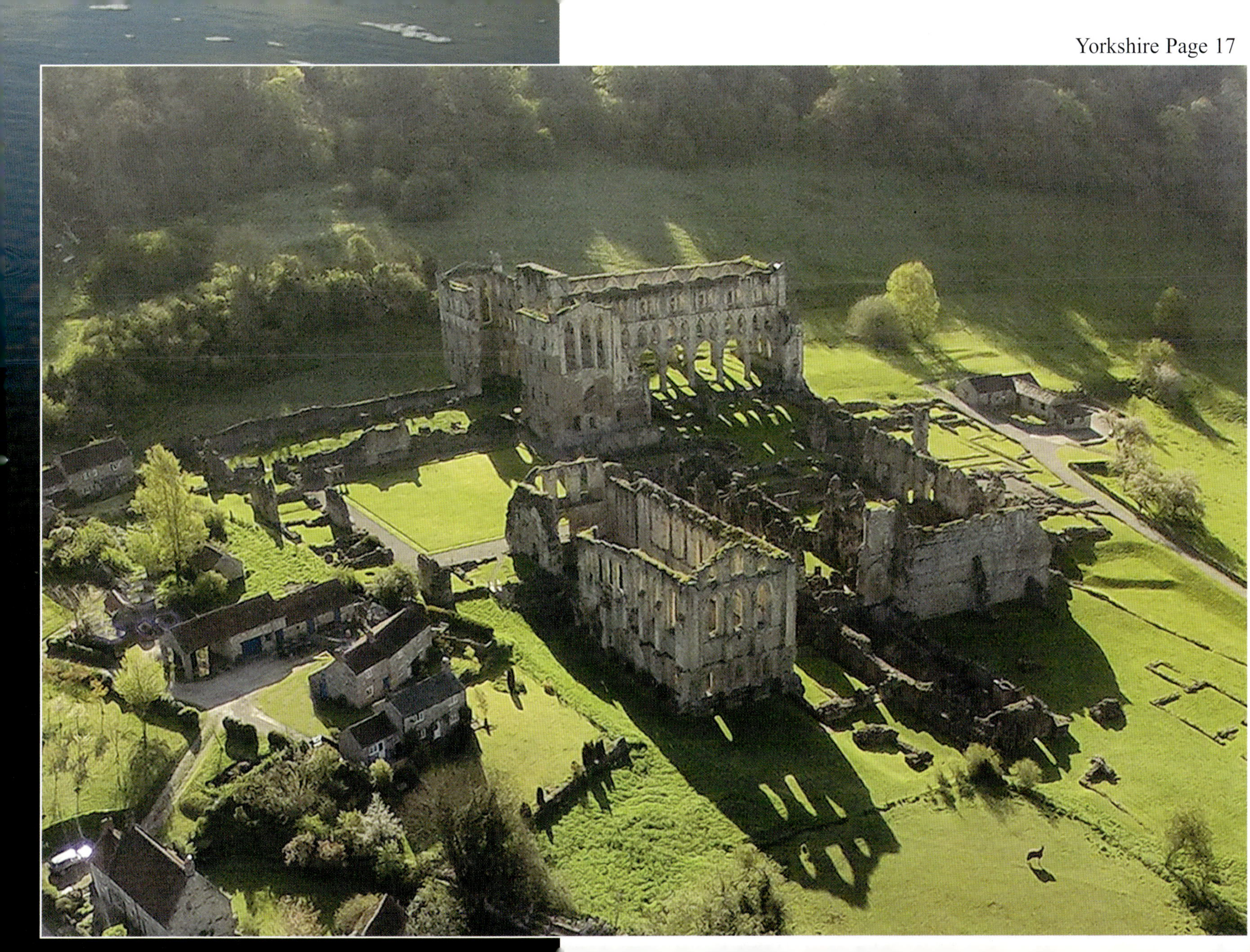

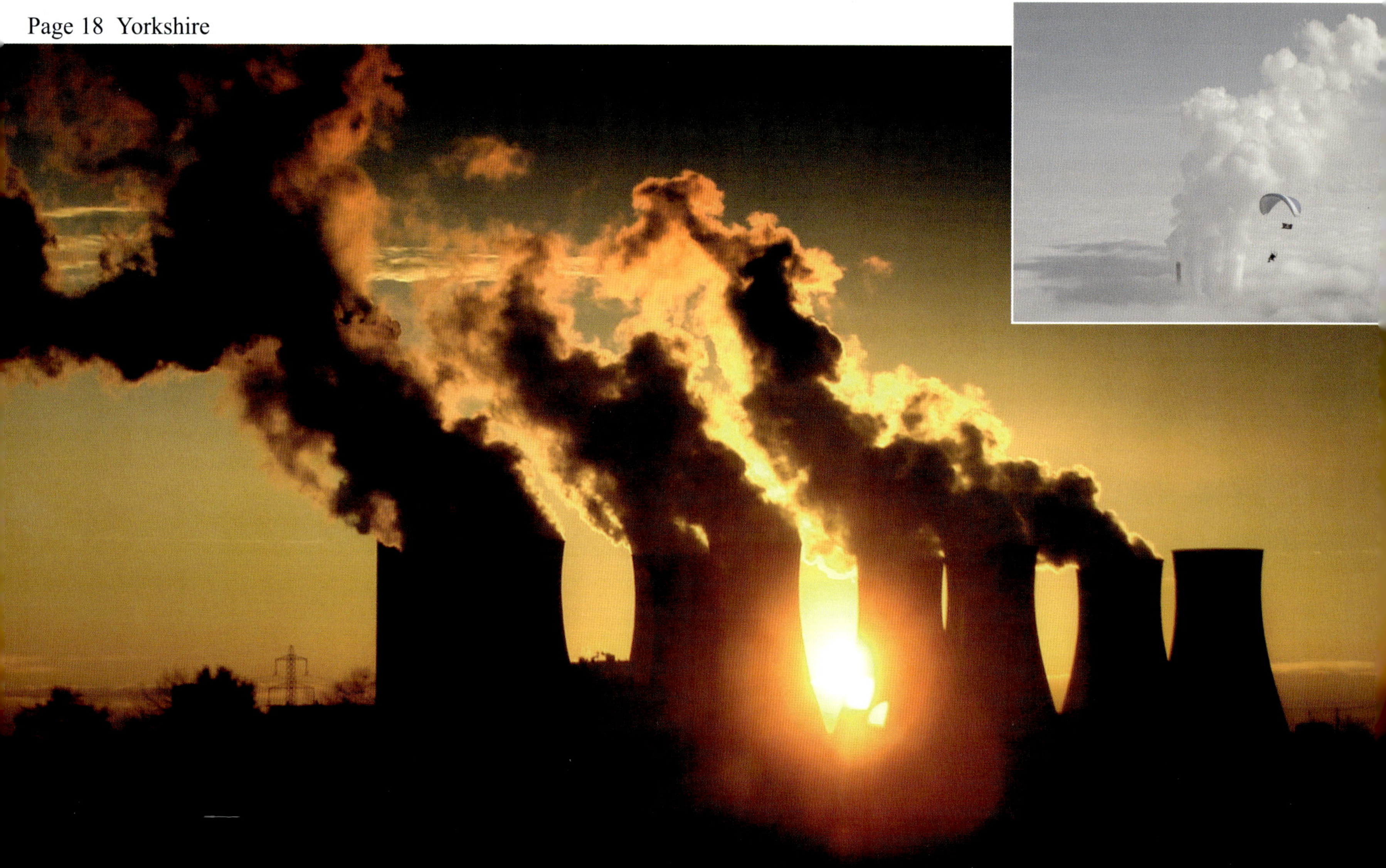

6.30 am

Early morning across Yorkshire where the first flyers are airborne in powered parachutes or hot air balloons to view a misty landscape where sleeping power stations, that almost define the river systems of Yorkshire, are powering to life.

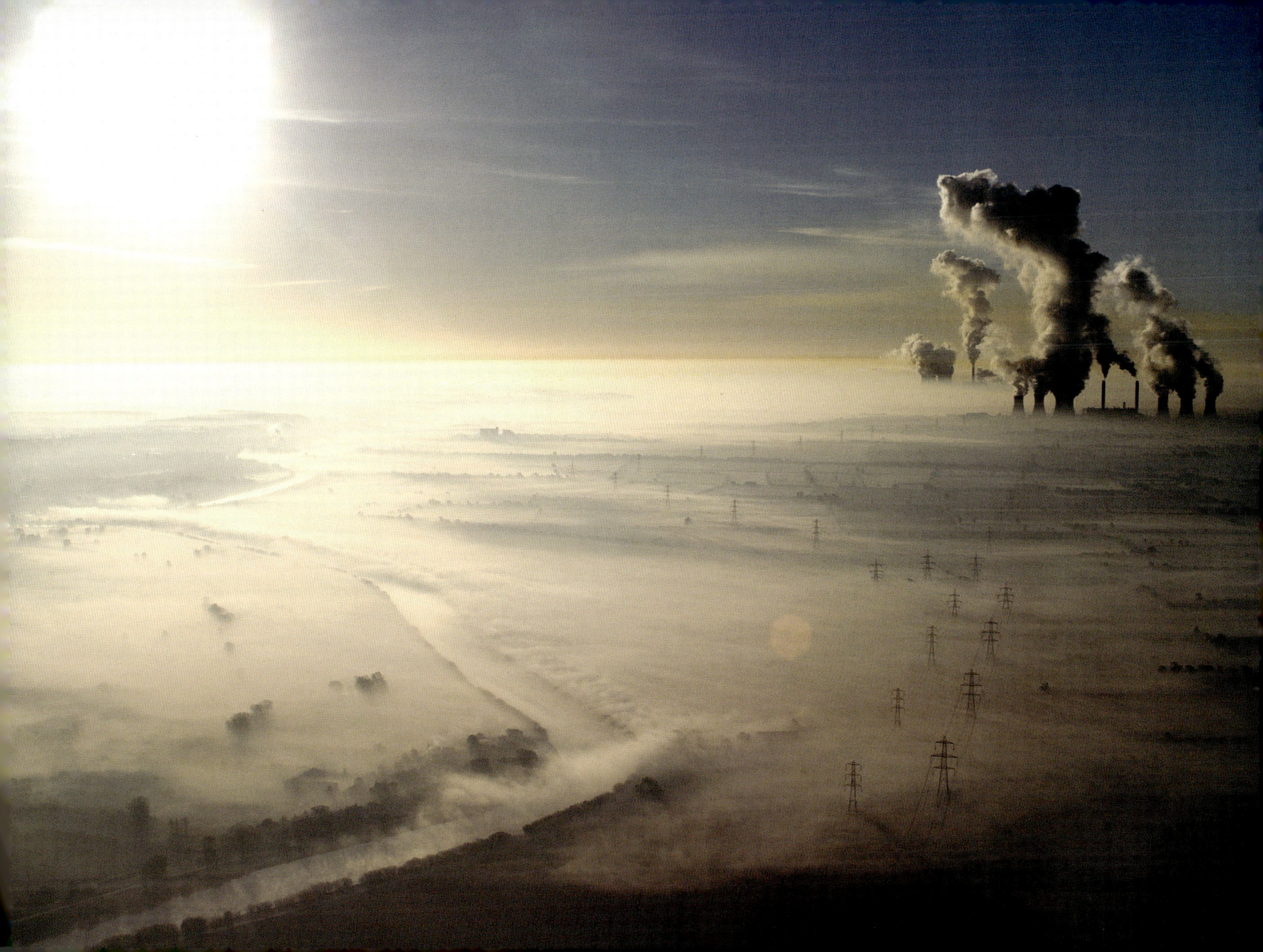

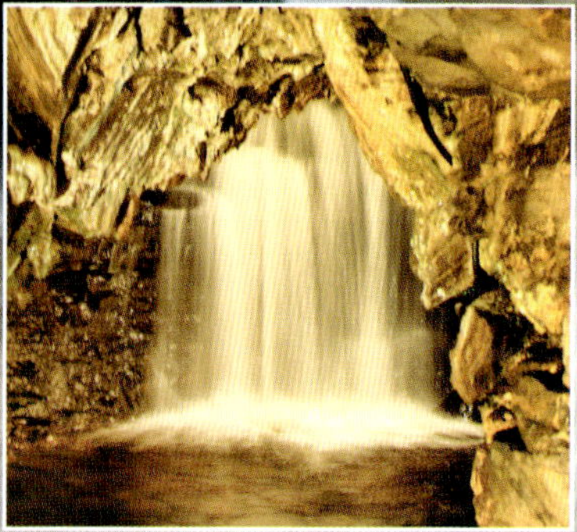

6.45 am

Yorkshire is blessed with abundant rainfall, which flows into vibrant rivers both on the surface and underground – seen here in Gaping Gill and White Scar caves. From rivulets on the hills, the streams grow to form, amongst the many rivers, the Ouse, Wharf, Ure,

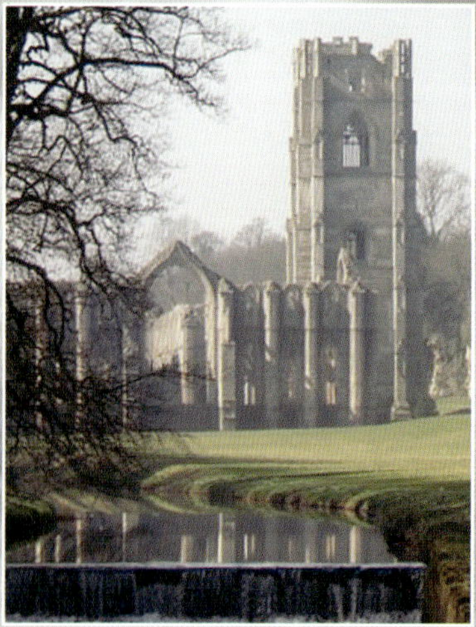

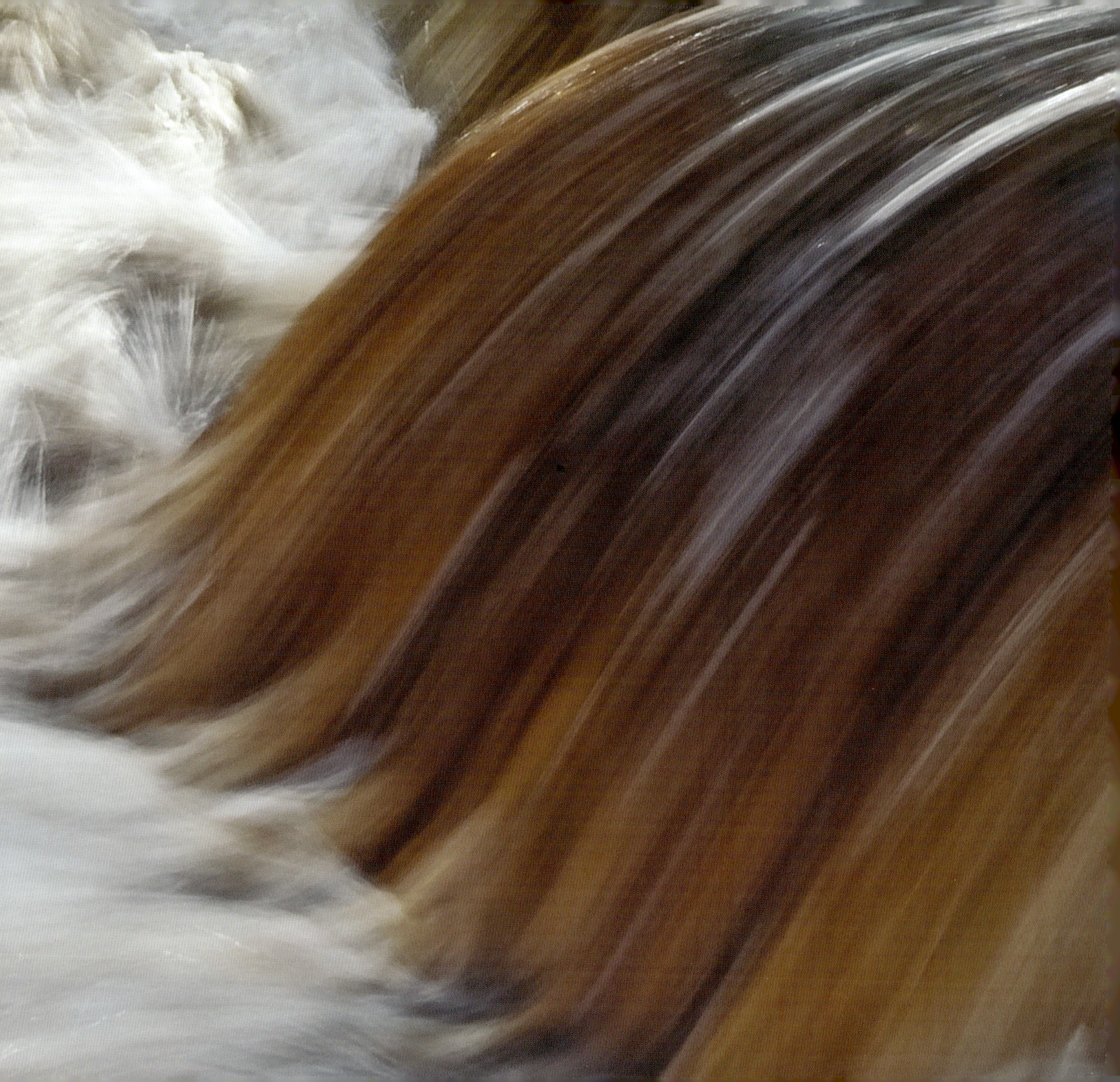

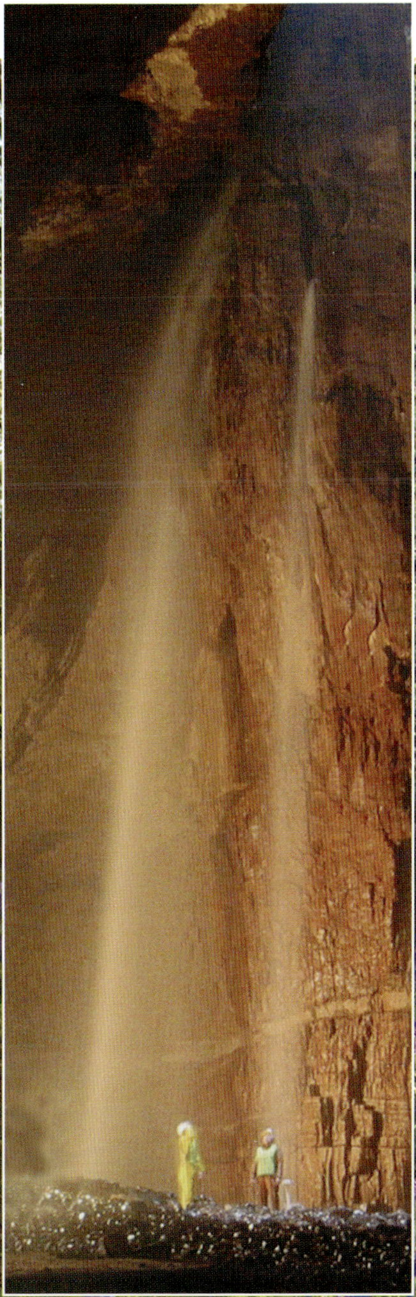

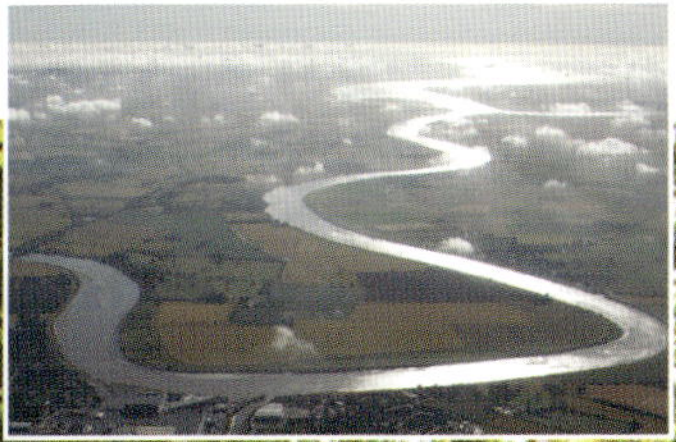

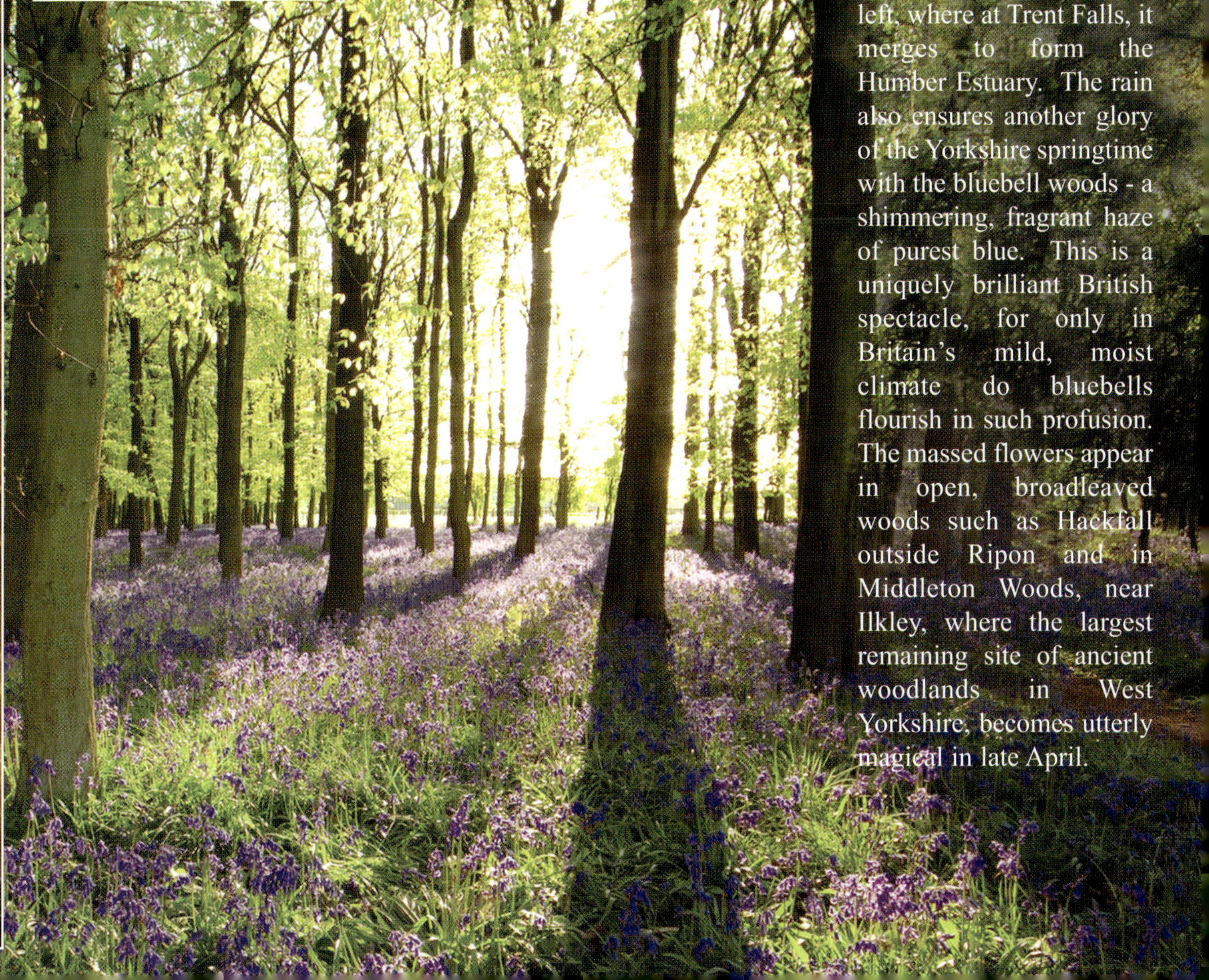

Nidd and Aire. In turn, these rivers form into the mighty Humber, shown left, where at Trent Falls, it merges to form the Humber Estuary. The rain also ensures another glory of the Yorkshire springtime with the bluebell woods - a shimmering, fragrant haze of purest blue. This is a uniquely brilliant British spectacle, for only in Britain's mild, moist climate do bluebells flourish in such profusion. The massed flowers appear in open, broadleaved woods such as Hackfall outside Ripon and in Middleton Woods, near Ilkley, where the largest remaining site of ancient woodlands in West Yorkshire, becomes utterly magical in late April.

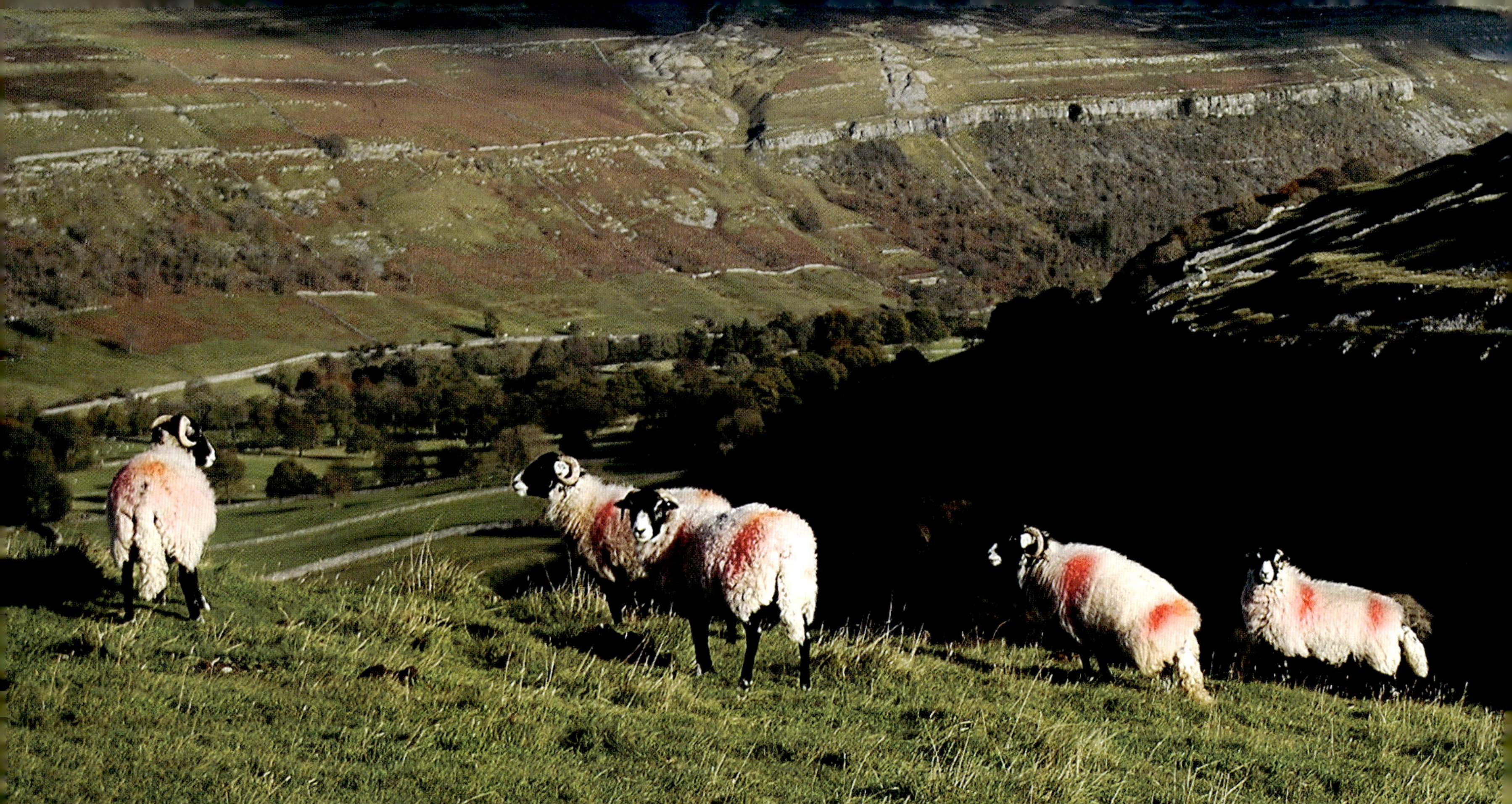

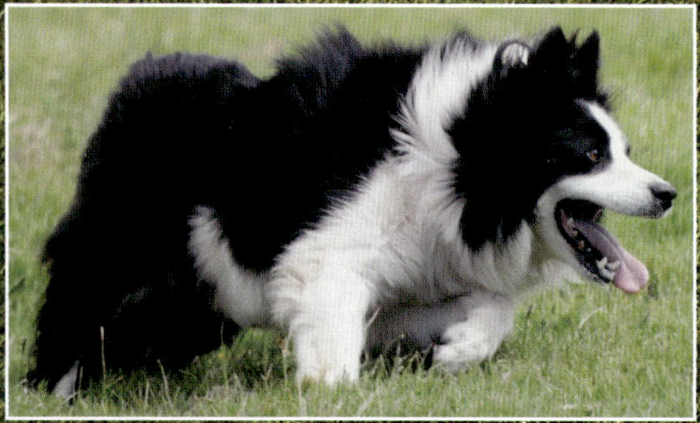

7 am.

Left, a Yorkshire sheepdog is hard at work on the hills above Wharfedale. The English National Sheepdog Trials are held at Bolton Abbey near Skipton or at Busby Hall near Stokesley. The training and sale of sheepdogs is now big business in the Dales with some dogs being sold for £6,000. Down in the valley, where warning signs mark the unfenced roads, sheep are separated prior to a journey to market.

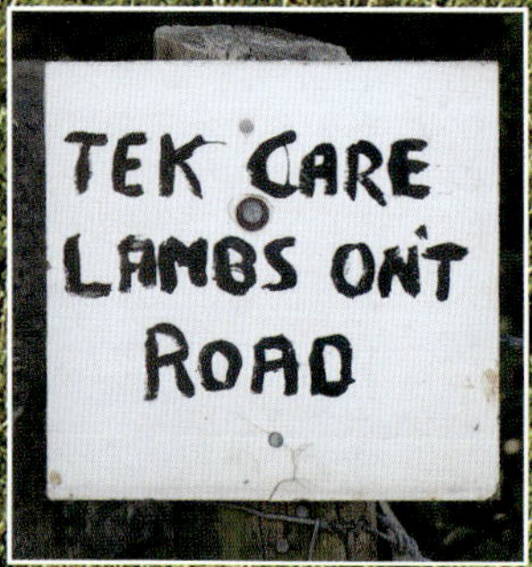

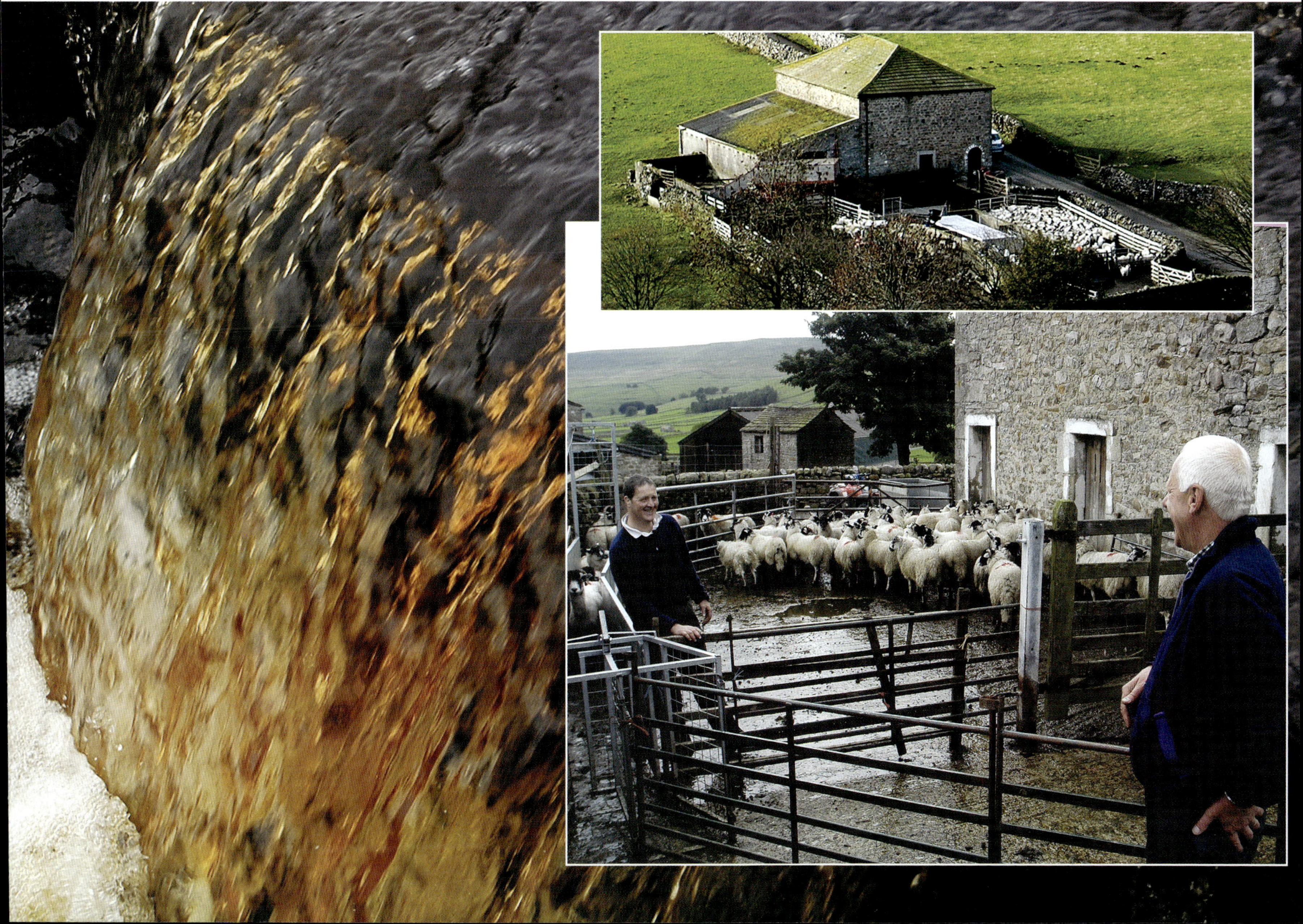

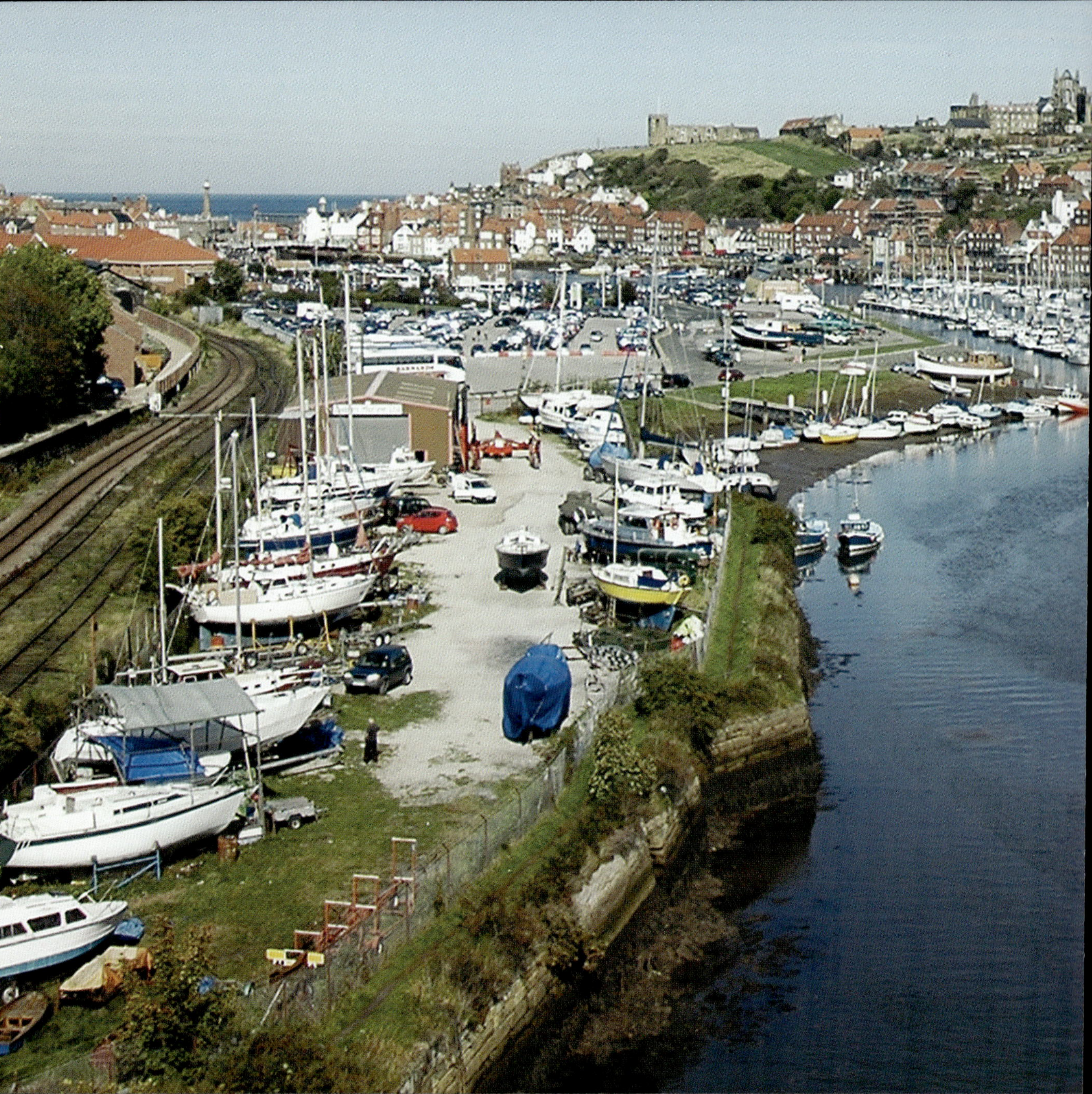

## 7.30 am

This photograph of Whitby, was taken from the new bridge spanning the River Esk. On the beach are fossilised dinosaur footprints and above Whitby are the dramatic ruins of the Benedictine Abbey, founded by St. Hilda in 657 A.D. The most famous son of Whitby is Captain Cook, shown below, who rose from cabin boy to become one of the most famous sailor-explorer-surveyors in the world. Captain Cook made three circumnavigations of the world discovering New Zealand, Hawaii and Alaska where the modern State Capital is

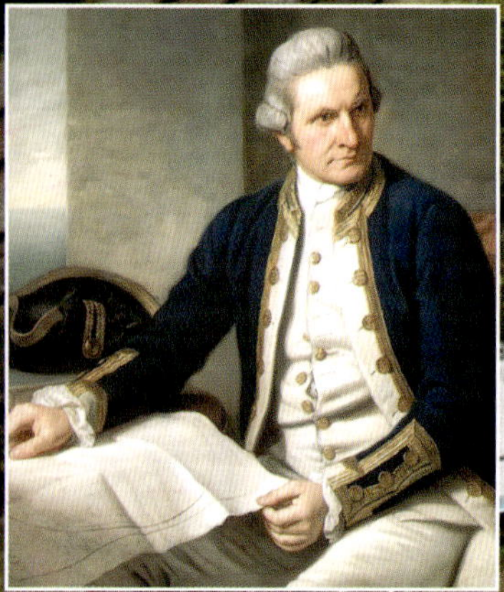

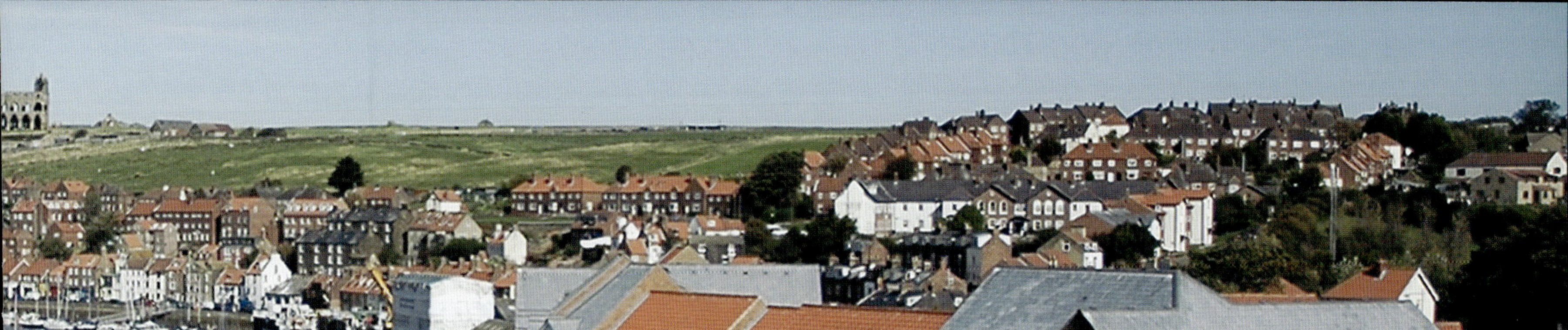

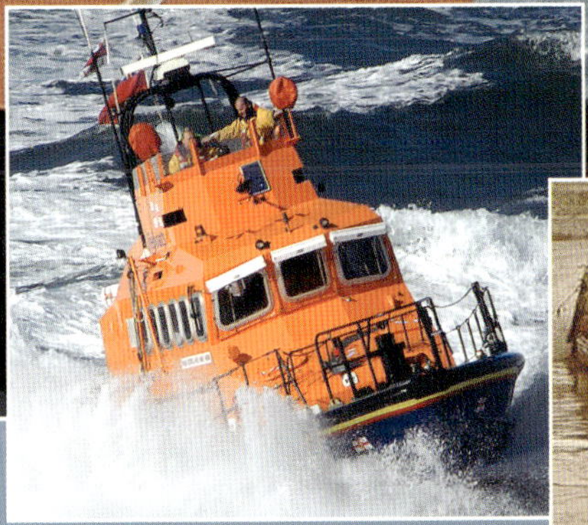

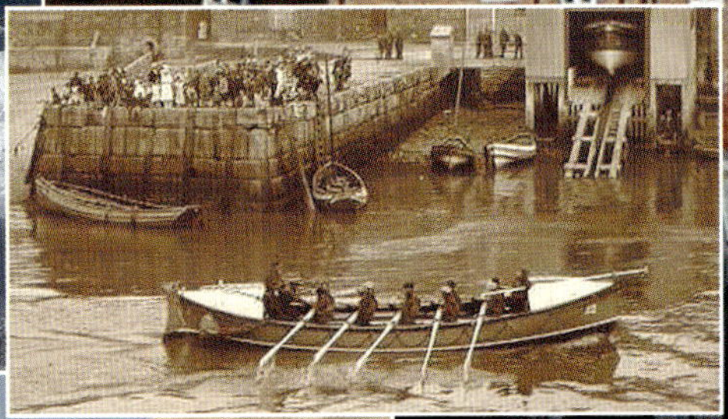

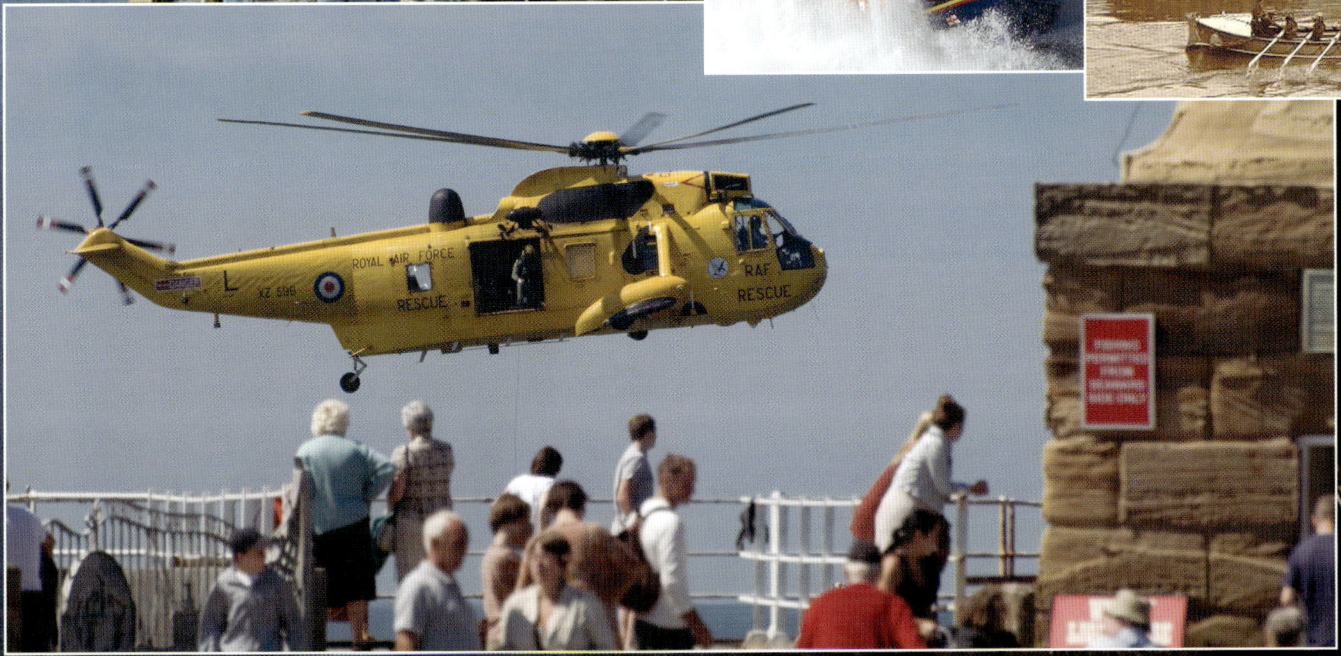


Anchorage. The Captain Cook Memorial Museum occupies the 17th Century house where Cook lodged prior to his epic voyages of exploration. For 150 years Whitby has hosted Regatta Day attracting thousands of visitors where Royal Air Force Sea King helicopters demonstrate rescue co-operation with the RNLI lifeboat off the harbour walls.

## 8 am

Leeds developed on the basis of wool, centred on the River Aire, shown opposite. Not even the impact of WWII stopped that development. In 1940, the Leeds 'Spitfire Fund' was launched and raised £30,000, enough for six Spitfires. One was named '*City Of Leeds*' and was flown by 609 '*West Riding*' Squadron based at RAF Yeadon, now Leeds-Bradford International Airport. During the Battle of Britain, 609 were the first Spitfire Squadron to shoot down 100 enemy aircraft. Today's pilots train on the Tucano, shown right, also named '*City of Leeds*'.

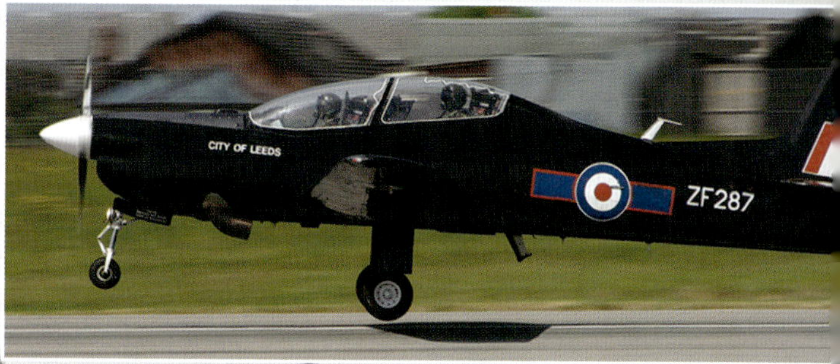


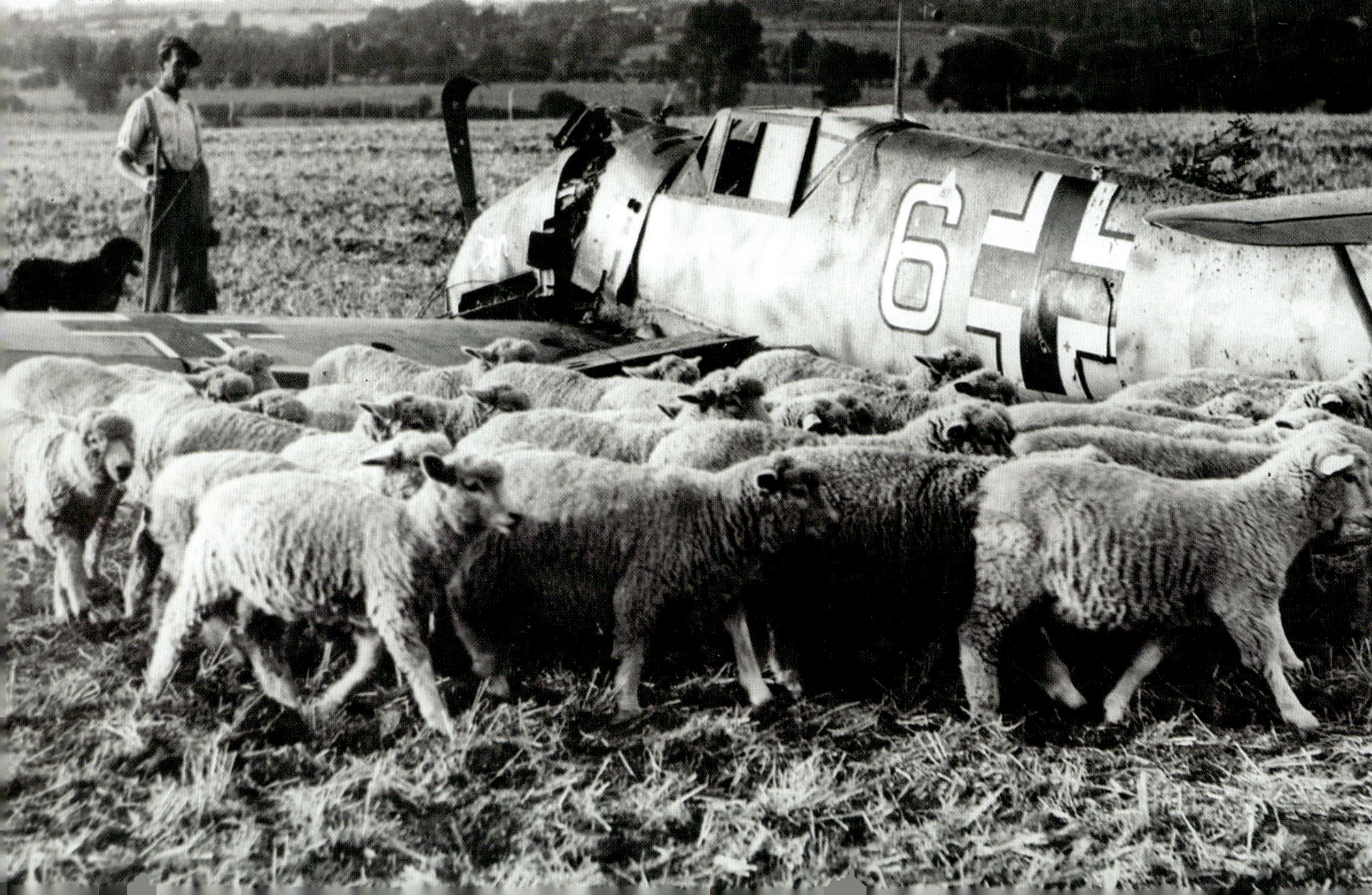

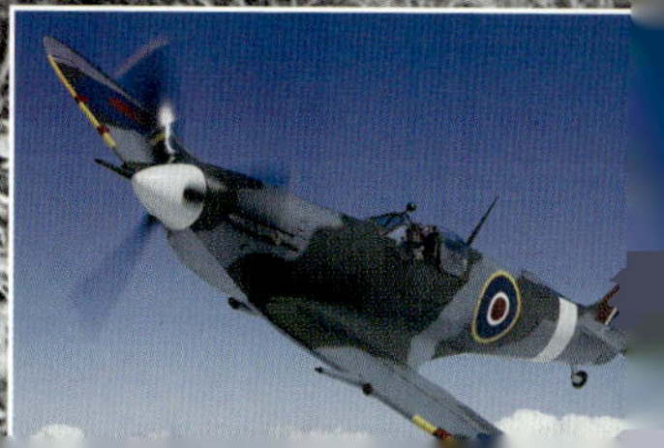

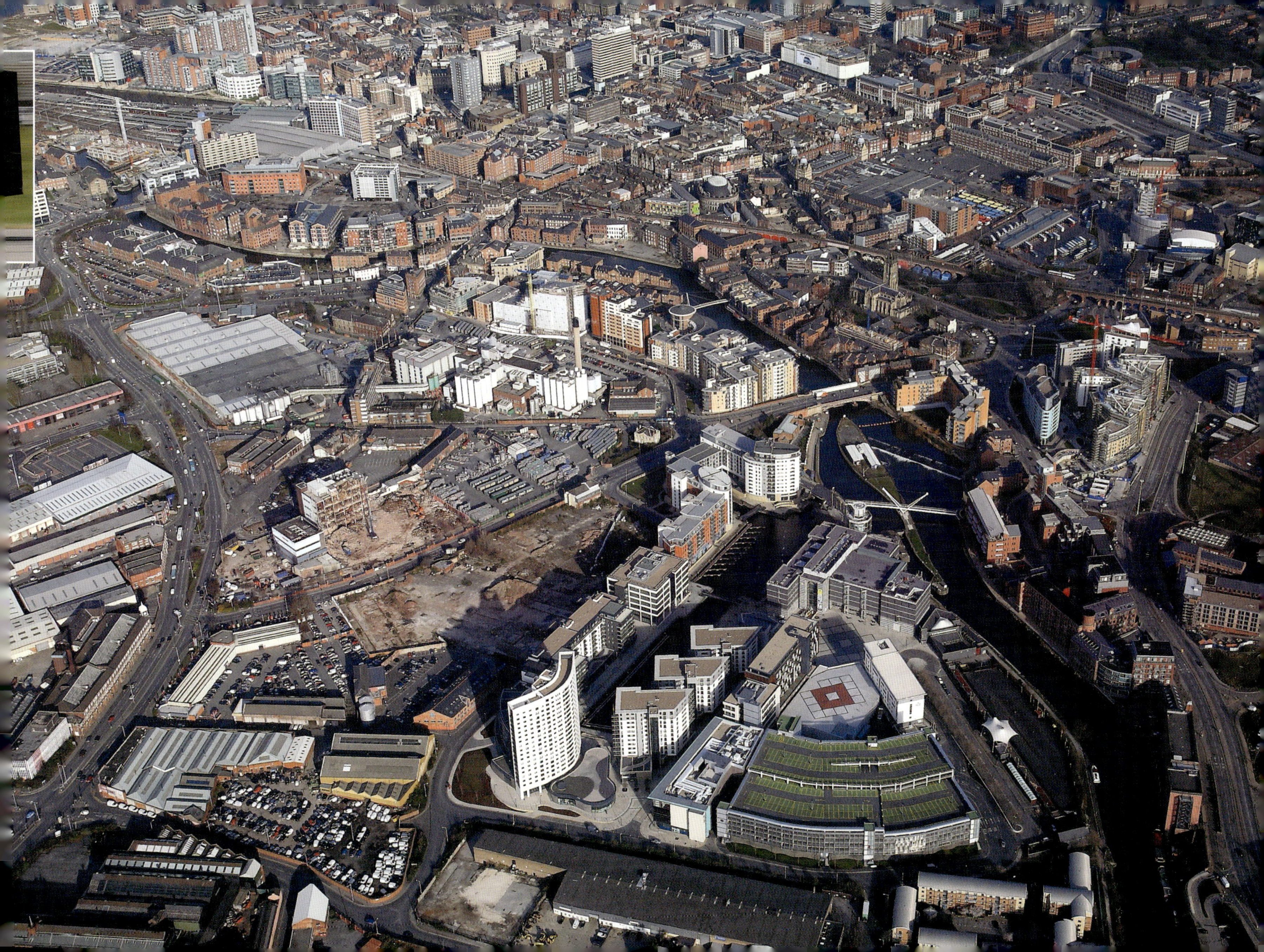

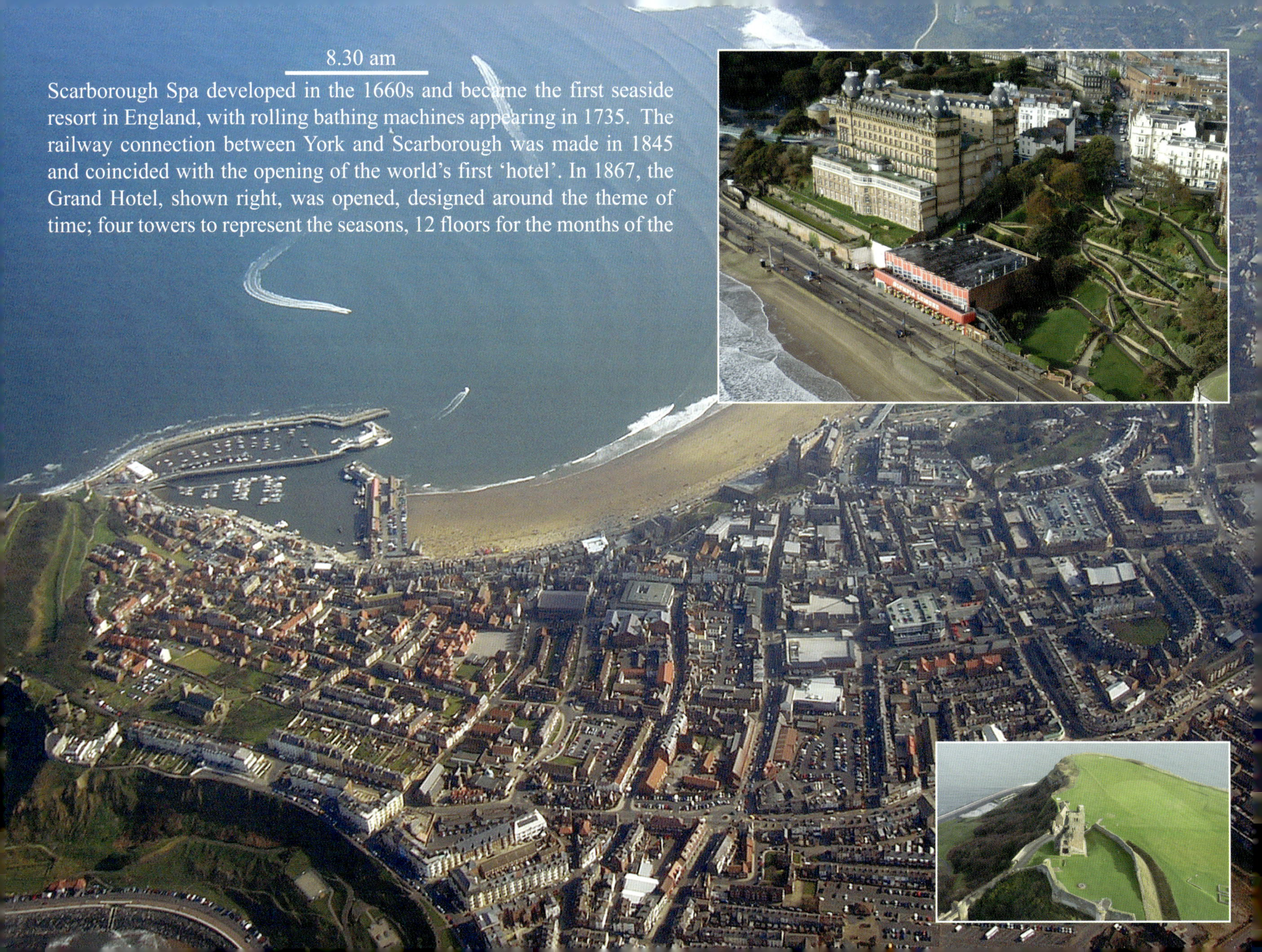

8.30 am

Scarborough Spa developed in the 1660s and became the first seaside resort in England, with rolling bathing machines appearing in 1735. The railway connection between York and Scarborough was made in 1845 and coincided with the opening of the world's first 'hotel'. In 1867, the Grand Hotel, shown right, was opened, designed around the theme of time; four towers to represent the seasons, 12 floors for the months of the

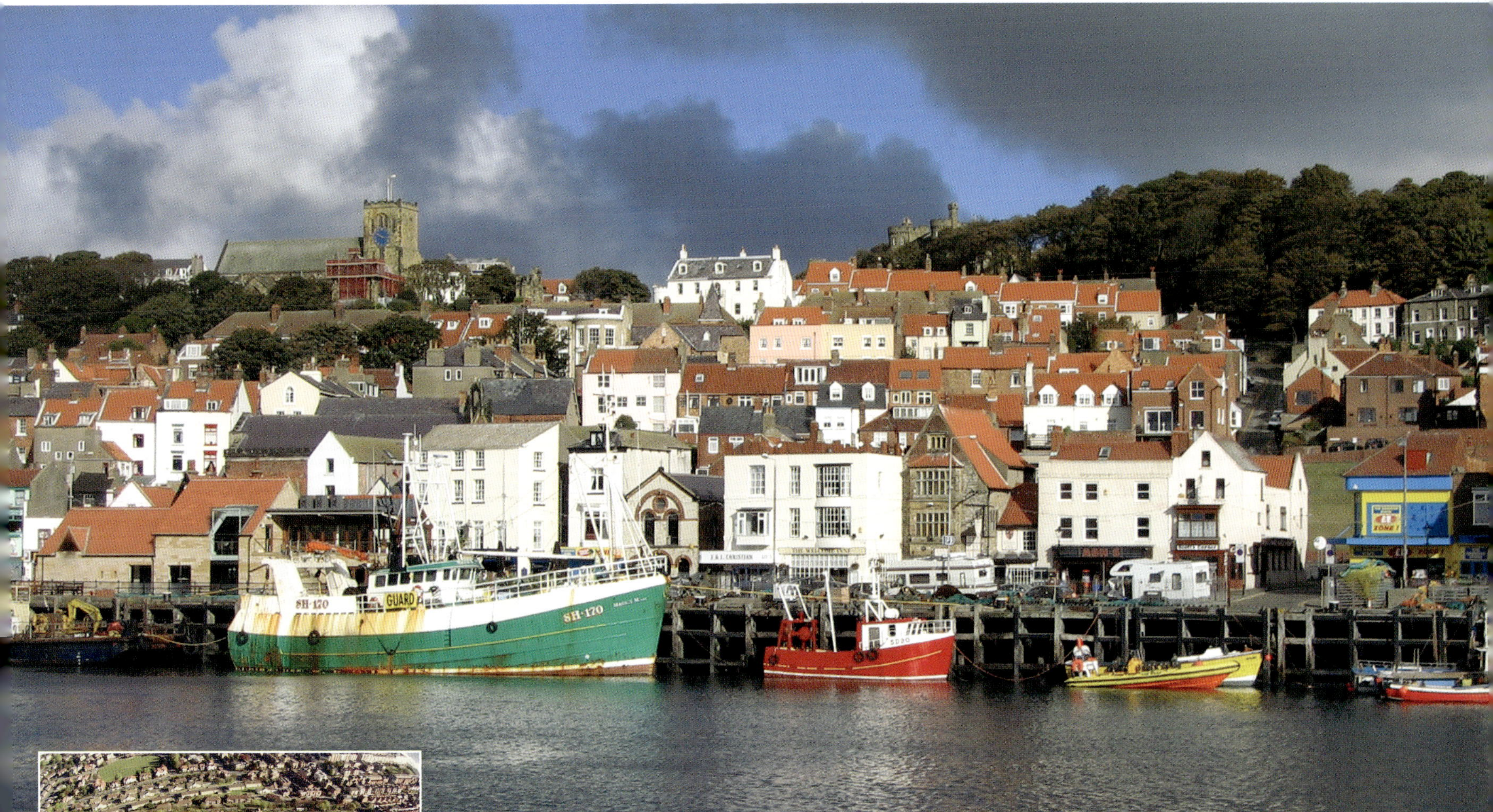


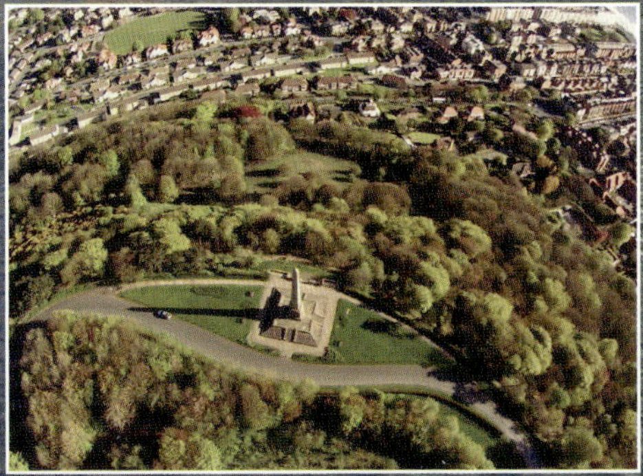

year, 52 chimneys symbolise the weeks, and originally there were 365 bedrooms, one for each day of the year. The hotel itself is in the shape of a 'V' in honour of Queen Victoria. Shown left is the Scarborough War Memorial on Oliver's Mount, named after Oliver Cromwell, which has been the venue for motorcycle races since 1946 and now the venue for music festivals.

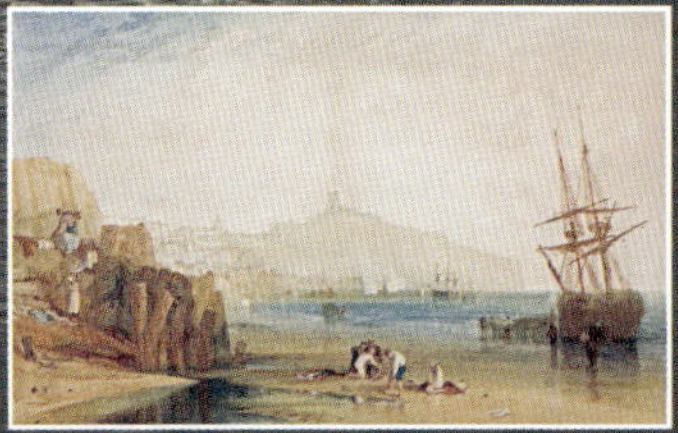

# Chapter 2

# Morning

## 9 am

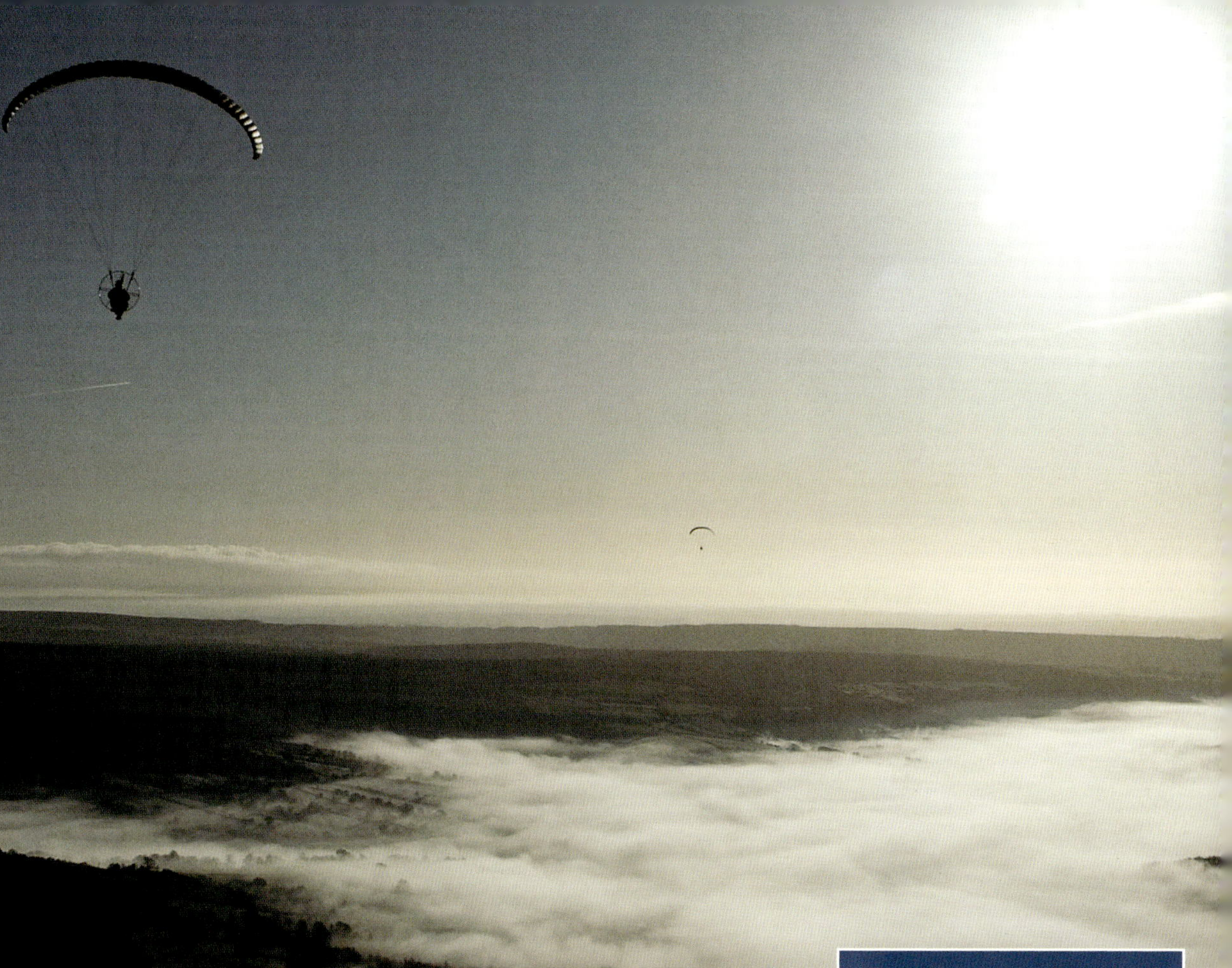

The River Tees is still the boundary between the old traditional counties of Yorkshire and County Durham. Here, the valley is still shrouded in mist which continues to burn off as the sun rises. On occasions the North Sea 'haar' or 'fret' continues to shroud Whitby Abbey. In the Vale of York, flying training has taken place for many years and the first RAF aircraft are now airborne, some in the climbing lane and reach 35,000 feet to perform high level aerobatics, just part of the diverse training of a modern pilot. Other pilots are practising their low level flying skills, needed in the modern combat role. These exercises provide thrills for photographers who climb the Pennines to capture the passing aircraft. As Neil Bates describes, '*Low Level*

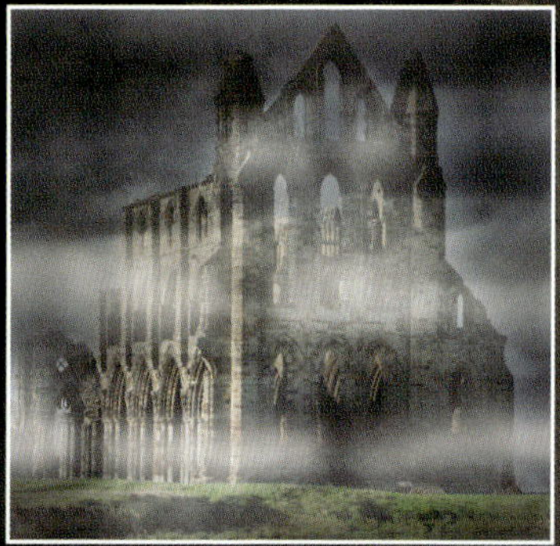

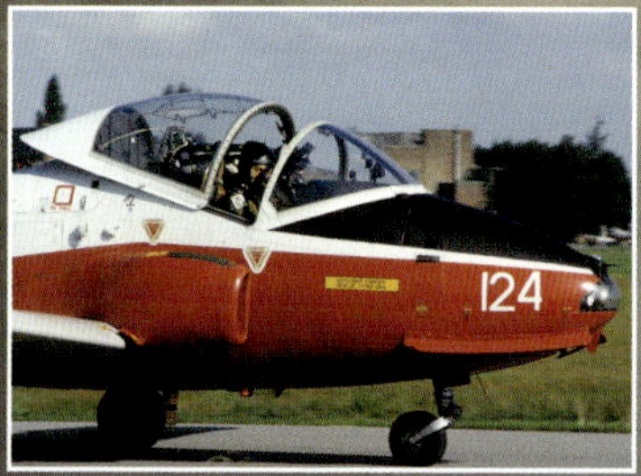


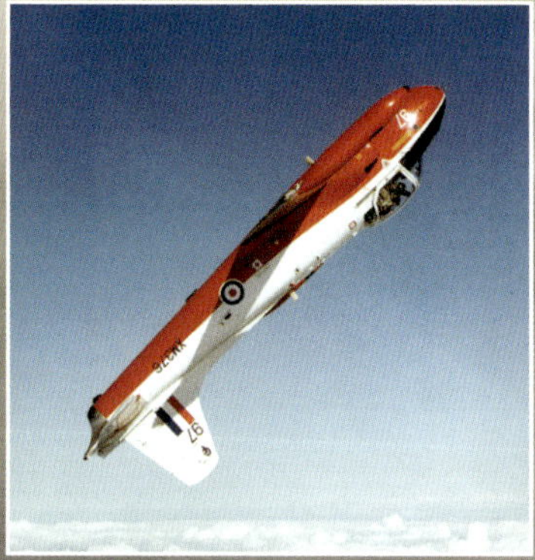

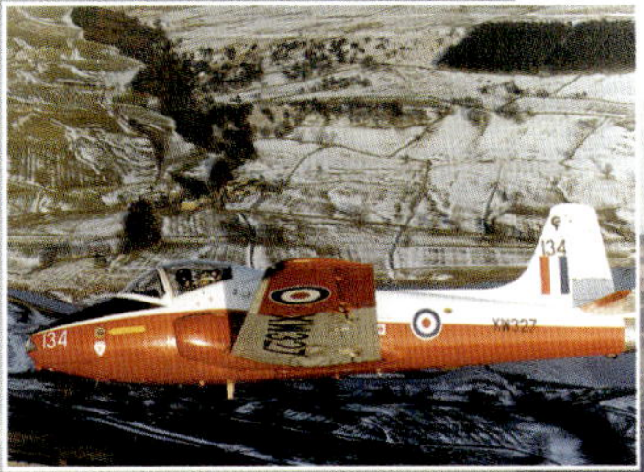

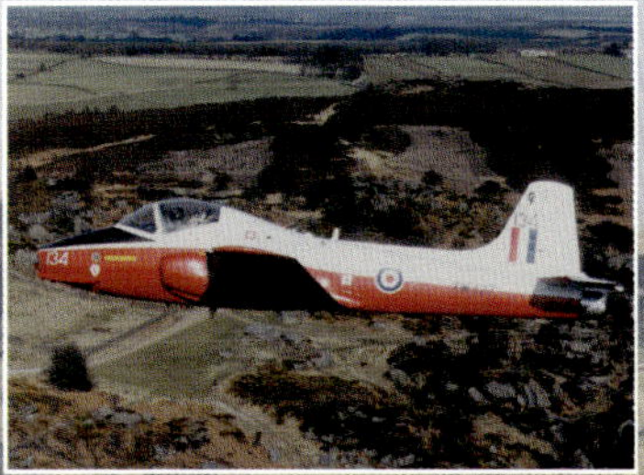

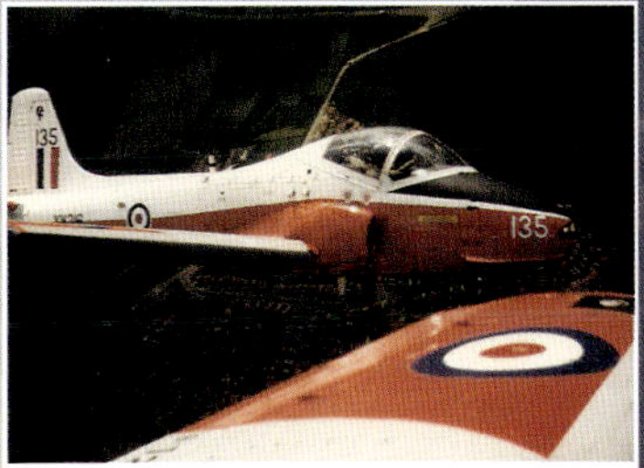

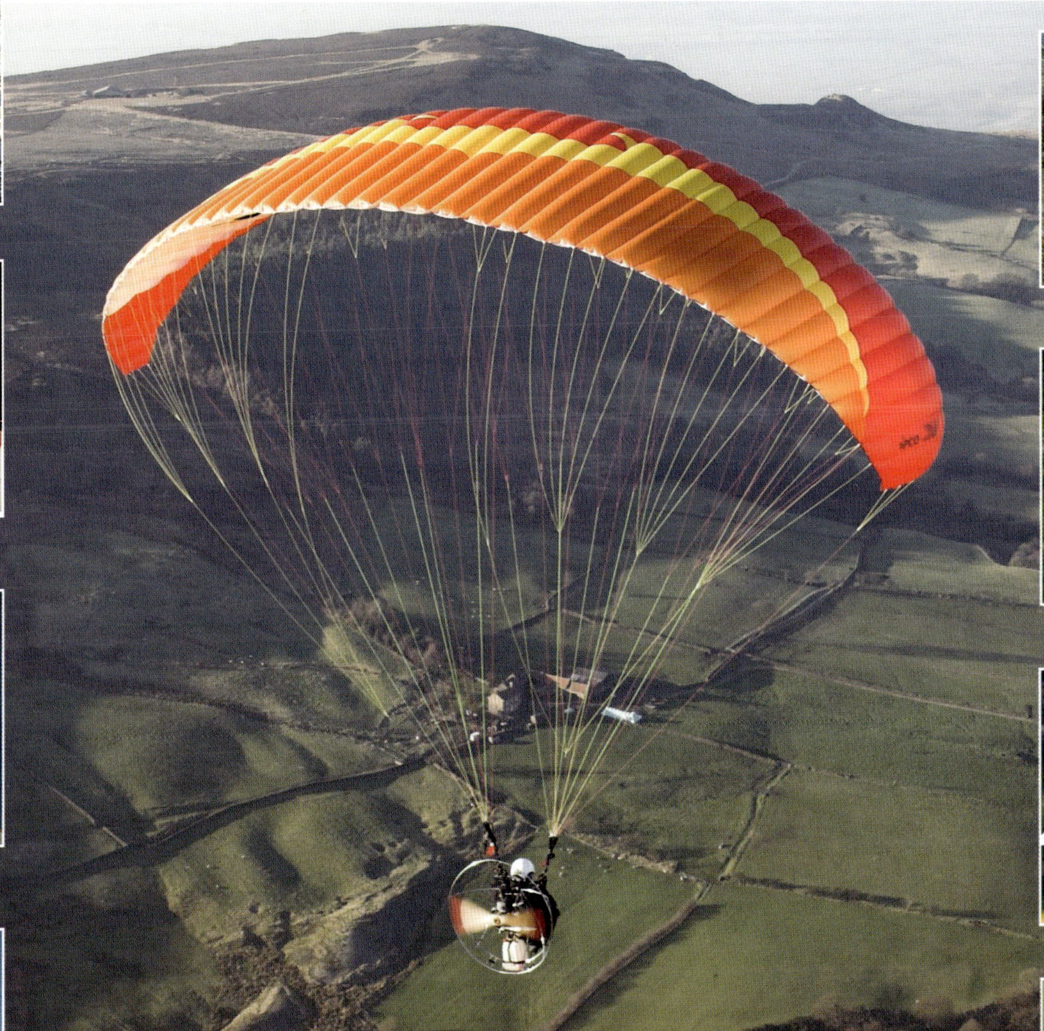

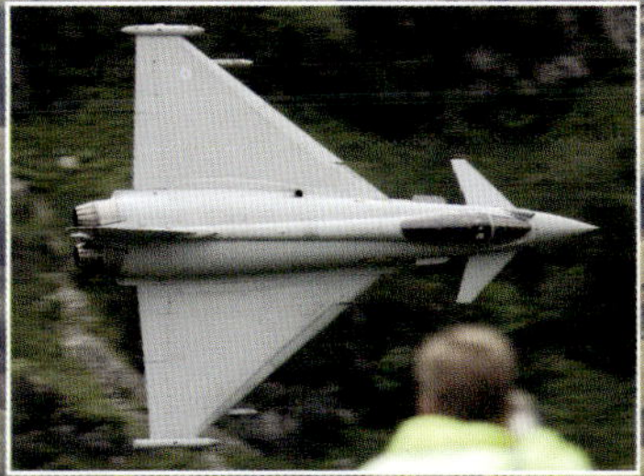

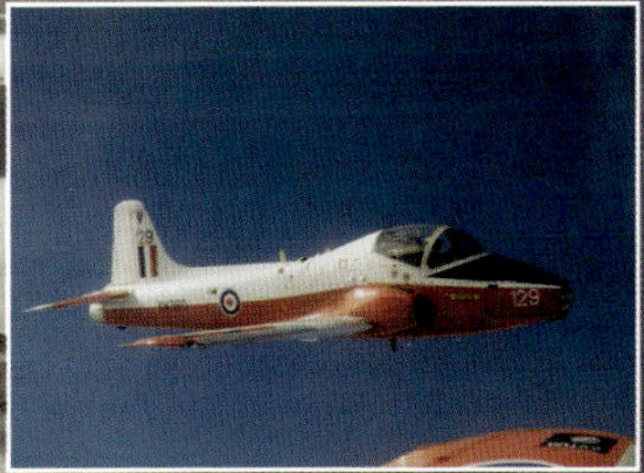

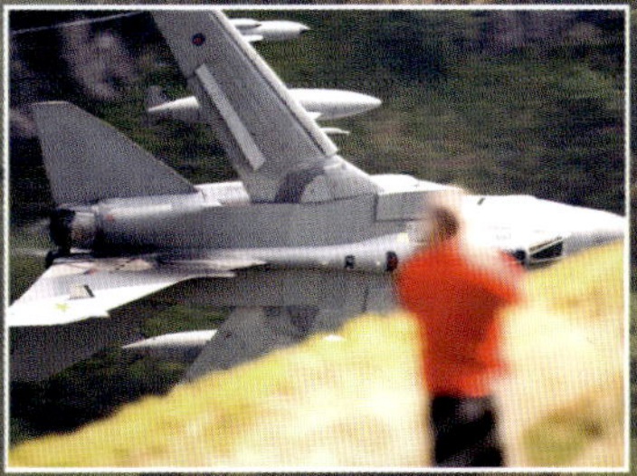

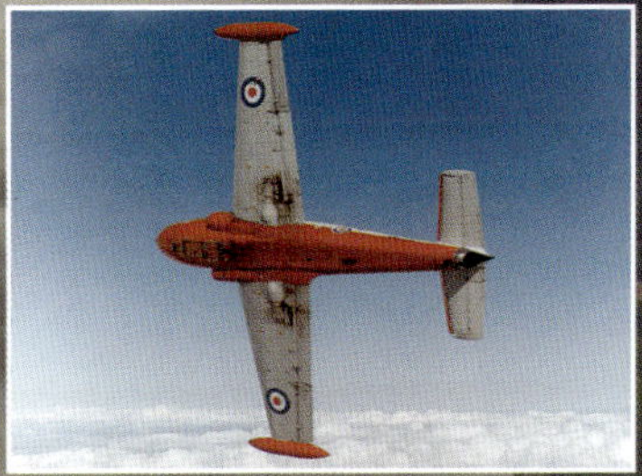

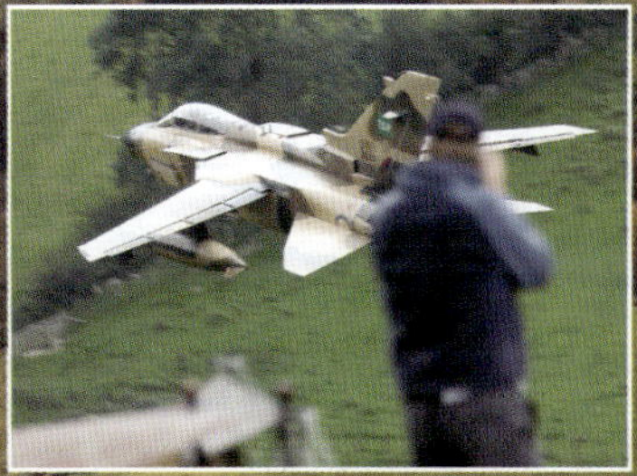

*photography is totally addictive .... there is a lot of waiting ... and waiting ... for literally seconds of a complete adrenalin rush as the jet comes zooming at 300kts out of the next valley ..... Hope you enjoy looking at the shots here as much as I have actually enjoyed climbing the hill sides and taking them!*

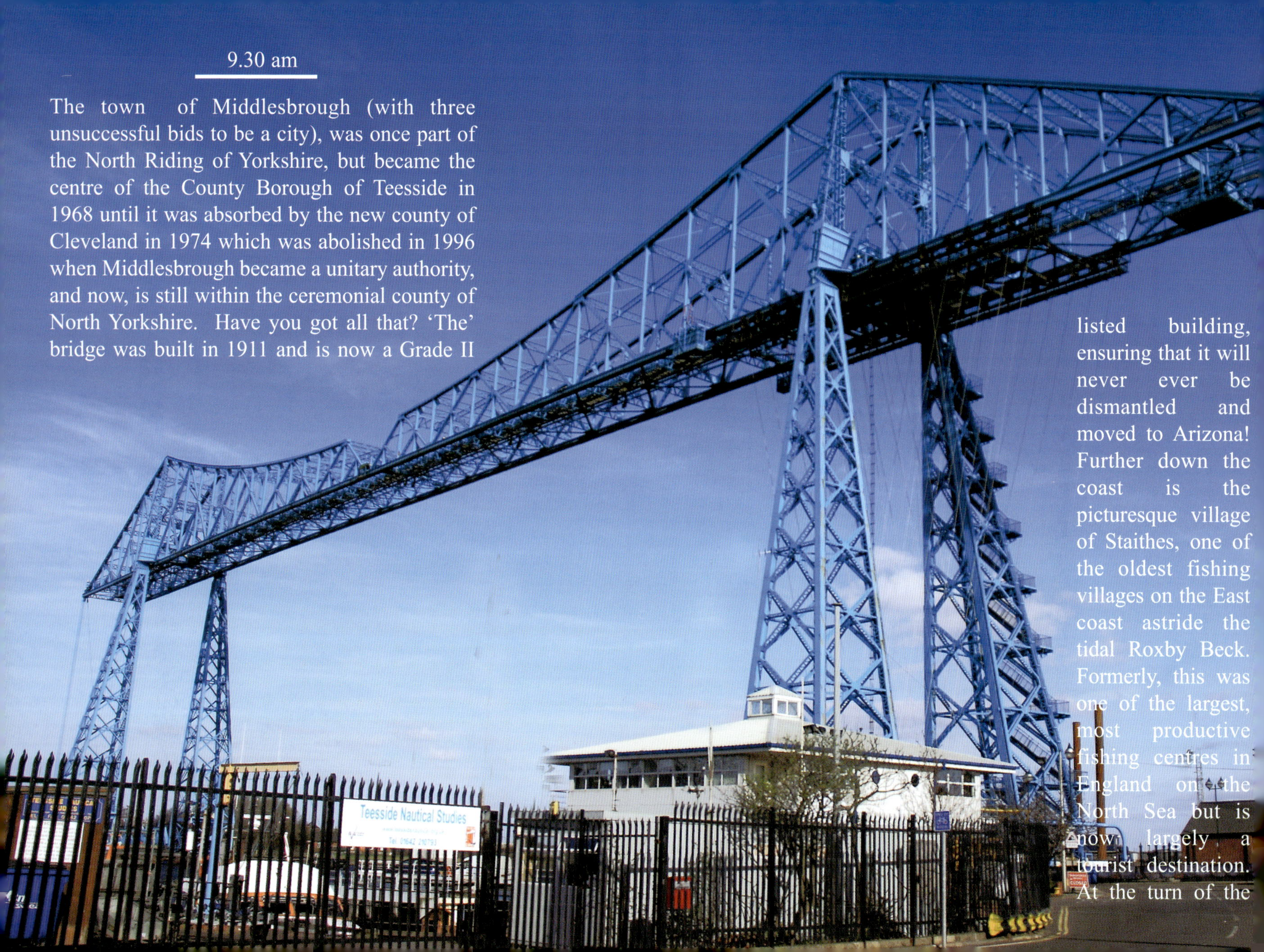


9.30 am

The town of Middlesbrough (with three unsuccessful bids to be a city), was once part of the North Riding of Yorkshire, but became the centre of the County Borough of Teesside in 1968 until it was absorbed by the new county of Cleveland in 1974 which was abolished in 1996 when Middlesbrough became a unitary authority, and now, is still within the ceremonial county of North Yorkshire. Have you got all that? 'The' bridge was built in 1911 and is now a Grade II listed building, ensuring that it will never ever be dismantled and moved to Arizona! Further down the coast is the picturesque village of Staithes, one of the oldest fishing villages on the East coast astride the tidal Roxby Beck. Formerly, this was one of the largest, most productive fishing centres in England on the North Sea but is now largely a tourist destination. At the turn of the

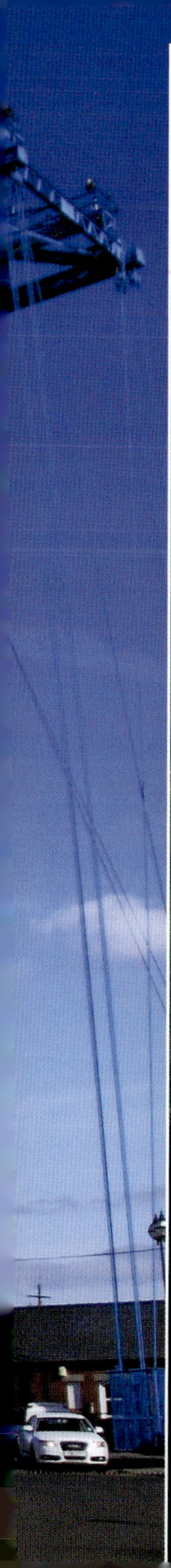

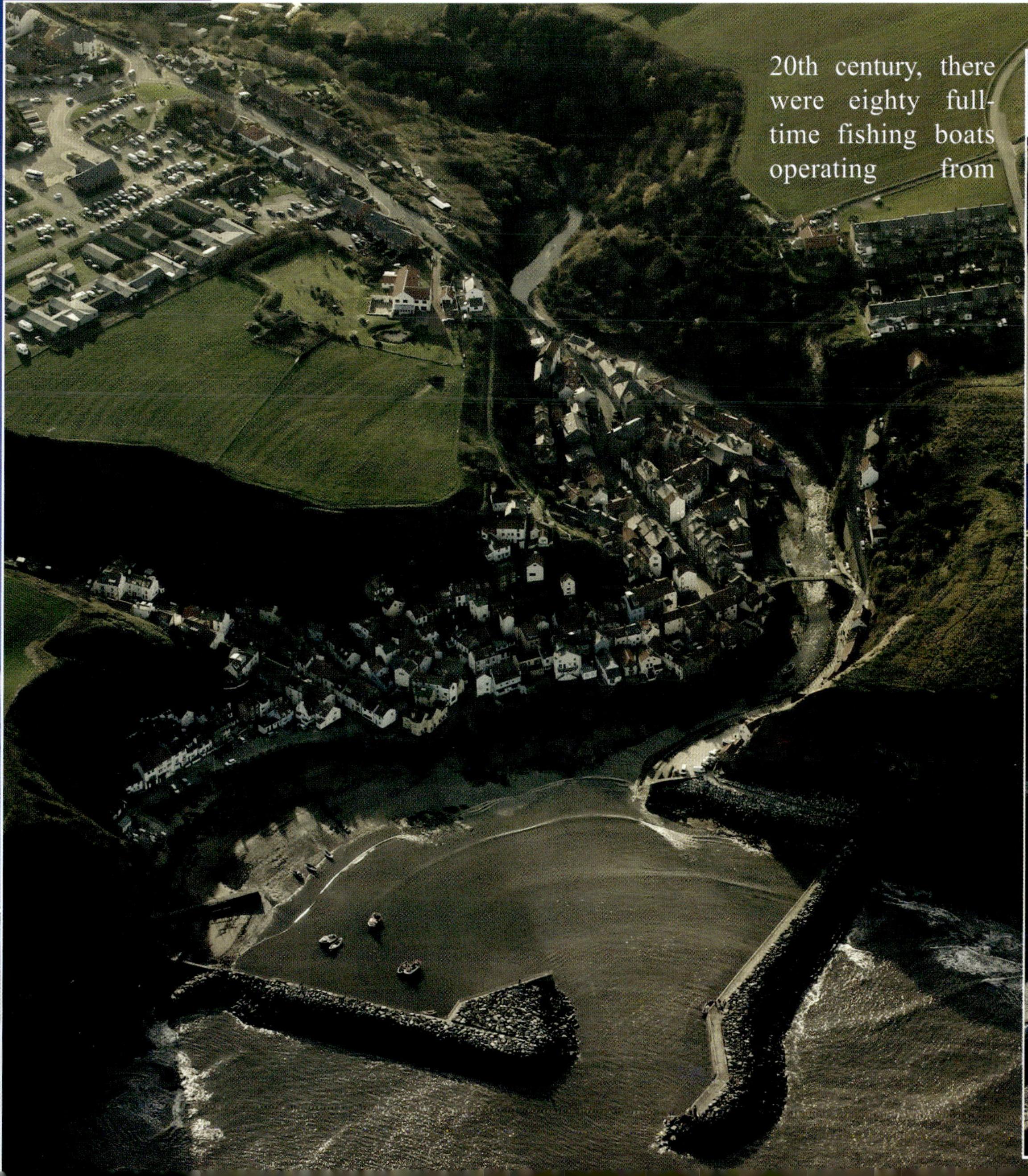

20th century, there were eighty full-time fishing boats operating from Staithes, now there is one, with the crew becoming part of the tourist scene.

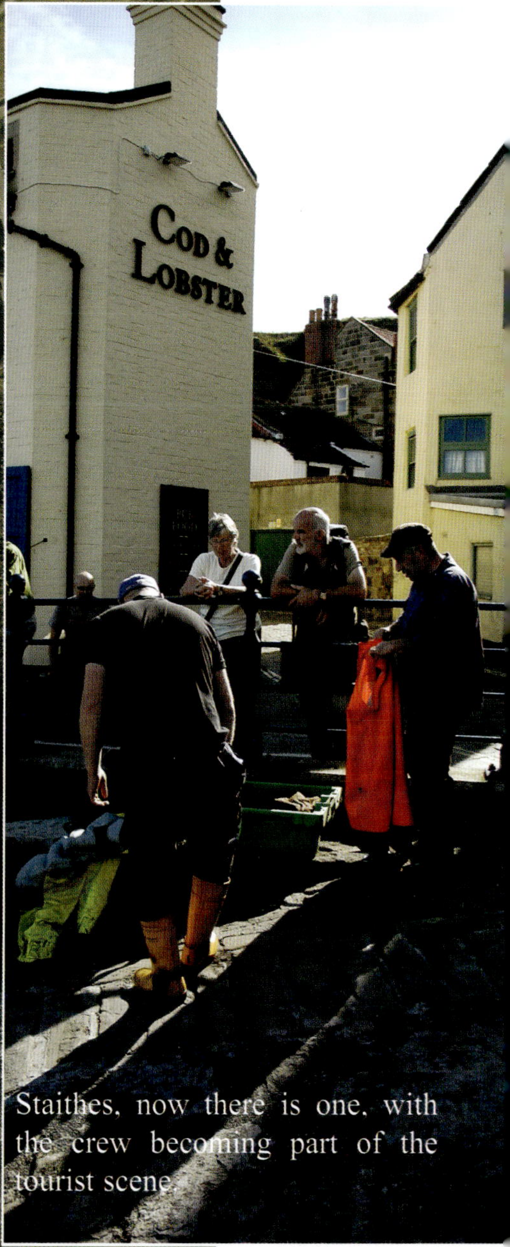

9.30 am

Hawdraw Falls are the highest single drop of any waterfall in England. Kevin Costner showered here in the 1991 film, 'Prince of Thieves'. The diverse legends of Robin Hood abound, usually portrayed in Sherwood Forest in their battles against the Sheriff of Nottingham. However, Robin Hood may have been based in Barnsdale Forest in what is now South Yorkshire. 16th century tradition tells that Robin was born in Loxley, South Yorkshire but long before that, the site of Robin Hodd's well in Skellow, South Yorkshire, has been known since 1422. Records show a man named Robin Hood lived in Wakefield, Yorkshire in the 13th and 14th centuries, that a 'Robert de Lockesly' appeared in the Royal Court in 1245 and his grave with headstone is at Kirklees Priory near Mirfield, West Yorkshire. Robin Hood is portrayed as a loyal supporter of the 12th-century King Richard-The-Lionheart, (1189-99) who was away on the 3rd Crusade. The most telling

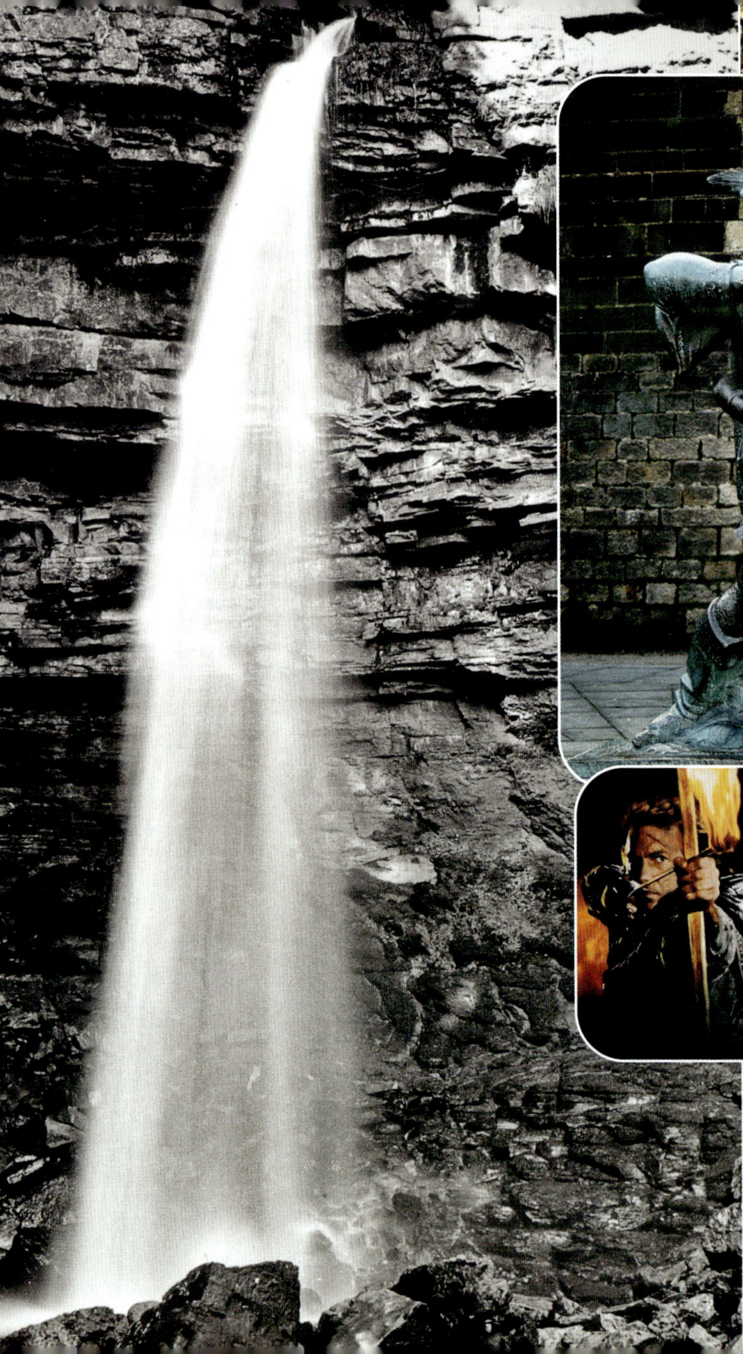

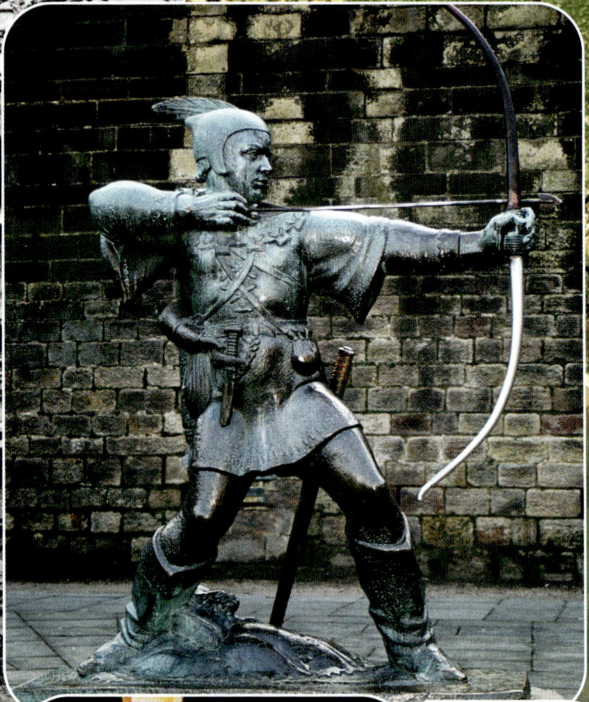

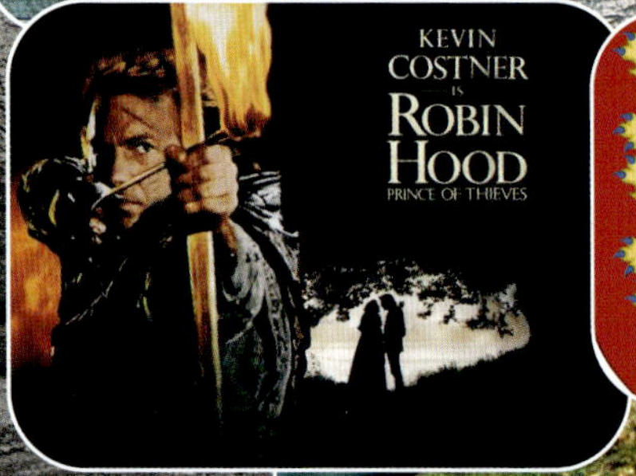


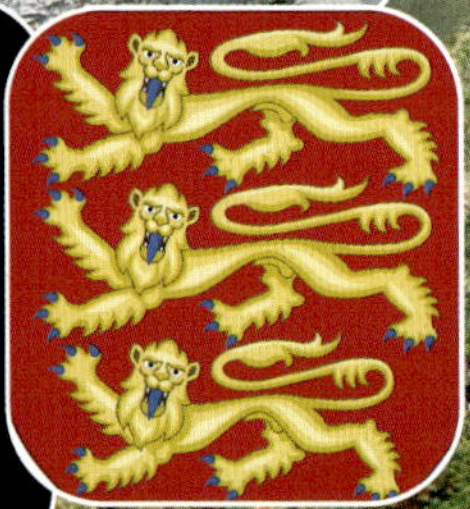

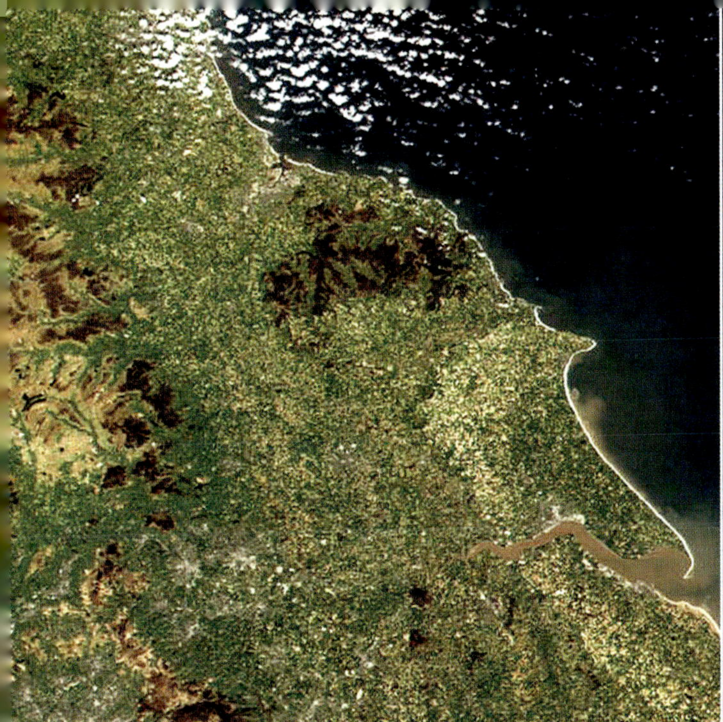

quote, made in 1439 to Parliament describes the band as; *'who having no liflode, ne sufficeante of goodes, gadered and assembled unto him many misdoers, beynge of his clothynge, and, in manere of insurrection, wente into the wodes in that countrie, as it hadde be Robyn Hude and his meyne'*. Many actors played the part of Robin including Errol Flynn, Douglas Fairbanks, Kevin Costner, Carey Elwes, Daffy Duck (voiced by the late Mel Blanc) and Sean Connery as Robin Hood with Audrey Hepburn as Maid Marian, portrayed the mature figures in their later years. Today, statues of Robin Hood stand beneath Nottingham Castle and in the terminal of Robin Hood International Airport at Doncaster.

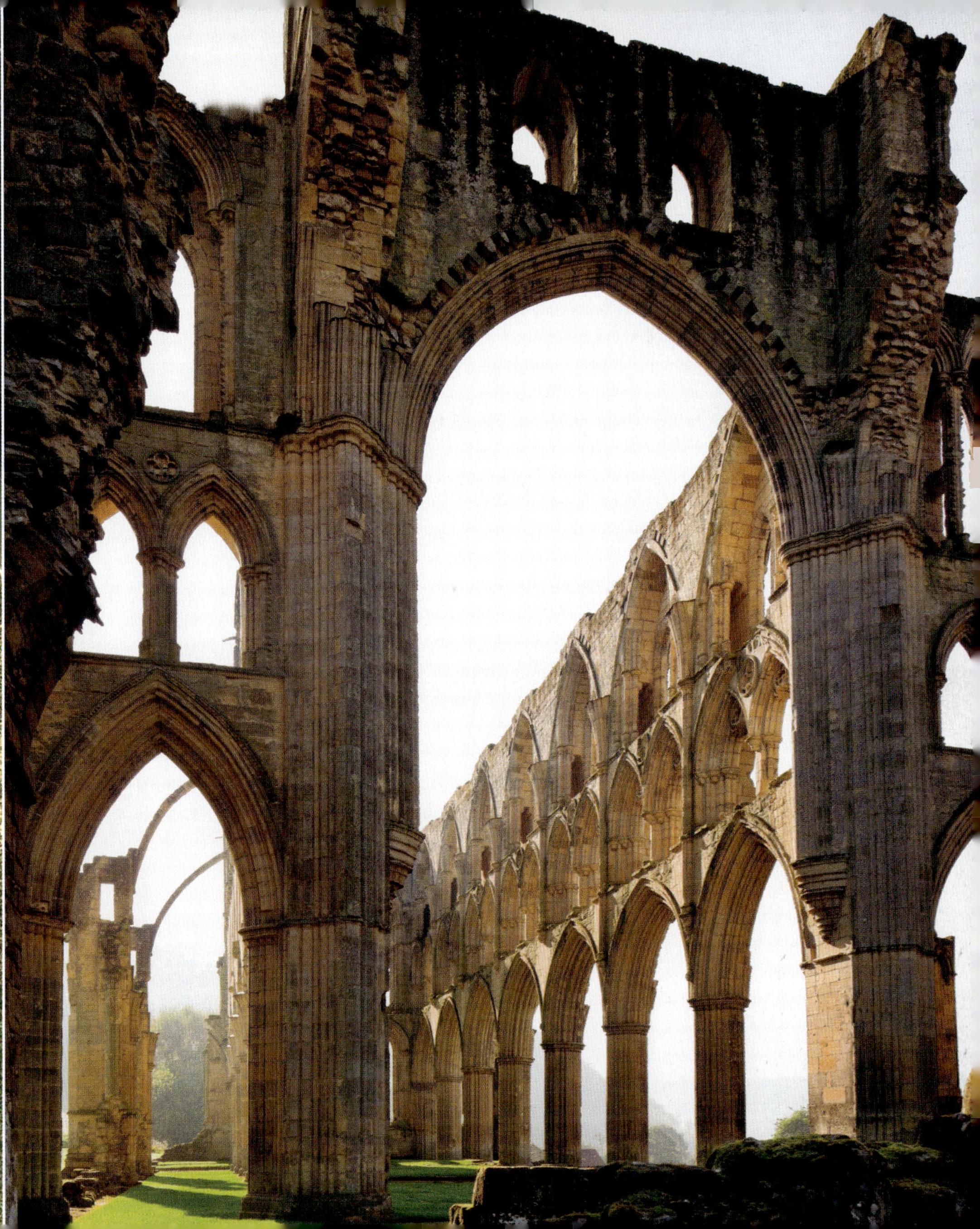

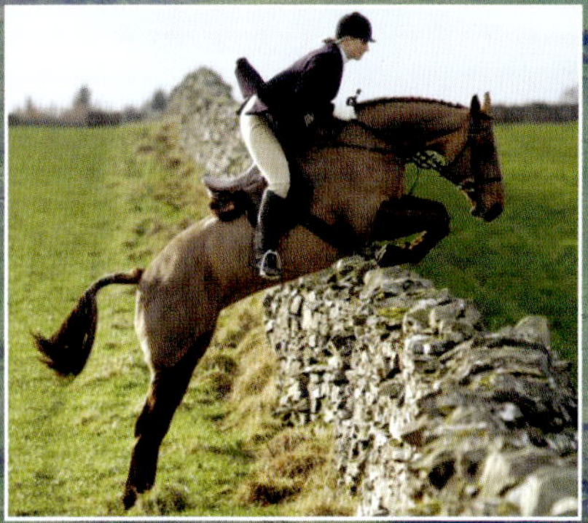

10.30 am

The imposing ruins of Middleham Castle, once the favourite home of King Richard III, dominates the village, now famous for the training of race horses. Lower down the Dale at Bedale, an adventurous rider takes off to clear a dry stone wall. Further down the Dale, beyond Leeming is the busy market town of Northallerton. To the north is the town of Richmond

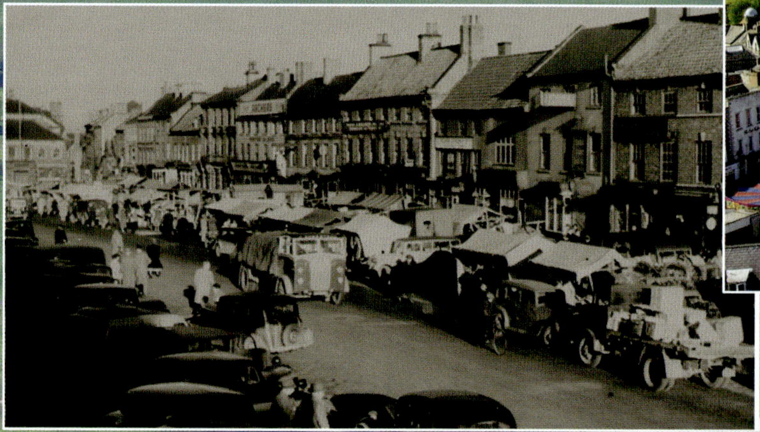

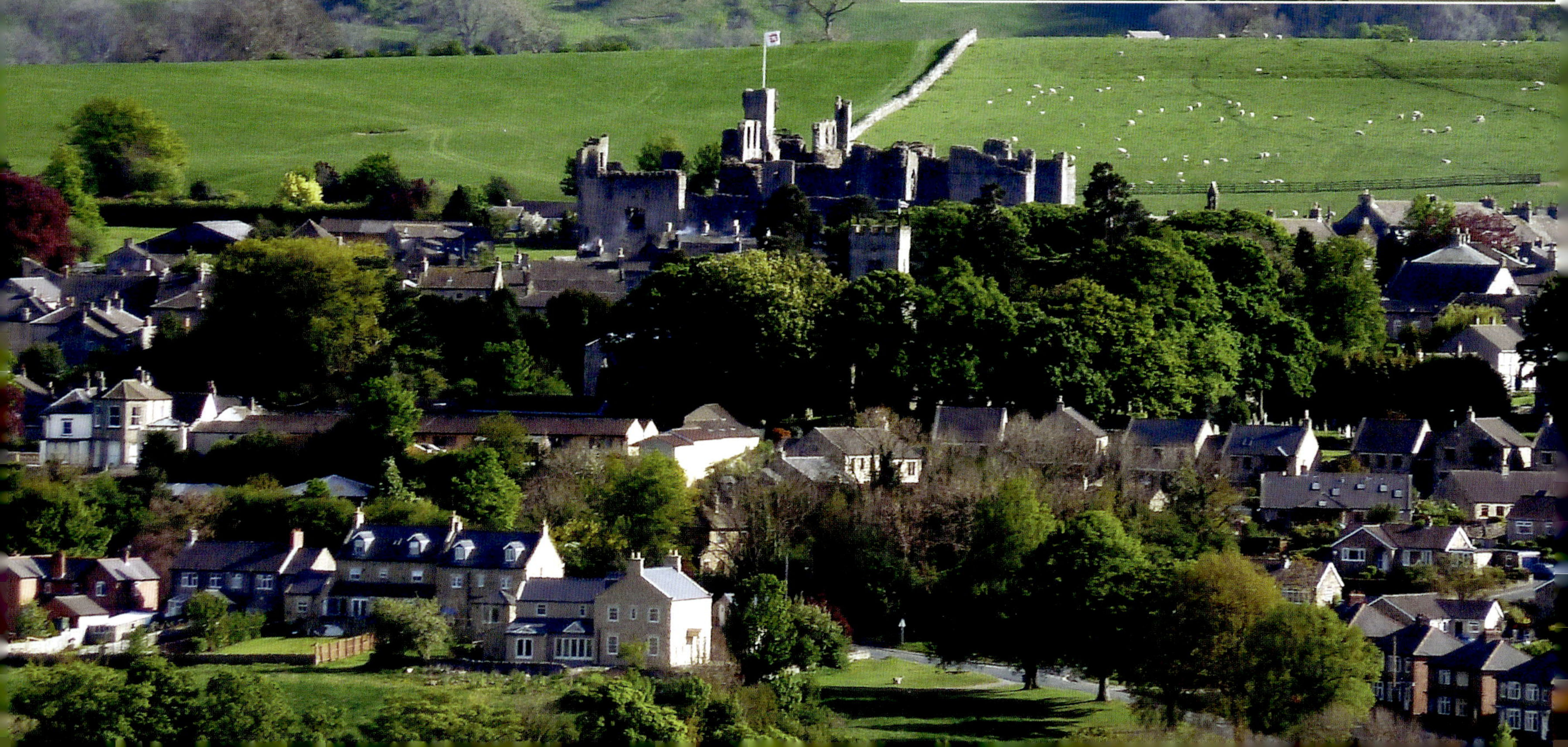

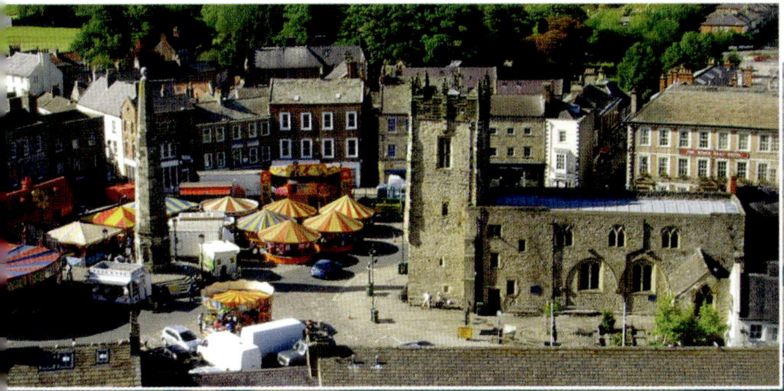

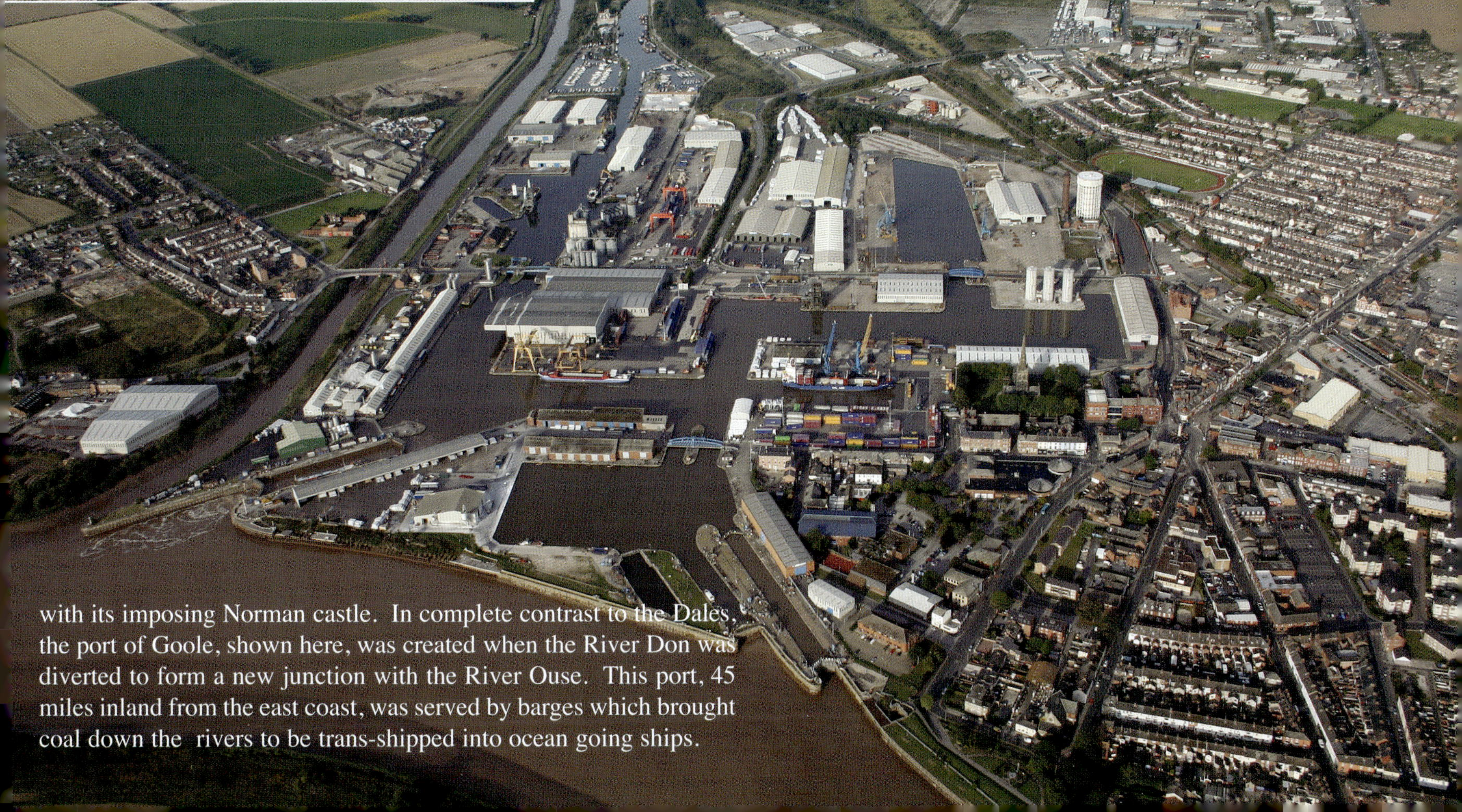

with its imposing Norman castle. In complete contrast to the Dales, the port of Goole, shown here, was created when the River Don was diverted to form a new junction with the River Ouse. This port, 45 miles inland from the east coast, was served by barges which brought coal down the rivers to be trans-shipped into ocean going ships.

## 11 am

On the 11th November 1951, the '*Pots & Pans*' War Memorial at Saddleworth stood in Yorkshire. I know, I climbed up to the site with my father and his wartime Royal Navy shipmates from Lancashire. The obelisk was built in 1923 on the site of the '*Pots and Pans Rocks*' - where erosion over thousands of years has created hollows which fill with water. Ironically, many thousands of

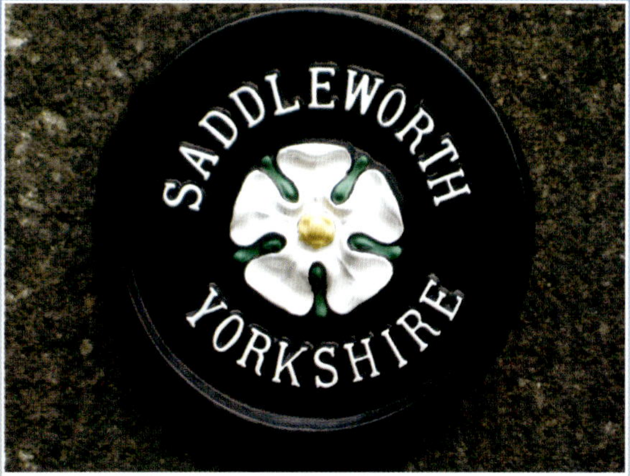


aluminium pots and pans were collected during WWII and recycled to build fighters. £5,000 was raised by workers at Ferranti Ltd to buy a Spitfire for the war effort. The cheque was presented to the Ministry of Aircraft Production on 27th April 1941 at a charity concert at the Empire Theatre in Oldham and the Spitfire was flown in combat by the Polish pilots of the RAF. Opposite, people climb every 11th

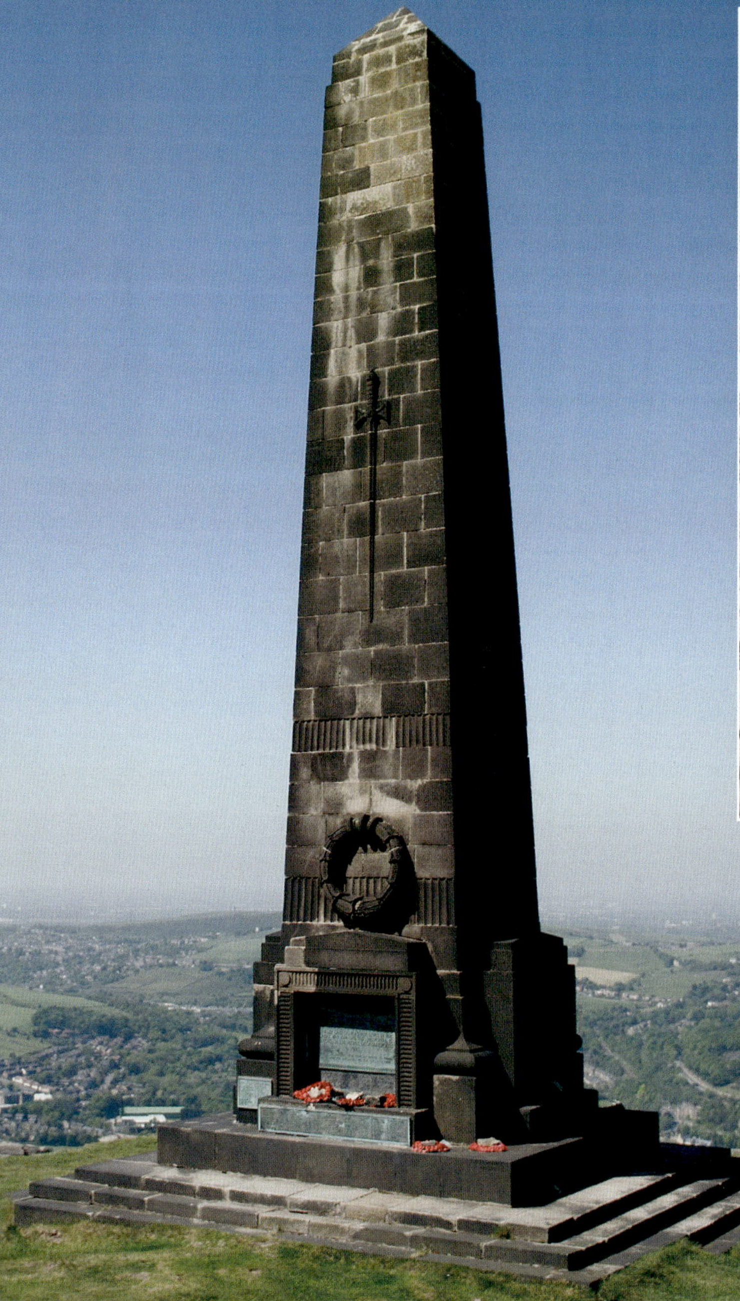

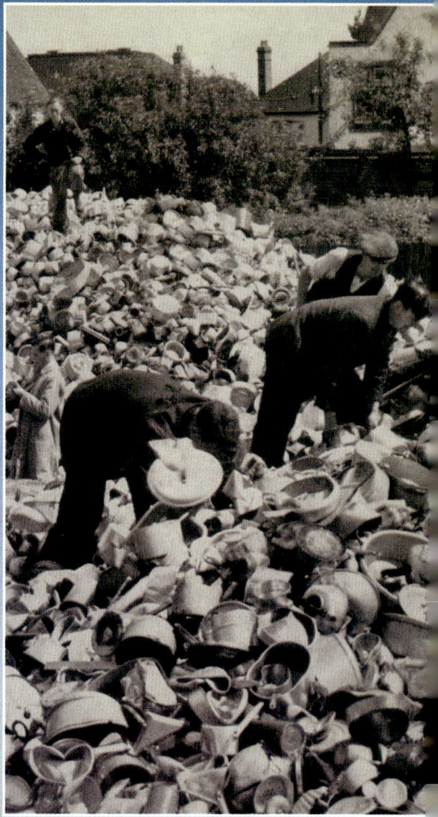

November for the memorial service to the fallen, commemorated by these cigarette cards showing the Yorkshire and Lancashire Regimental flags. In addition to the many rolls of honour, the following inscription on the Saddleworth '*Pots & Pans*' Memorial reads;

'*True love by life - true love by death is tried. Live thou for England - we for England died*'.

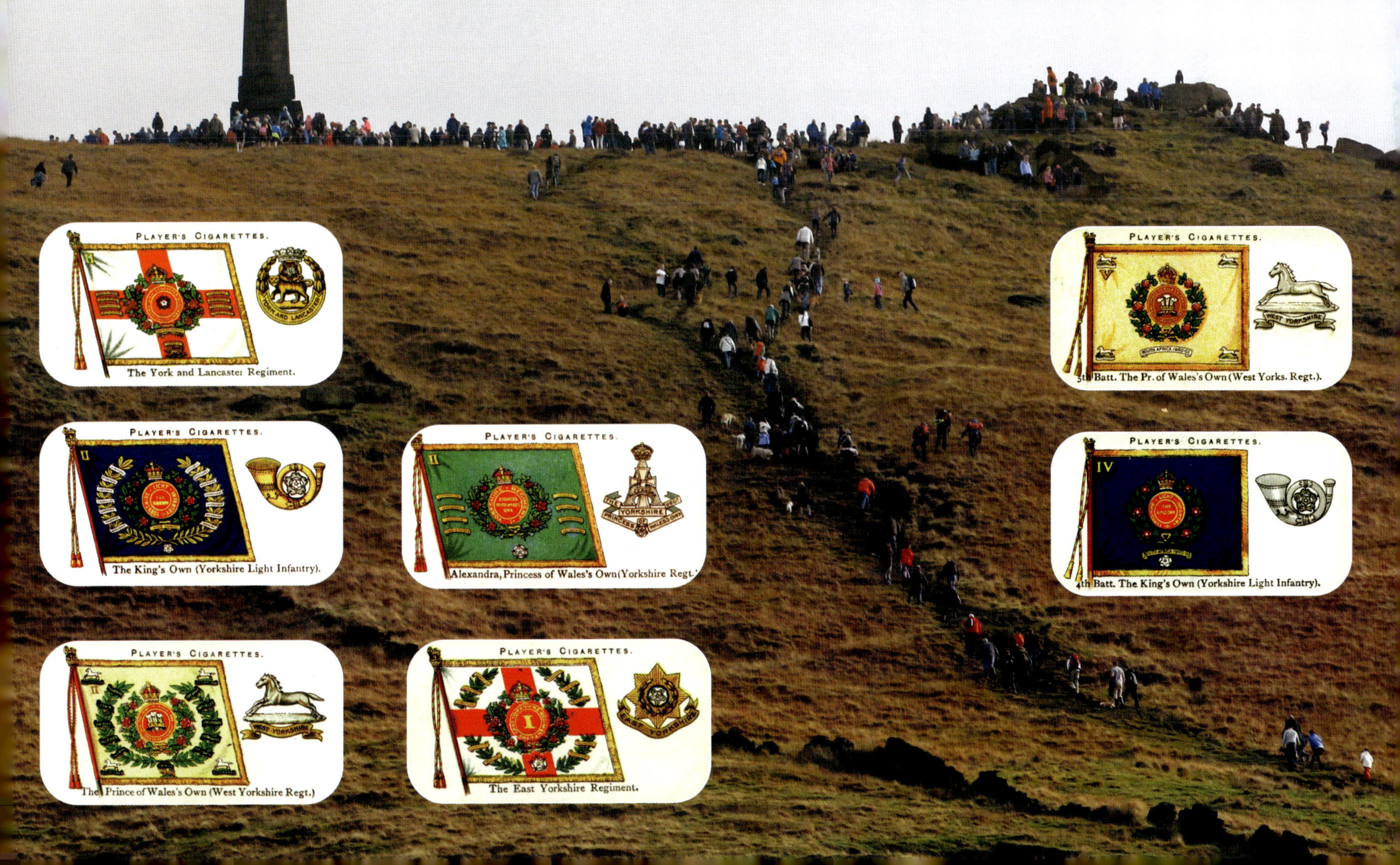

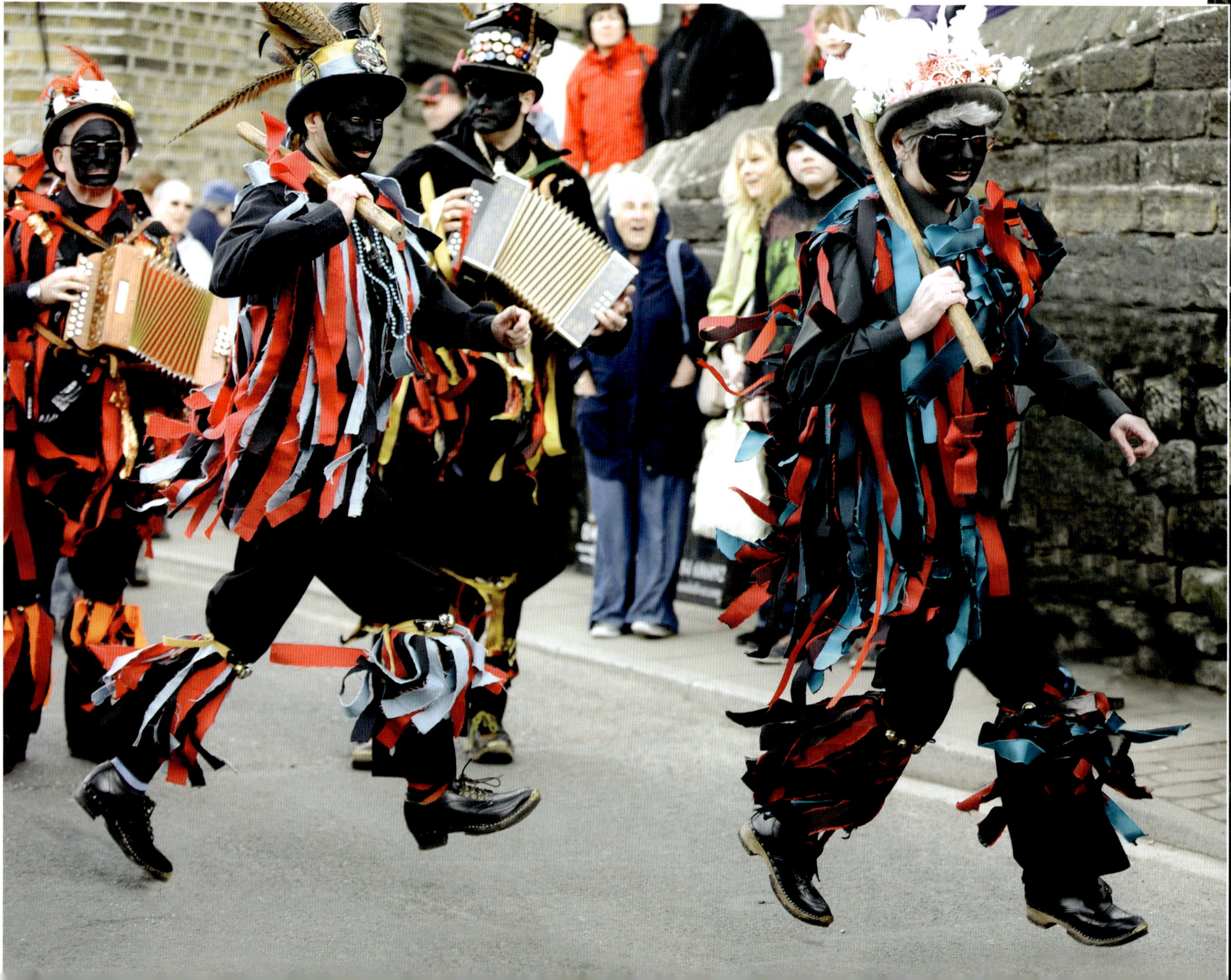

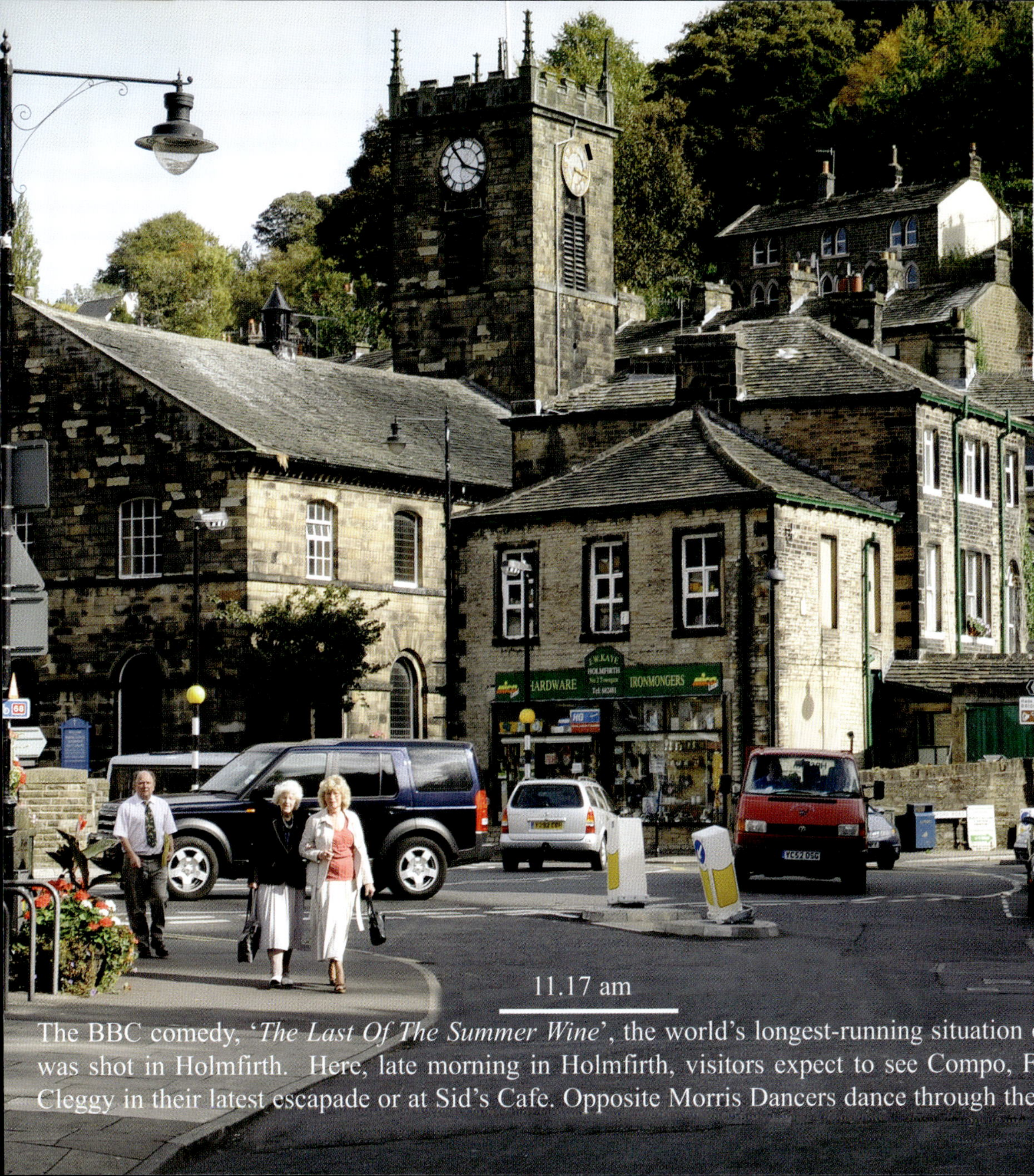


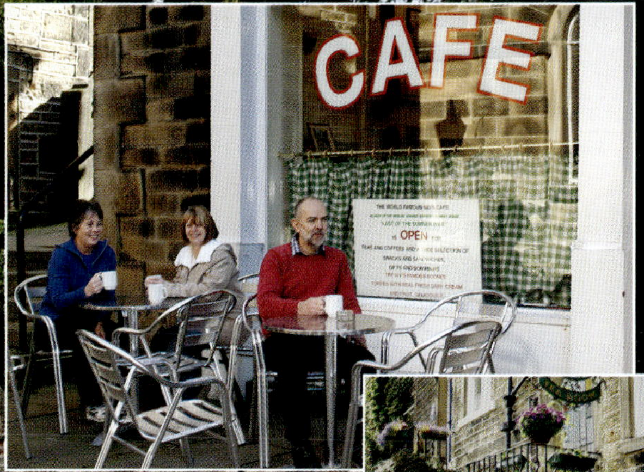


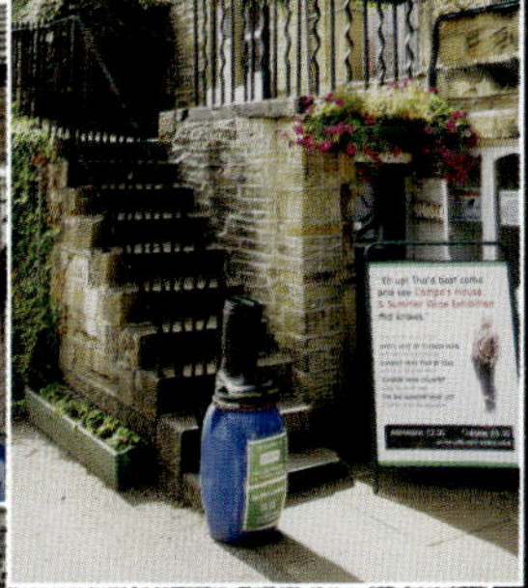

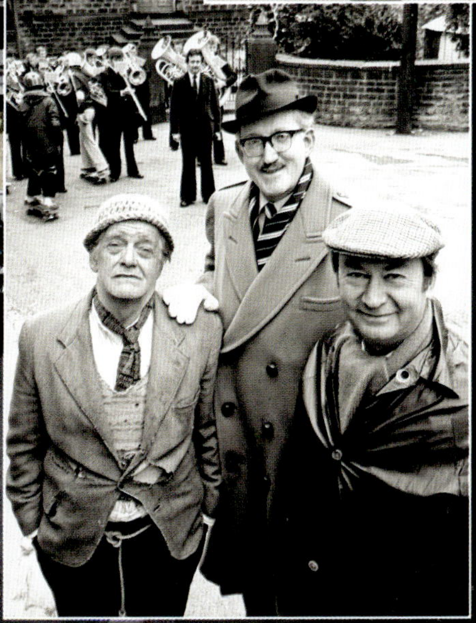

11.17 am

The BBC comedy, '*The Last Of The Summer Wine*', the world's longest-running situation comedy, was shot in Holmfirth. Here, late morning in Holmfirth, visitors expect to see Compo, Foggy & Cleggy in their latest escapade or at Sid's Cafe. Opposite Morris Dancers dance through the town.

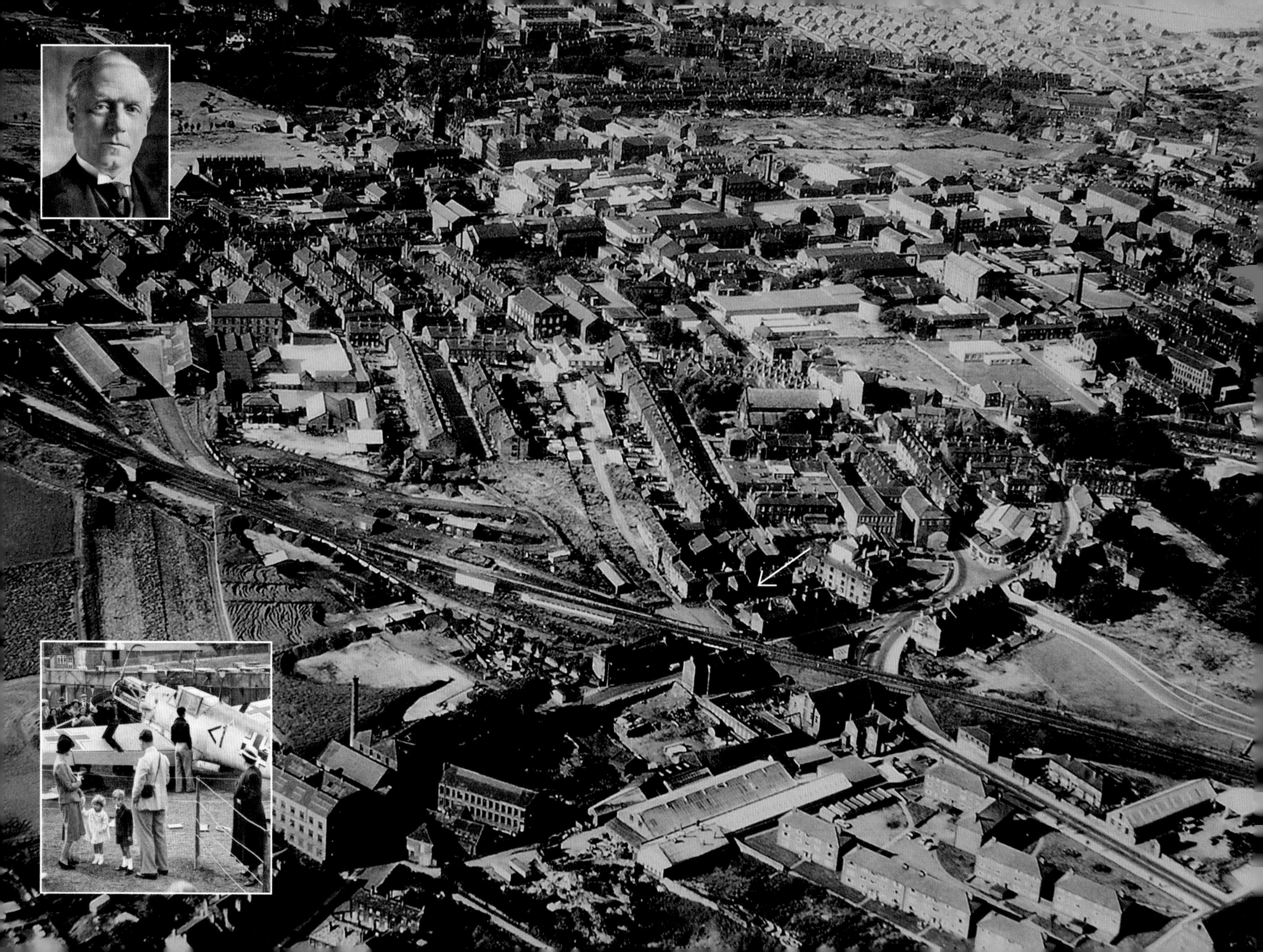

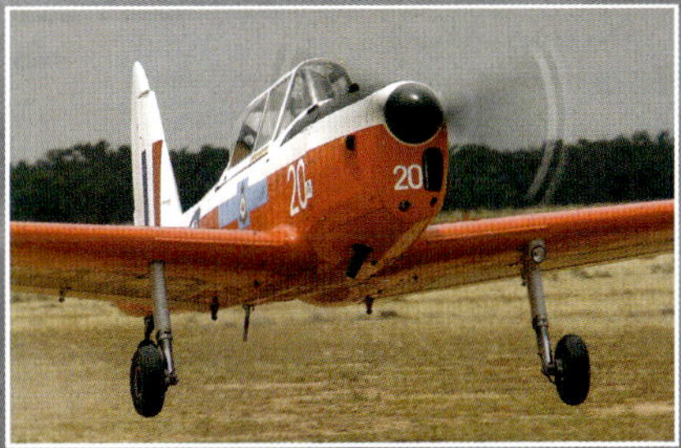

## 11.30 am

Opposite page is an aerial view of Morley taken on 22nd August 1968 with an arrow pointing to where the author was born in 1941 at the height of World War II. An early experience was to view a shot-down ME109. The price to view was 6 pence (10p today's money) which contributed to the Borough of Morley Spitfire Fund. £5,000 was raised and 'our' Spitfire flew with with 610,

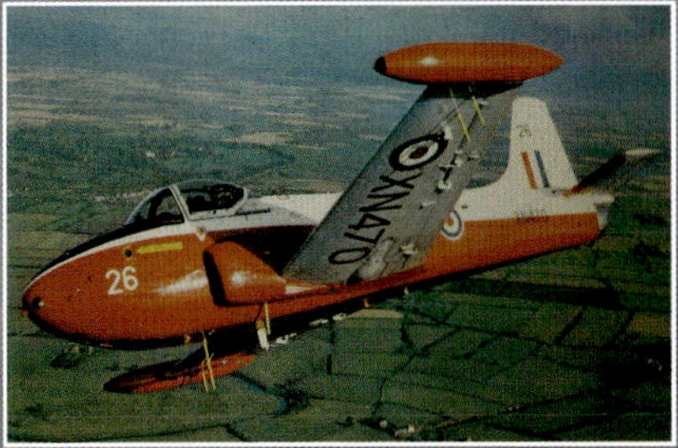

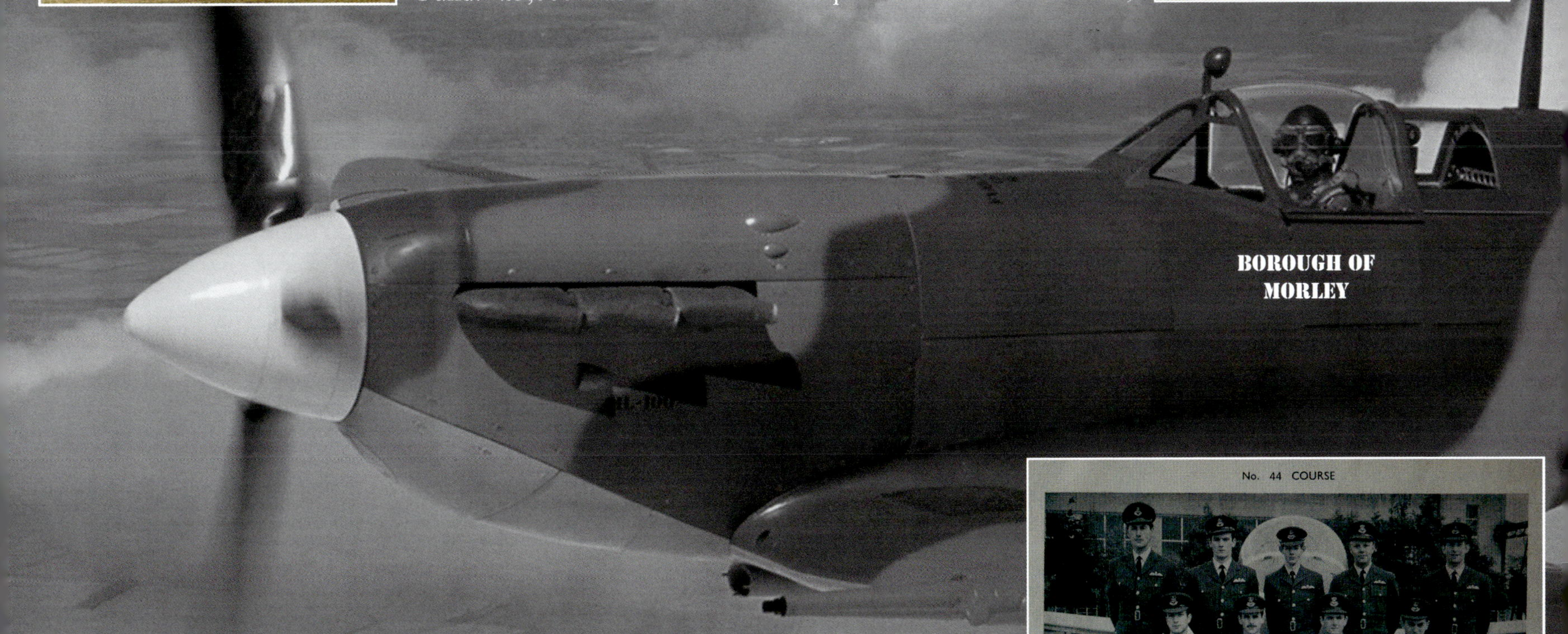


15, 266, 124 and 54 Squadrons shooting down ME109s and German bombers. Herbert H. Asquith, Prime Minister from 1908 to 1916, shown upper left was born in Morley in 1852 and 101 years later, Her Majesty Queen Elizabeth II visited Morley after her coronation in 1953. When the author was 14, he went for his first flight in a De Havilland Chipmunk and embarked on a flying career. He returned to RAF Leeming joining Number 44 Course (shown right) and completed jet training on the Jet Provost Mk III and MkVs.

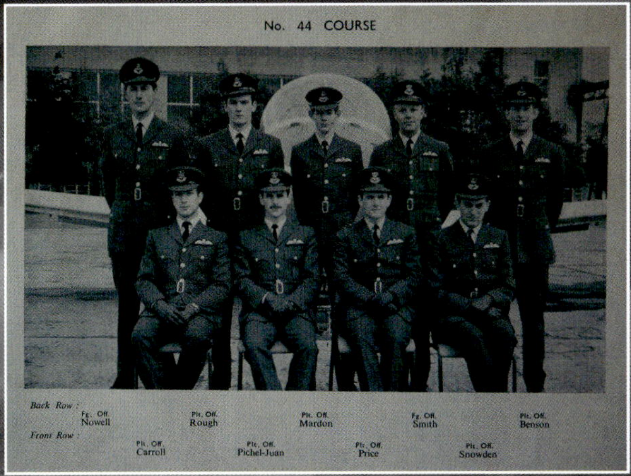

11.45 am

Titus Salt was born in Morley on 20th September 1803, attended Heath Grammar School then joined the family firm in 1824 and became the firm's wool buyer. Between 1801 and 1851 the population of Bradford grew from 13,000 to 104,000 but with over 200 factory chimneys churning out black, sulphurous smoke, Bradford gained the reputation of being the most polluted town in England. In 1848, Salt became Mayor of Bradford and in 1850, Salt built a new industrial community called Saltaire on the banks of the River Aire. His new mill was the largest and most modern in Europe. He also built 850 houses, with individual outside toilets, for his workers plus school, hospital, library and shops. Salt died on 29th December 1876, having given away over £500,000 to good causes. Newspapers noted 'Titus was the greatest captain

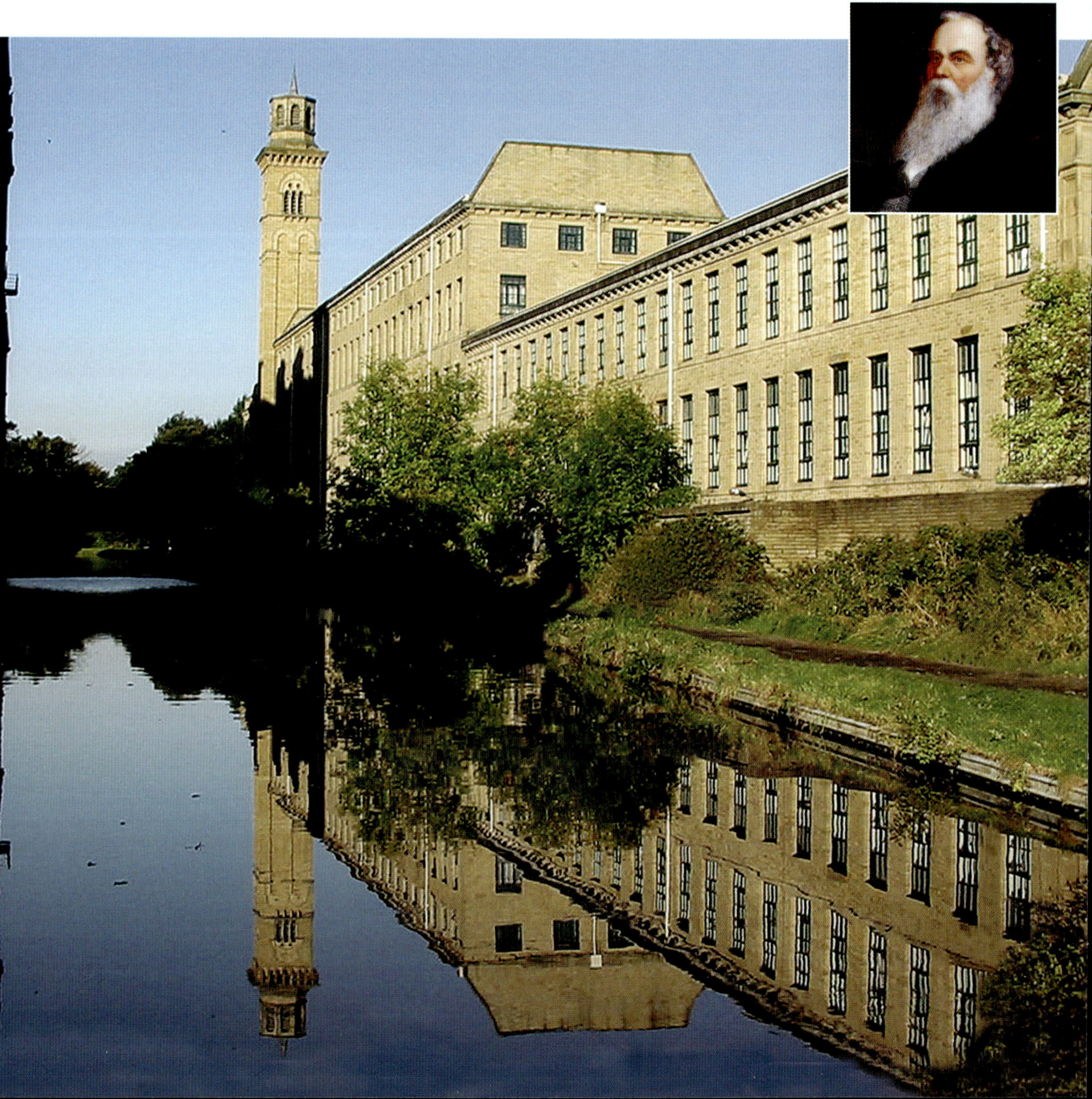

of industry in England and the best representative of the employer class in this part of the country if not the whole kingdom.' Only a few miles north of Bradford is Ilkley, the striking historic location not only of mysterious carvings on Ilkley Moor but also the setting of the Yorkshire National Anthem - 'On Ilkla Moor B'aht 'at', a song that has been sung by this author in far-away places such as the Australian Mess on the Cocos Islands, the Mormon Tabernacle in Salt Lake City and the US Navy Mess at Sangley Point in the Philippines. It may, at first, be somewhat surprising that a Yorkshire song should be included within a book whose primary purpose and theme is aviation. The answer lies in some of the additional lines that are inserted and sung in some versions. The additional lines such as some singers add the responses 'without no kegs on' (from the Goon Show) meaning 'no trousers on' after the fourth line of each verse, and 'where the sheep fly backwards' or 'where the ducks fly backwards', after the seventh. The Yorkshire dialect lyrics follow. For a translation, ask any Yorkshireman - such as Alan Titchmarsh, born in Ilkley, seen below left!

'Wheear 'ast tha bin sin' ah saw thee, ah saw thee?
On Ilkla Mooar baht 'at
Wheear 'ast tha bin sin' ah saw thee, ah saw thee?
Wheear 'ast tha bin sin' ah saw thee?
On Ilkla Mooar baht 'at
On Ilkla Mooar baht 'at
On Ilkla Mooar baht 'at'.

Tha's been a cooartin' Mary Jane
Tha's bahn' to catch thy deeath o` cowd
Then us'll ha' to bury thee
Then t'worms'll come an` eyt thee up
Then t'ducks'll come an` eyt up t'worms
Then us'll go an` eyt up t'ducks
Then us'll all ha' etten thee
That's wheear we get us ooan back

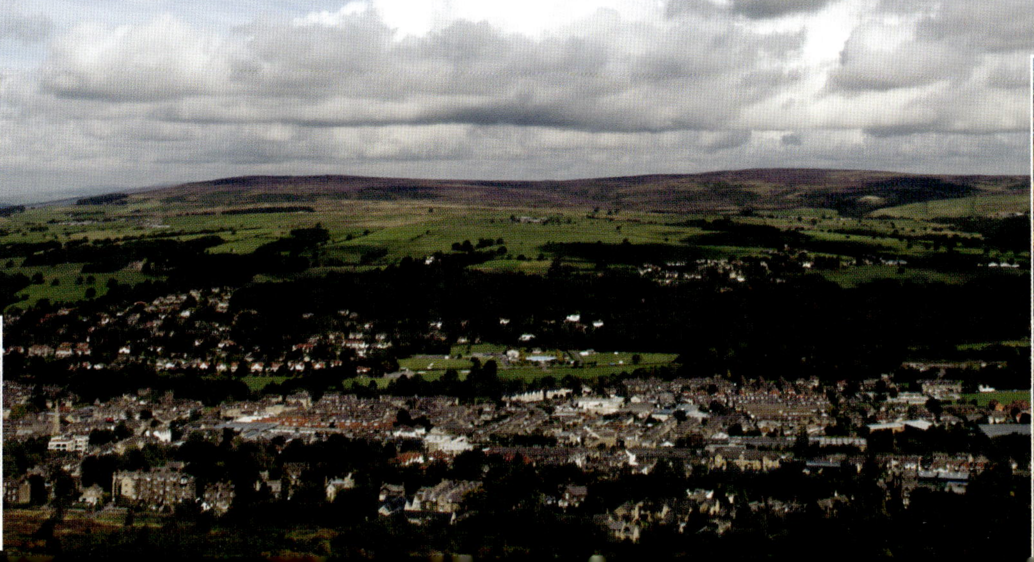

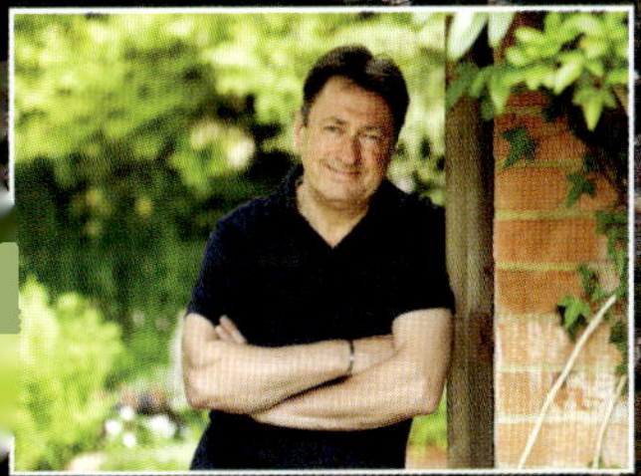

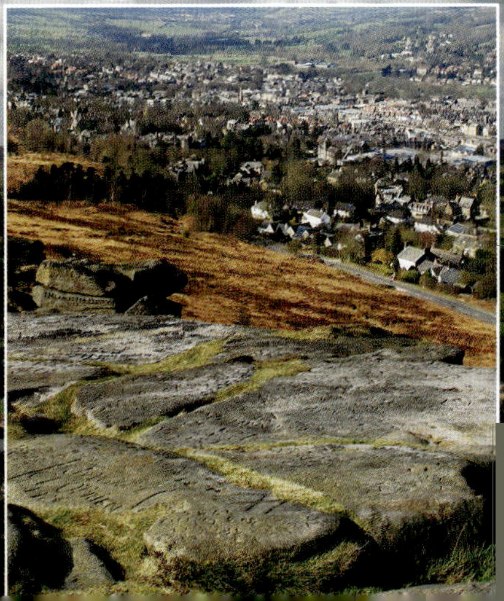

# Chapter 3

# Midday

## 12 pm

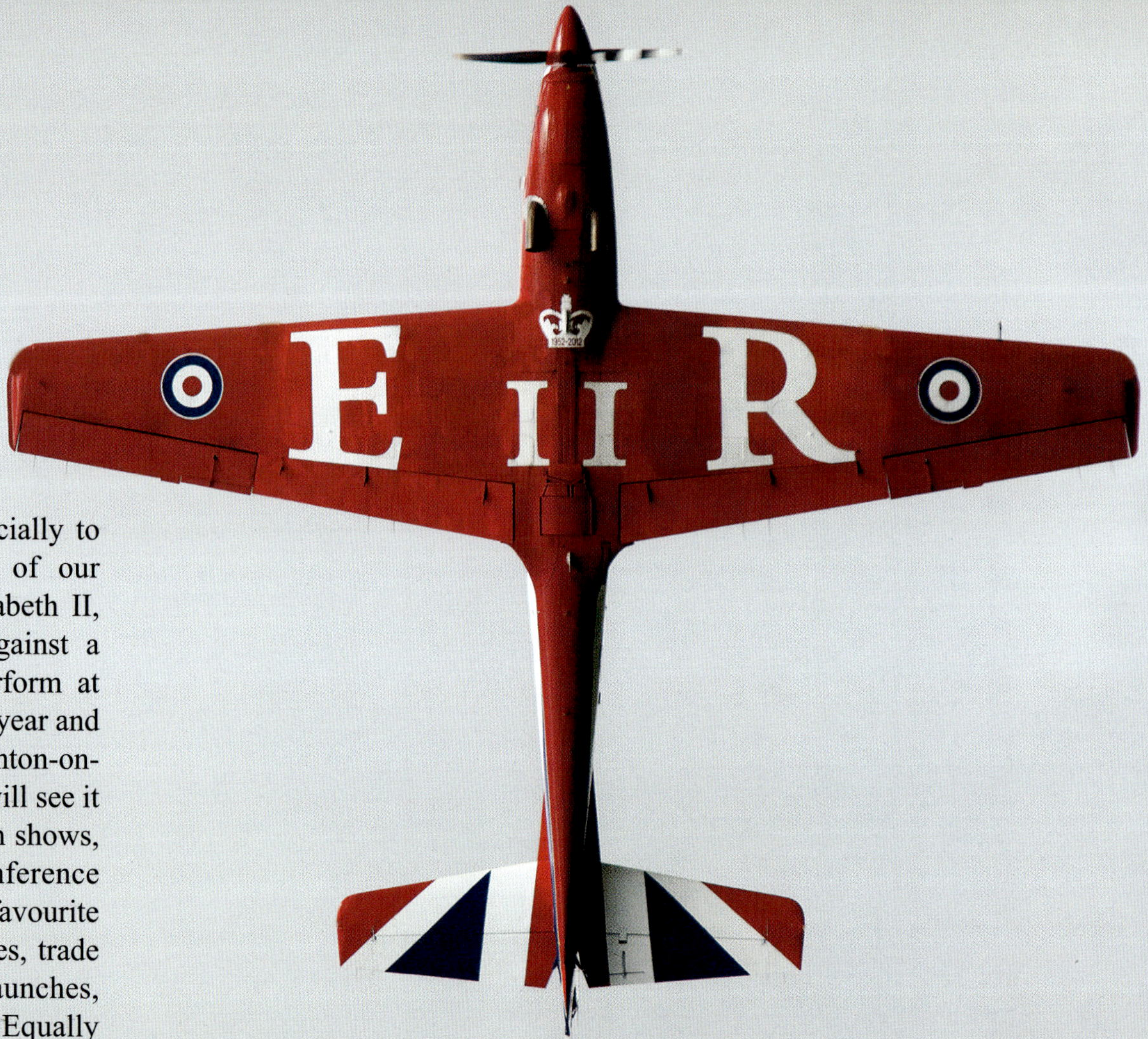


The 'EIIR' Tucano, painted especially to celebrate the Diamond Jubilee of our Queen, Her Majesty Queen Elizabeth II, zooms high across Harrogate against a grey sky. This Tucano will perform at many airshows during the Jubilee year and since it is based at nearby RAF Linton-on-Ouse, the residents of Harrogate will see it often. Right, the aerial photograph shows, Harrogate International Conference Centre (HIC), one of the UK's favourite venues for exhibitions, conferences, trade fairs, public shows, product launches, banquets and entertainments. Equally famous is the Majestic Hotel behind the HIC and beyond is another Victorian classic, the Cairn Hotel, where Paul the barman (now retired), was a Polish fighter pilot flying Hurricanes on 306 Squadron in WWII based at RAF Church Fenton.

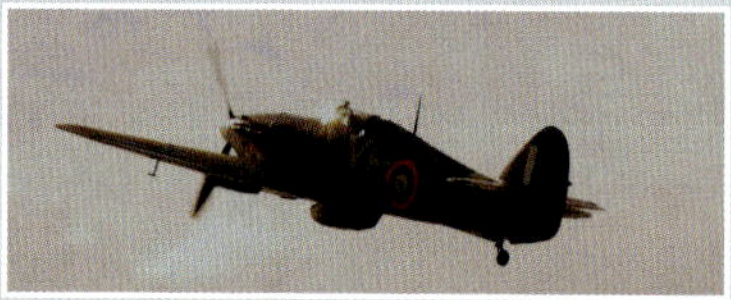

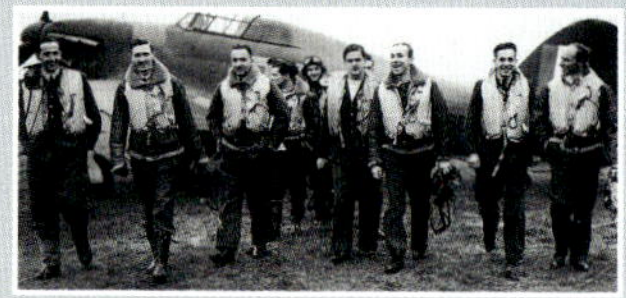

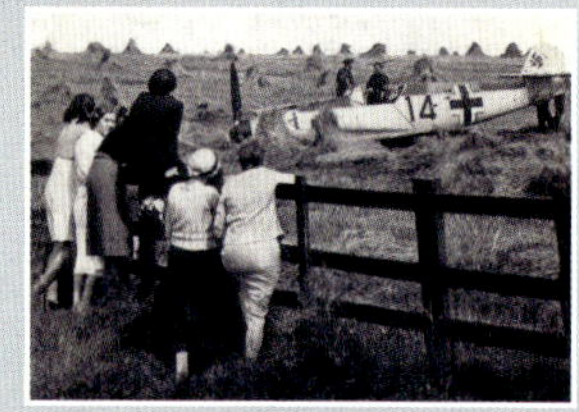

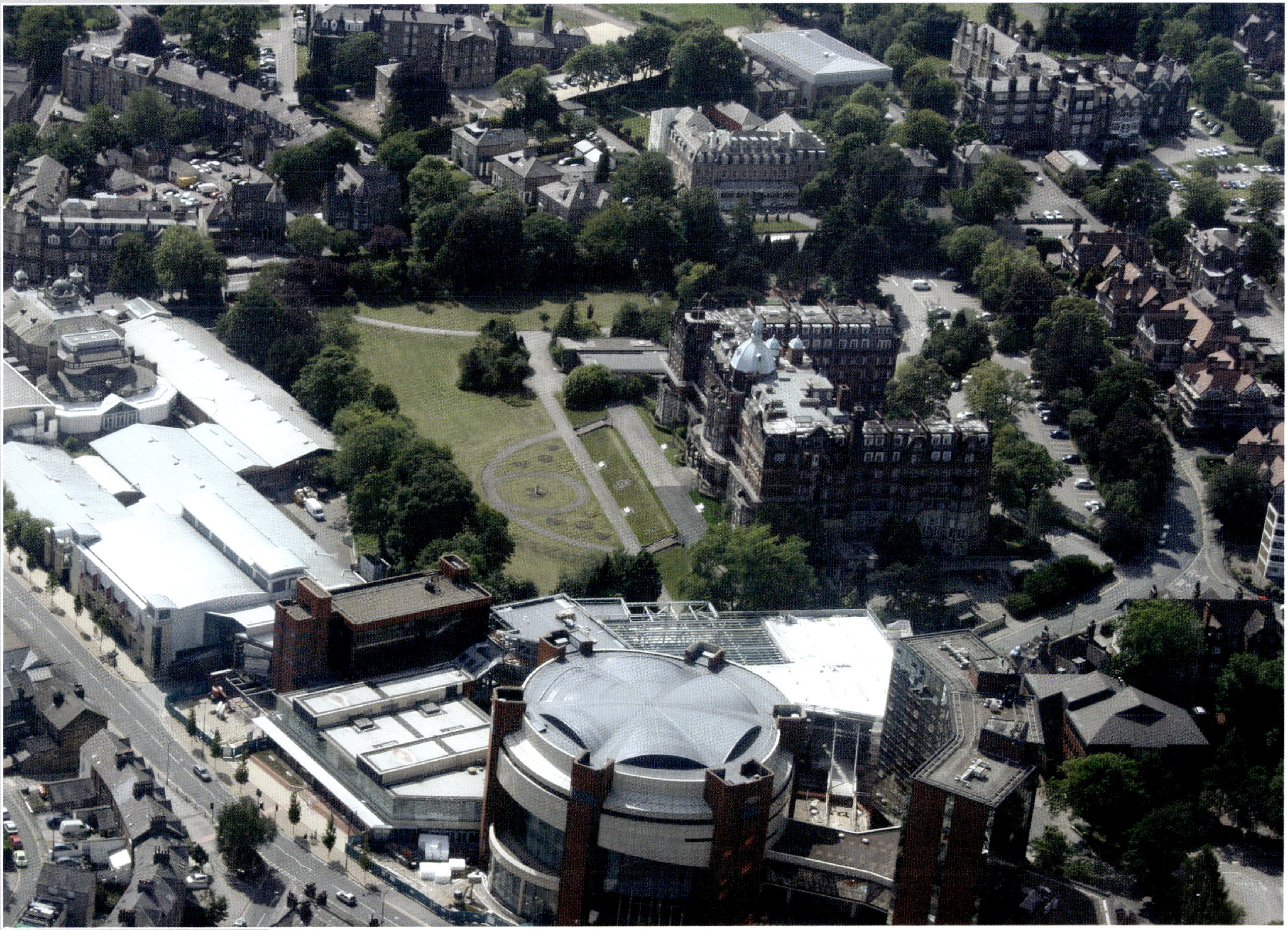

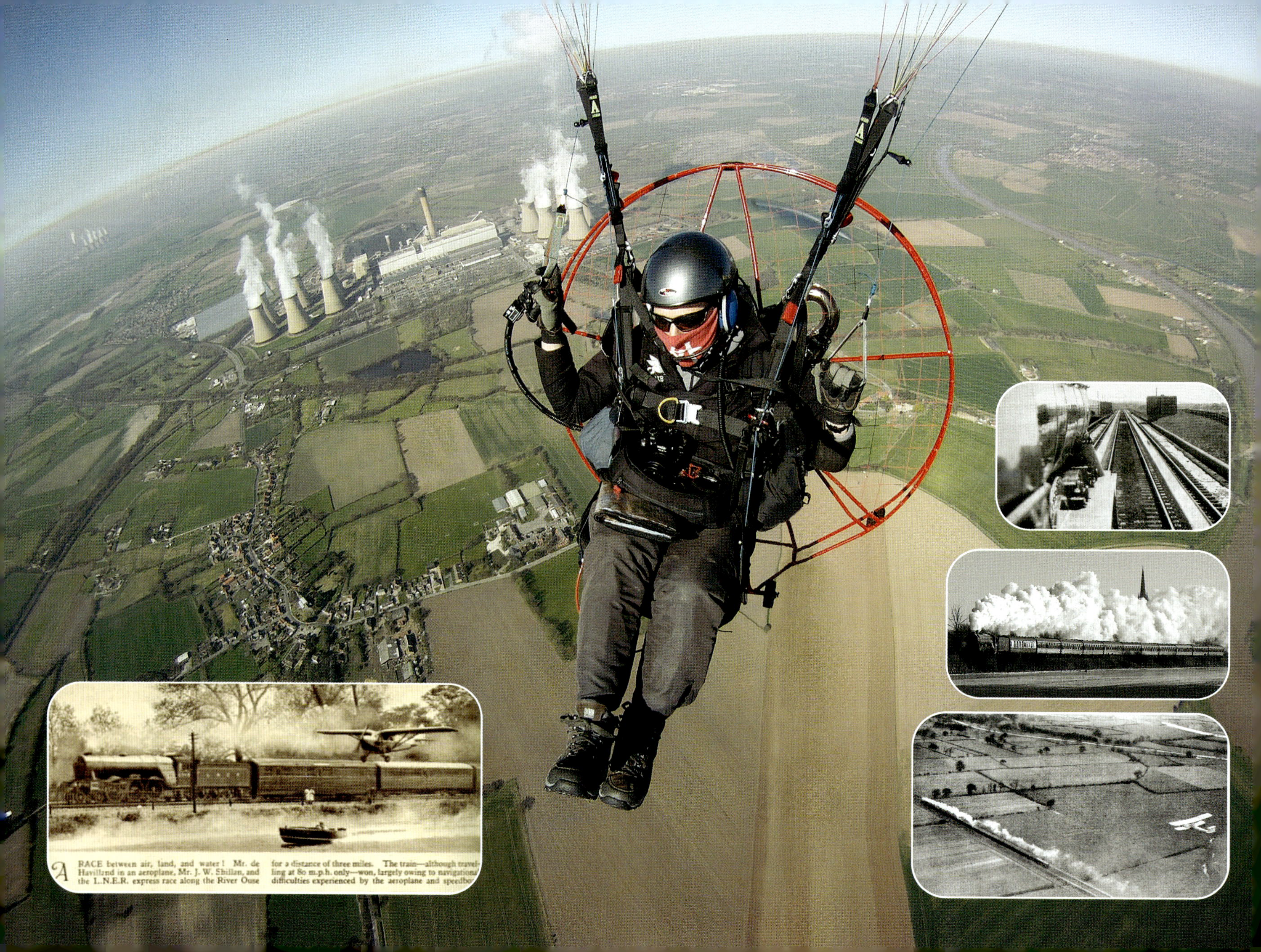

A RACE between air, land, and water! Mr. de Havilland in an aeroplane, Mr. J. W. Shillan, and the L.N.E.R. express race along the River Ouse for a distance of three miles. The train—although travelling at 80 m.p.h. only—won, largely owing to navigational difficulties experienced by the aeroplane and speedbo

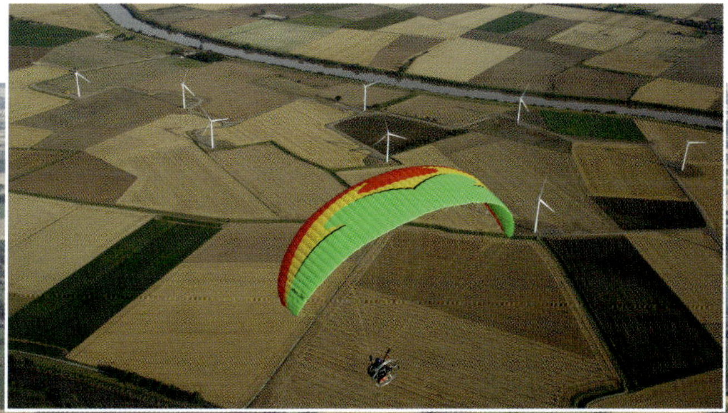

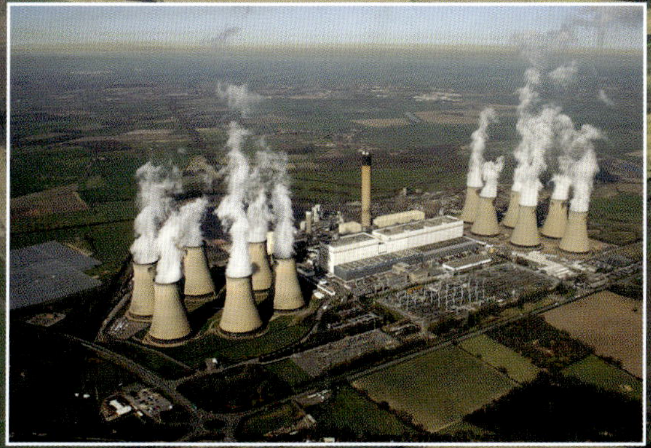

## 12.15 pm

Around midday on a warm day, the Drax power station is idling with plumes of steam rising gently from the cooling towers. A few miles west of here is the East Coast main line railway where in the 1930s, the steam-powered Flying Scotsman set new records for non-stop, scheduled services from London Kings Cross to Edingburgh beating the Imperial Airways Heracles aircraft of the day in a publicity race. The original newsreel filming by Pathe News is available to view on www.britishpathe.com/video/in-the-van (showing the Flying Scotsman v Heracles) and www.britishpathe.com/video/speed-1/query/aircraft+train+boat+race (showing the plane v boat v train race).

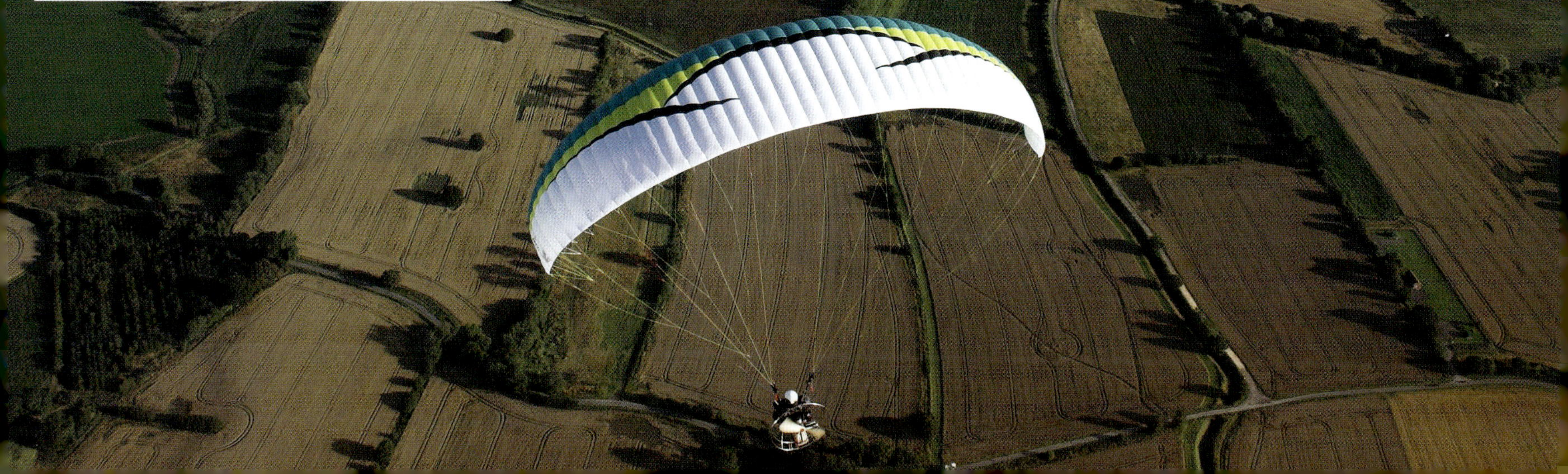

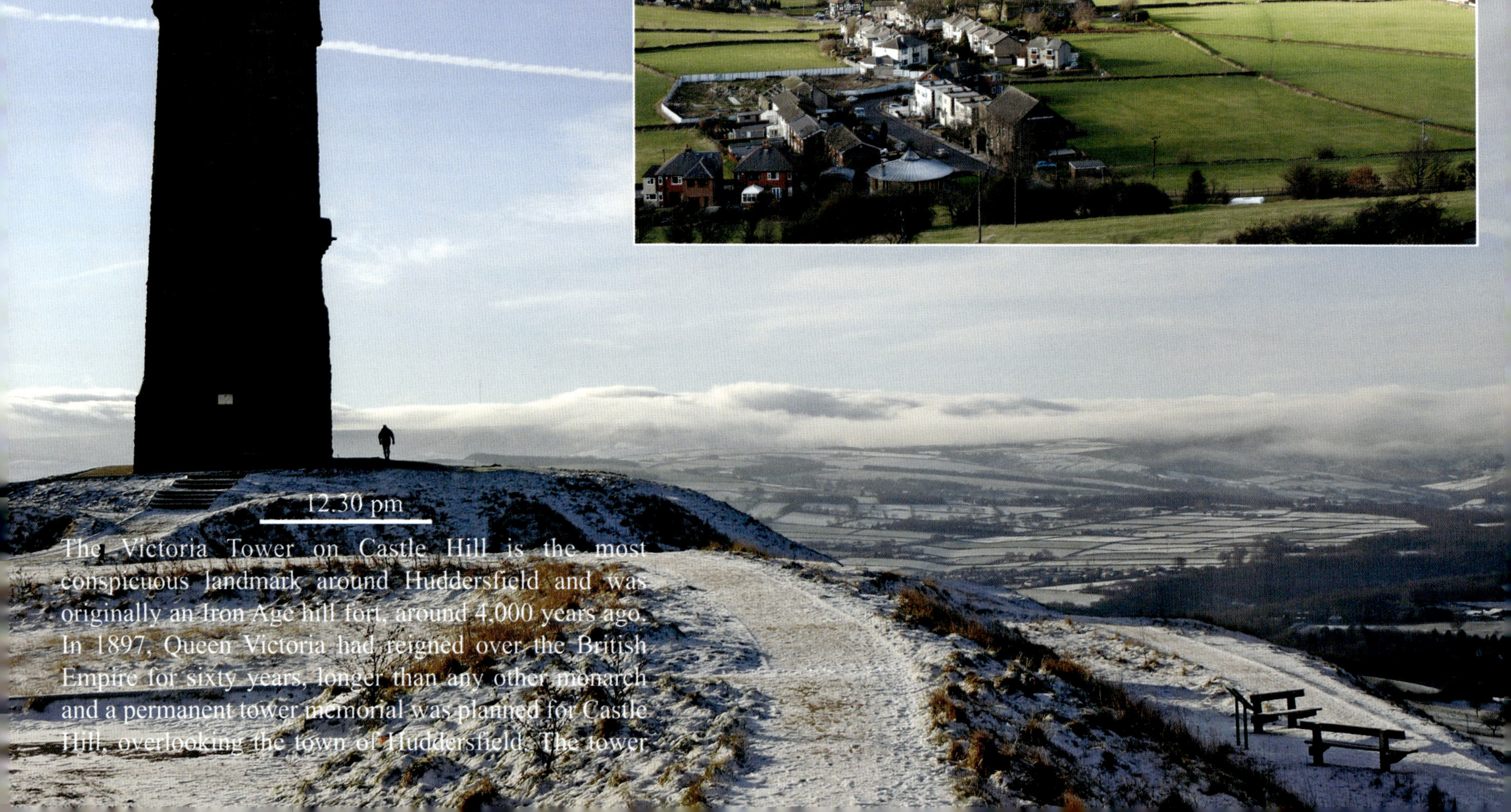

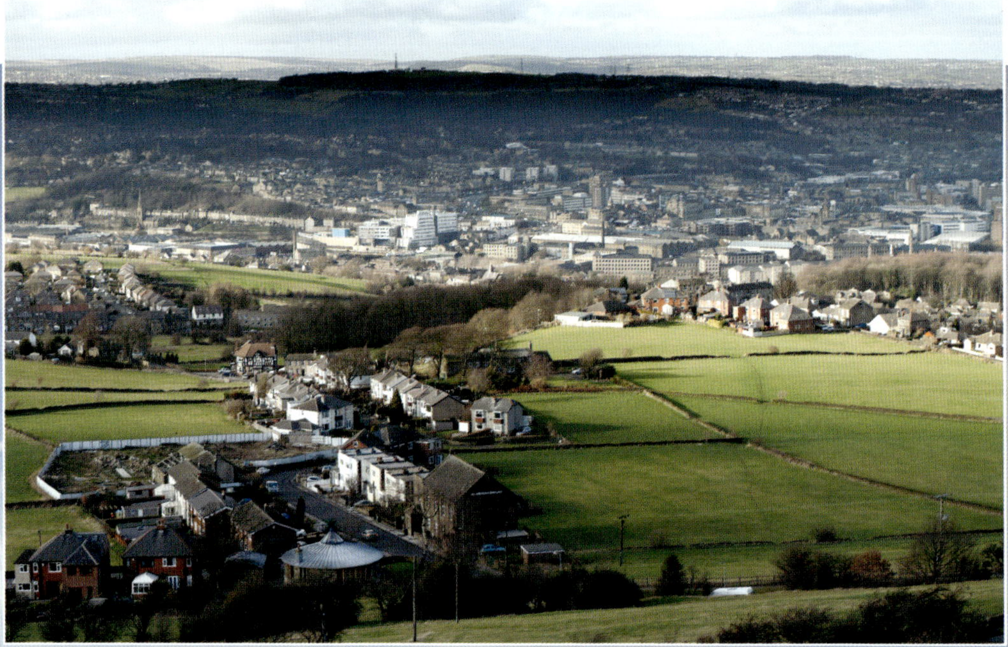

12.30 pm

The Victoria Tower on Castle Hill is the most conspicuous landmark around Huddersfield and was originally an Iron Age hill fort, around 4,000 years ago. In 1897, Queen Victoria had reigned over the British Empire for sixty years, longer than any other monarch and a permanent tower memorial was planned for Castle Hill, overlooking the town of Huddersfield. The tower

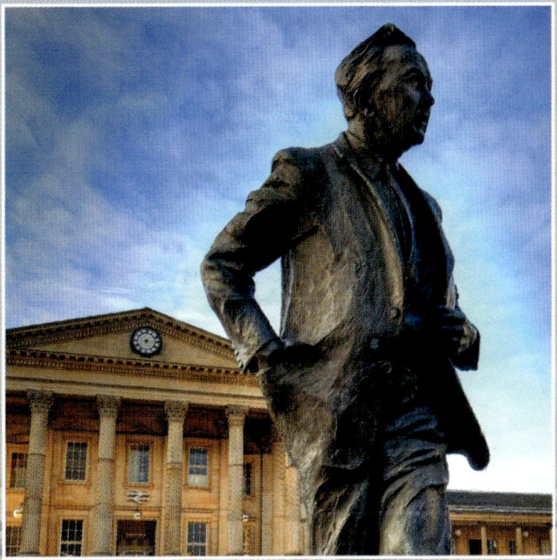

was opened by the Earl of Scarborough on 24th June 1899. Often referred to as the 'Jubilee Tower', the correct name is the Victoria Tower - designed by Isaac Jones, built by Ben Graham and Sons of Folly Hall using Crosland stone, costing £3,298, 106 feet (32.3m) high, making the top 1,000 feet (305m) above sea level. Down in the city, this statue of Harold Wilson, twice Prime Minister of the UK during the 1960s and 70s winning four general elections, was unveiled by Tony Blair, former Prime Minister, and stands outside Huddersfield railway station. Harold Wilson, who was born in Huddersfield on 11th March 1916, died on 24th May 1995. He became Baron Wilson of Rievaulx, KG, OBE, FRS, FSS, PC. Across the valley, the Emley Moor transmitter is the tallest free-standing structure in the UK at 328m (agl), 1084 ft. The elegant tapered concrete tower opened in 1971 and covers more than 4 million people in Doncaster, Leeds, Bradford, Sheffield, Elland and Huddersfield.

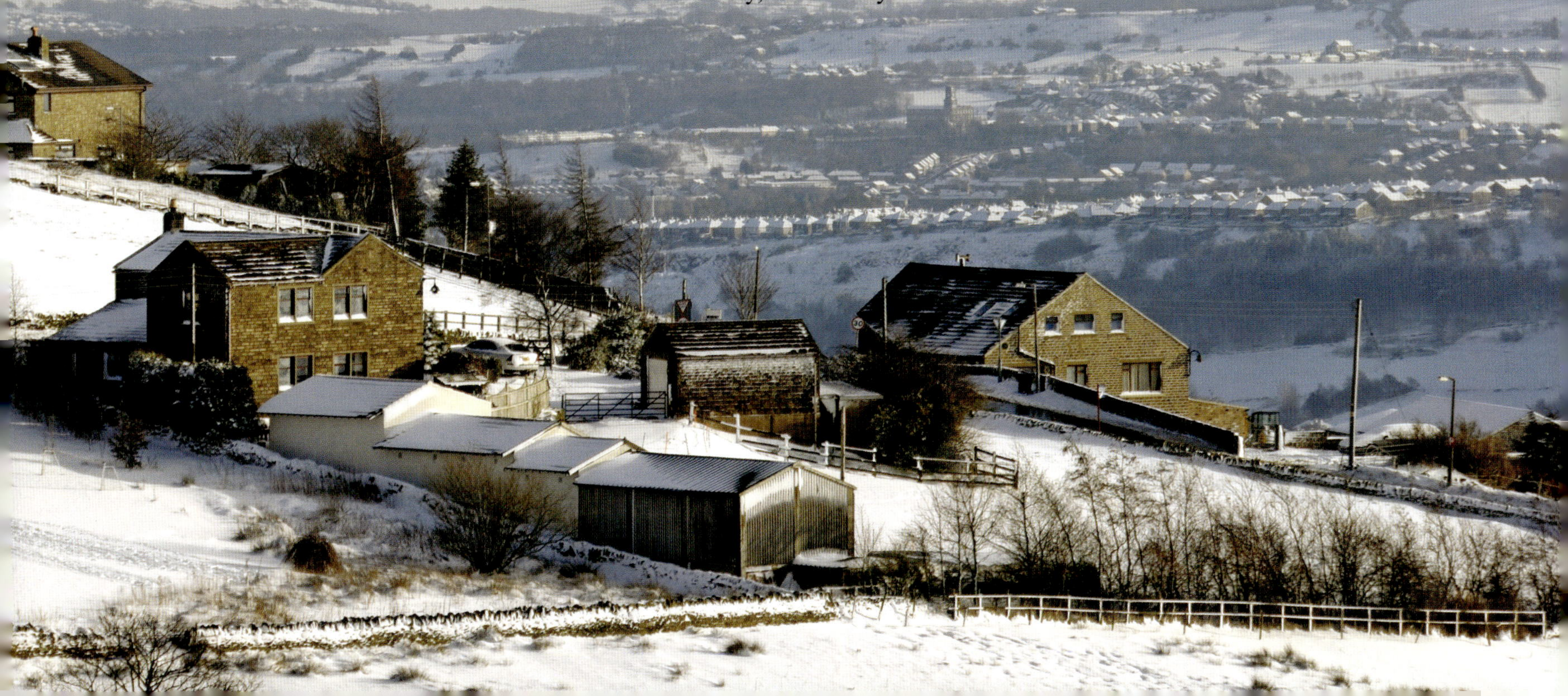

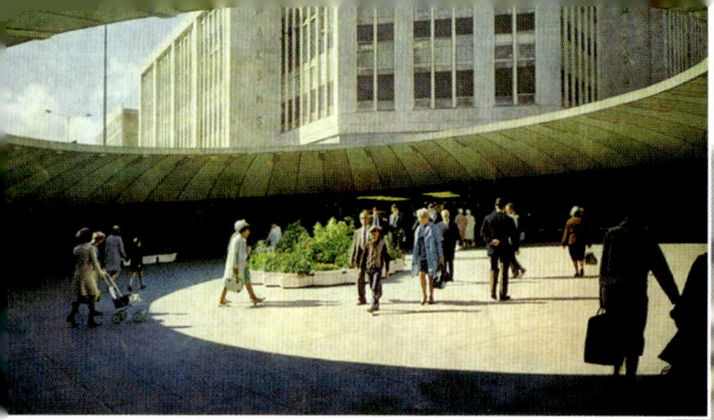

1.00 pm

Above, Castle Square in Sheffield photographed in the early 1970's and featured in the opening sequence of the film, '*The Full Monty*'. Sheffielders were not impressed and this subway was rapidly re-christened as '*The Hole in the Road*'. This was simply because there is no castle and it's not a square. This vernacular name was adopted in a semi-official way and, in 1981, *The Sheffield Scene* published a German guide for tourists which neatly described the Hole as the '*Fussgangerunterfuhrung*'. This

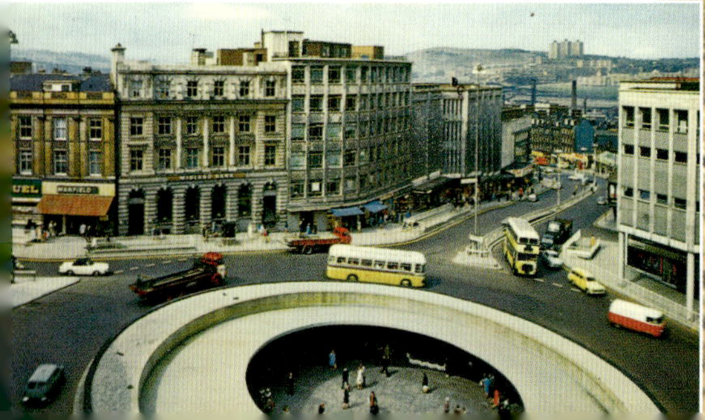

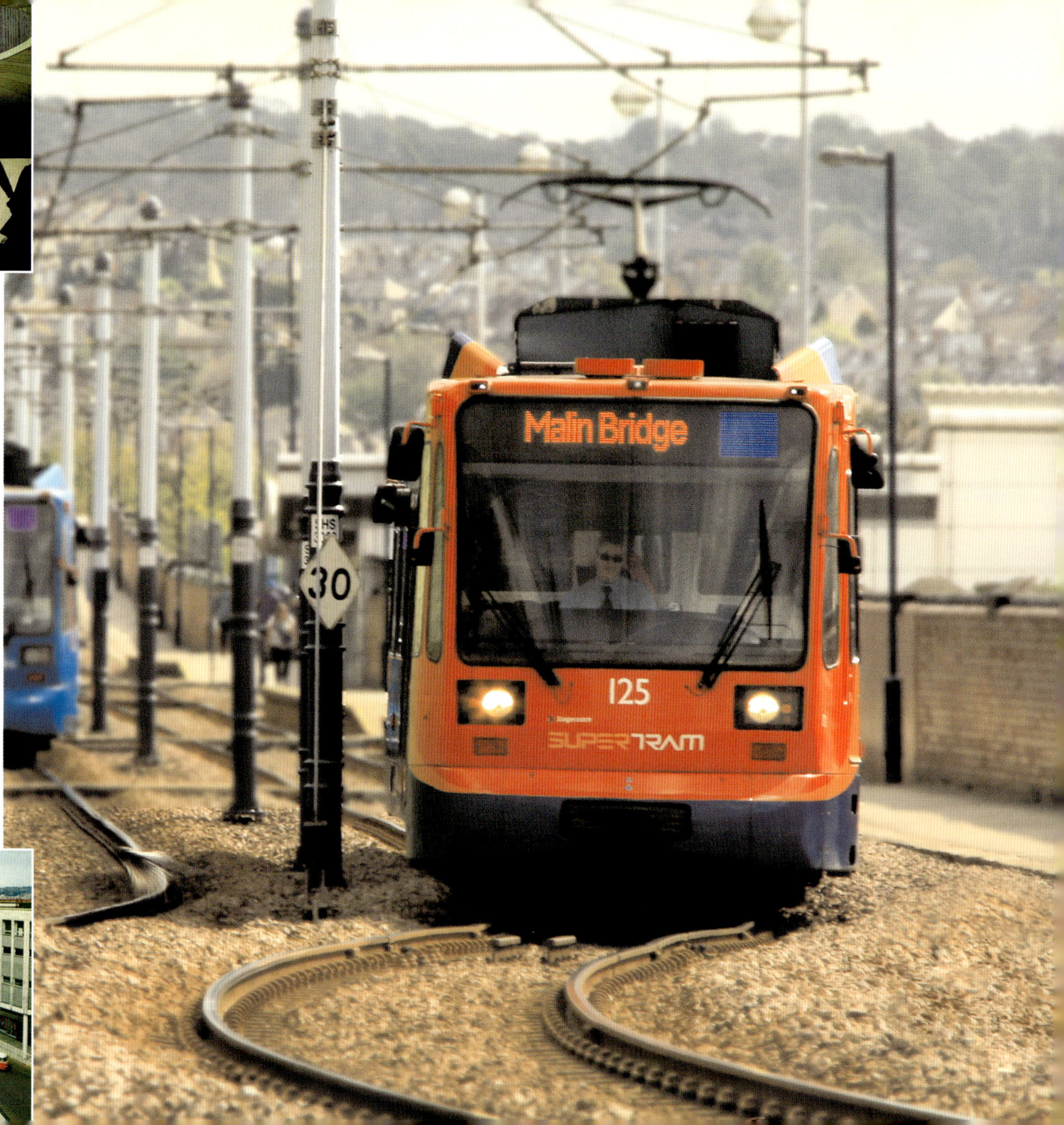

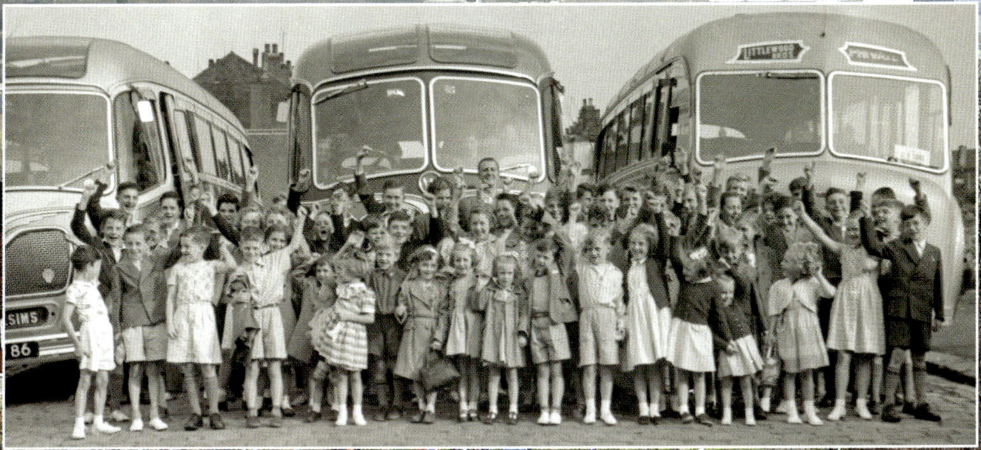

particular view of the city centre came to represent Sheffield's modernity and could be described as iconic. It's also a view that is remembered by many Sheffielders with affection. From the mid 1990's onward both trams and pedestrians have returned to this junction of High Street and Angel Street. The modern red tram was photographed in 2007. Below, 'Now & Then' - children's outings.

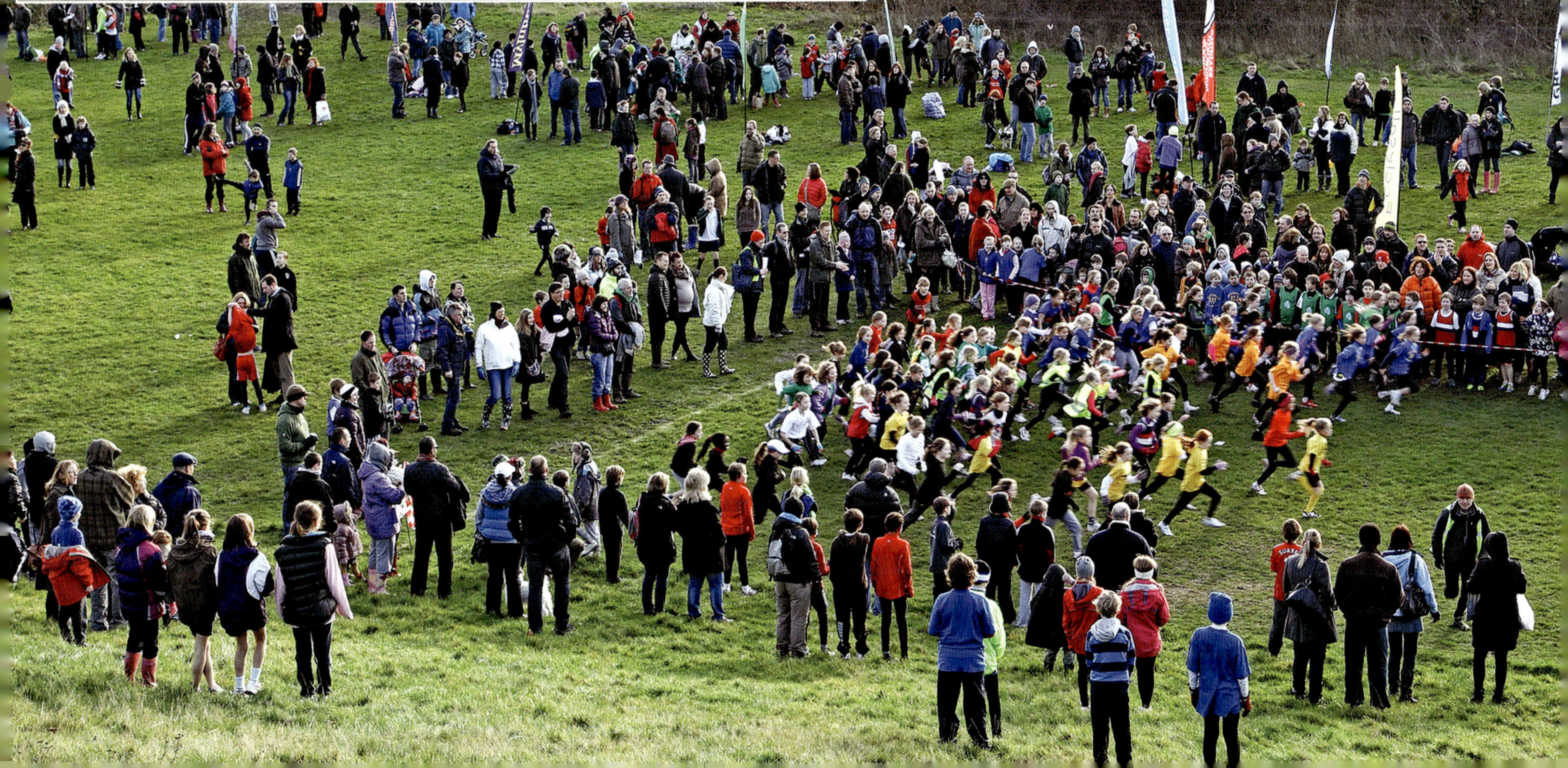

1.15 pm

Hill-climbing photographers receive a wave from a Typhoon of the RAF as it passes down the valley past Kettlewell on a training mission. It was here that the film 'Calendar Girls' was actually filmed. It was based on a true story of a group of ladies living in Rylstone, three miles north of Skipton. They produced a calendar of themselves to raise

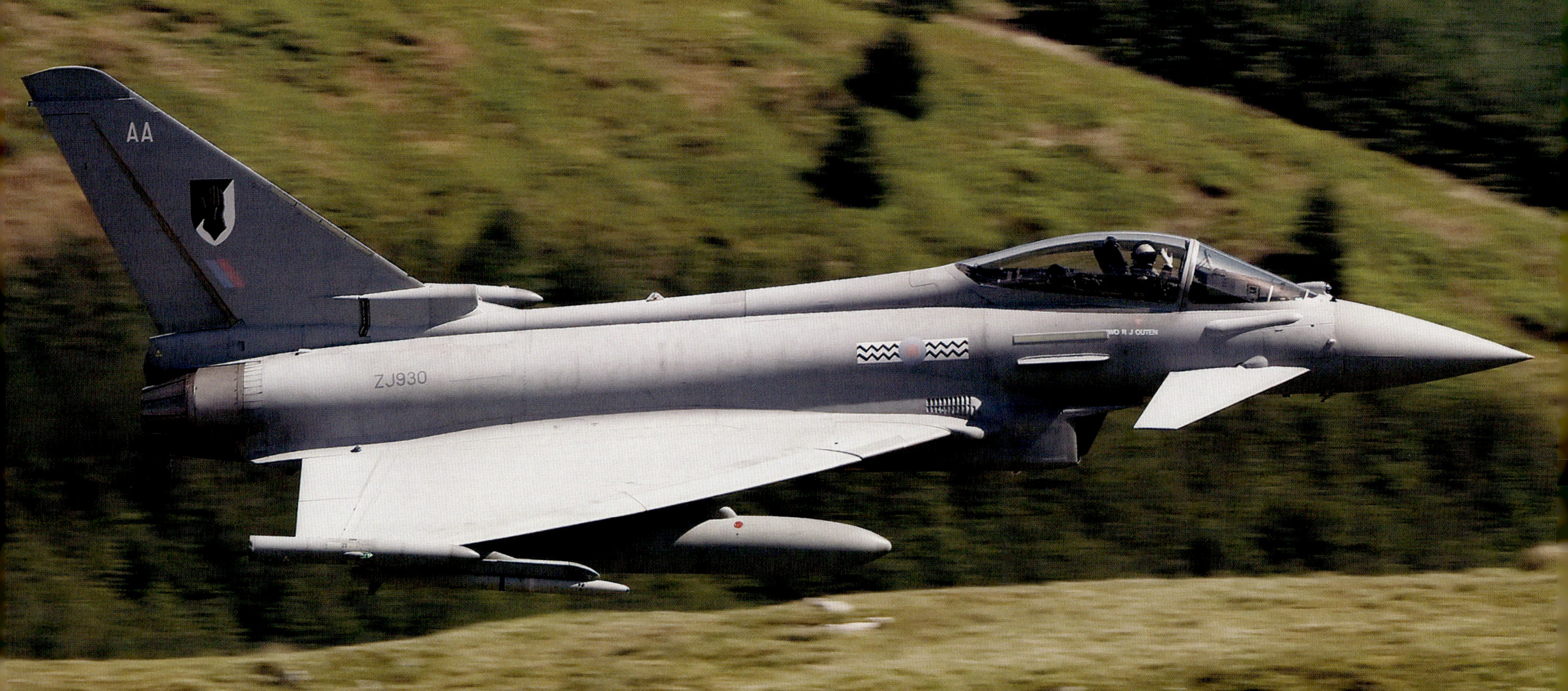


money for Leukaemia research under the auspices of the Women's Institute in April 1999. The story was produced as a film in 2003 by Touchstone Pictures with a budget of US$10 million and eventually grossed almost US$100,000,000! The fundraising phenomenon of the Calendar Girls was inspired by the death of John R. Baker, a Yorkshire Dales National Park Officer who died from lymphoma at the age of 54 in 1998. The calendar was released on 12th April 1999 and sold out in the first week. 10,000 additional copies were printed, all of which were sold within three weeks. Nine months after its launch, having sold 88,000 copies, it was adapted as an American version and the ladies were invited to appear on the Jay Leno Show. That year the calendar sold 202,000 copies. Proceeds from the calendar were used to fund lymphoma and leukaemia research in new laboratories at the University of Leeds where a plaque dedicated to John Baker reads, '*The work in this laboratory is dedicated to the memory of John Baker in recognition of the exceptional fundraising achievements of 'The Calendar Girls' of the Rylstone & District Women's Institute*'. The calendar continues to be produced every year to raise more funds for research.

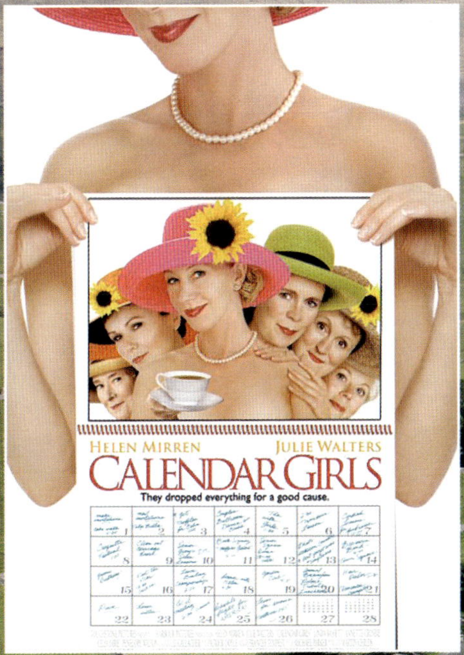


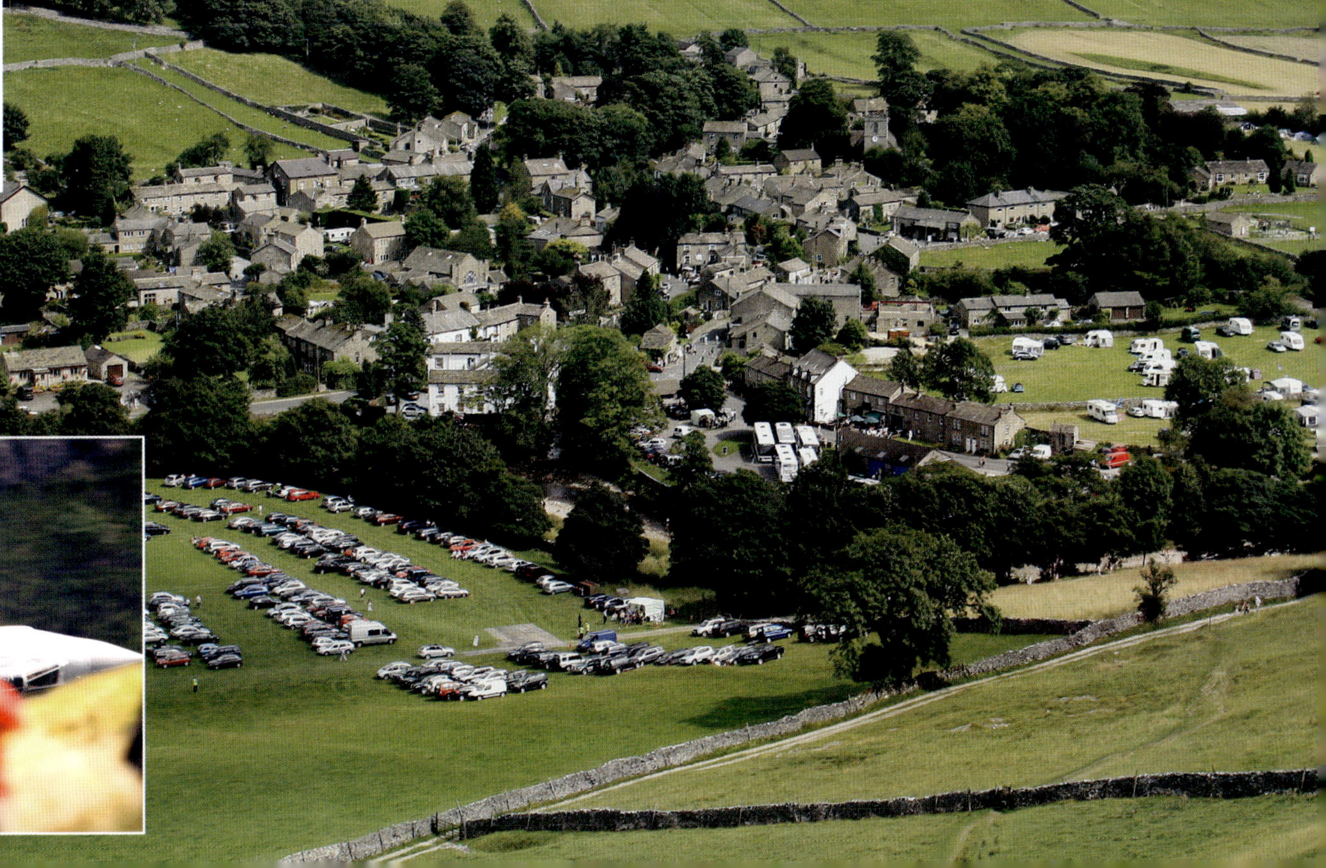

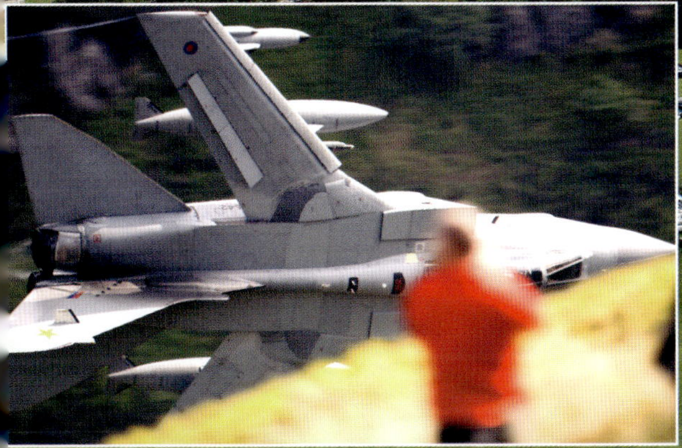

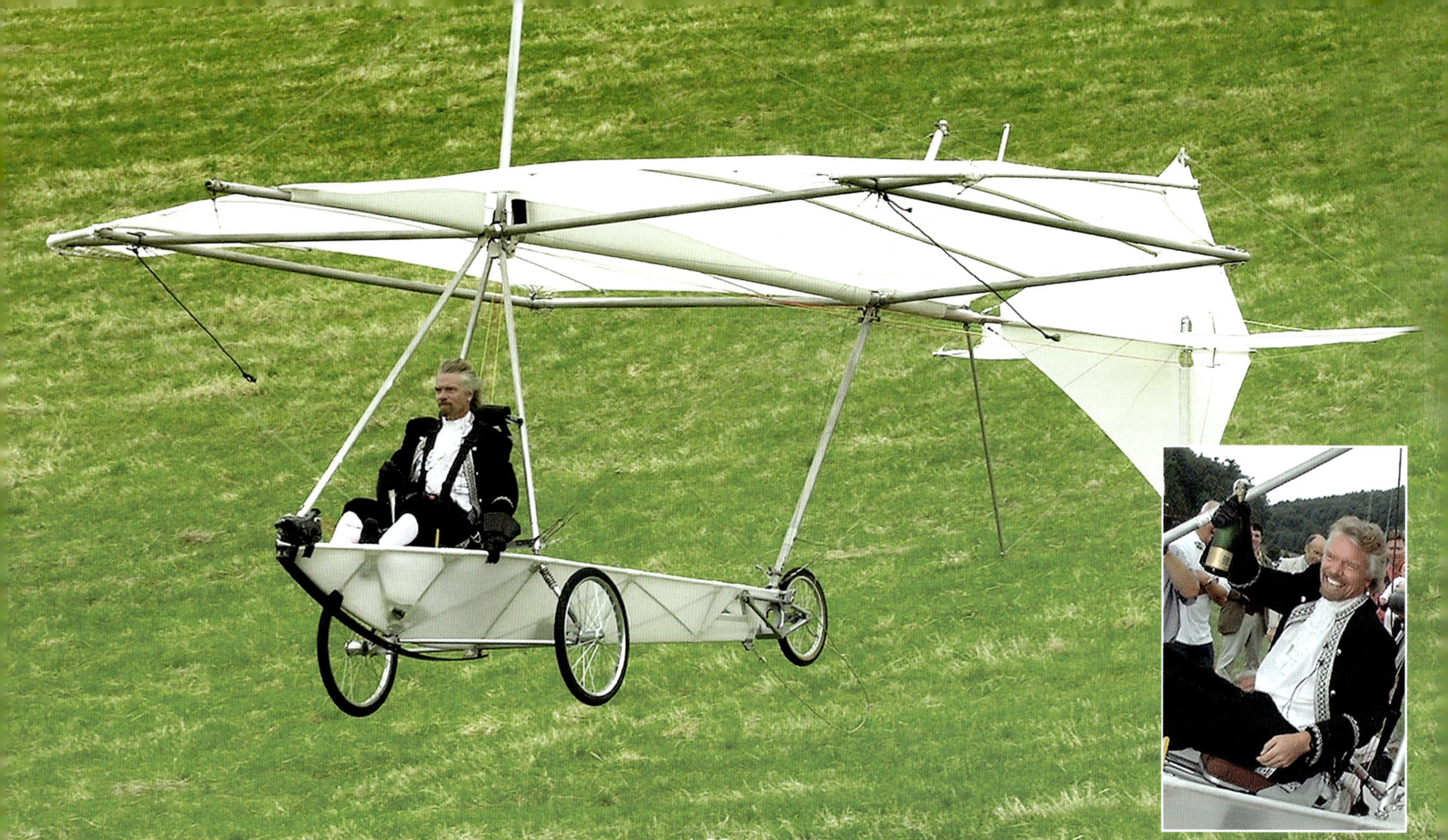

1.30 pm

Above, Sir Richard Branson commemorates in elegant style, the first ever flight by the coachman of Sir George Cayley in 1853. Sir George Cayley was born on 27th December 1773 and, as one of the most important men in the science of aeronautics, is now known as 'The Father of Aerodynamics'. As a 10 year-old boy, Cayley developed an understanding of the principles of flight by watching birds and making a careful study of how they fly. He observed that there were two modes of bird flight - to gain lift, birds flapped their wings or glided. At the age of 19, his father died and he became the 6th Baron of Brompton. He discovered and identified the four aerodynamic

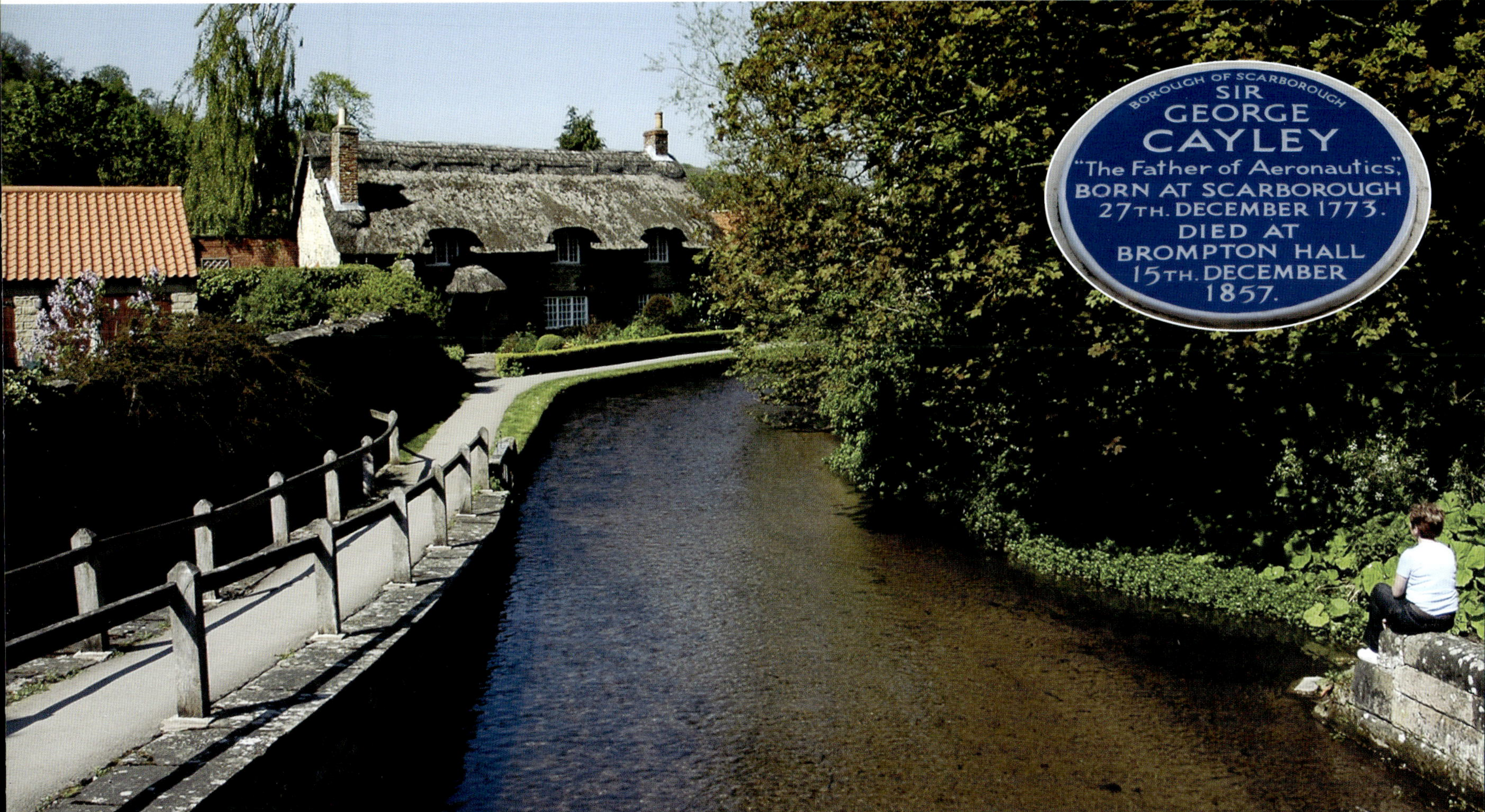


forces of flight: weight, lift, drag and thrust, which act on any flying machine. Modern aircraft design is based on those discoveries including cambered wings. He is credited with the first major breakthrough in heavier-than-air flight and he worked over half a century before the development of powered flight, being acknowledged by the Wright Brothers. Sir George died on 15th December 1857 at the age of 84. Today, his workshop, built in Greek temple style with classical references, in the grounds of Brompton Hall School in Brompton-by-Sawdon, near Scarborough has been reopened by a group of enthusiasts - a workshop where Sir George followed the dream of making a man fly 60 years before the Wright brothers were even heard of.

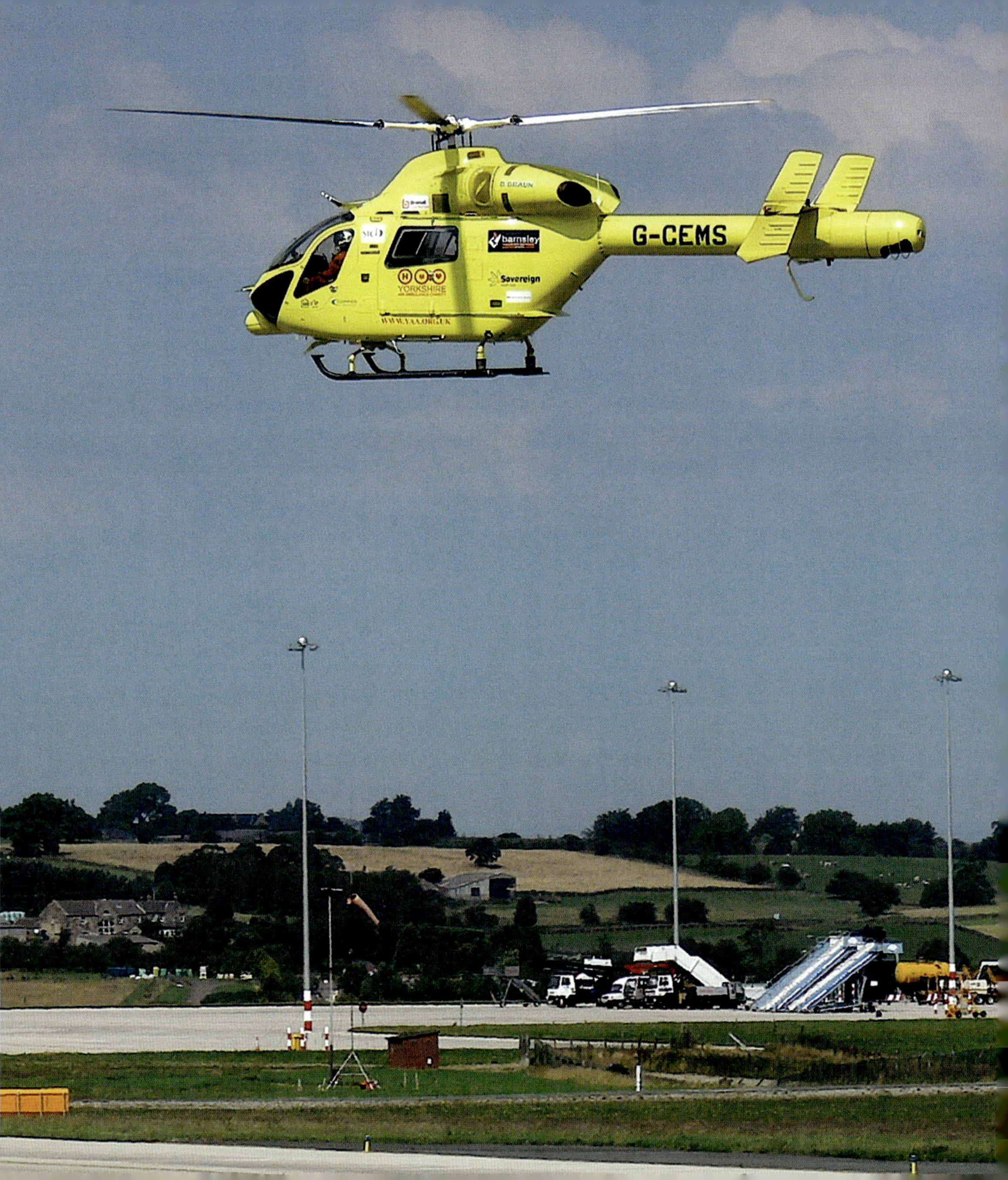


2.0 pm

At the end of the second mission of the day, the Yorkshire Air Ambulance, a MD902 NOTAR, hovers above Leeds-Bradford International Airport, waiting for the Jet2 Boeing 737 to get airborne. When the Air Ambulance is on a rescue mission, all other air traffic gives way - including Royal Flights! The two YAA helicopters cover 5 million people across Yorkshire. Opposite is the blue plaque to Robert Blackburn who built biplanes at the Olympia Works at Roundhay - a site now occupied by Tesco where literally hundreds of people pass by this blue plaque every day. After WWI, Blackburn Blackburn started the first

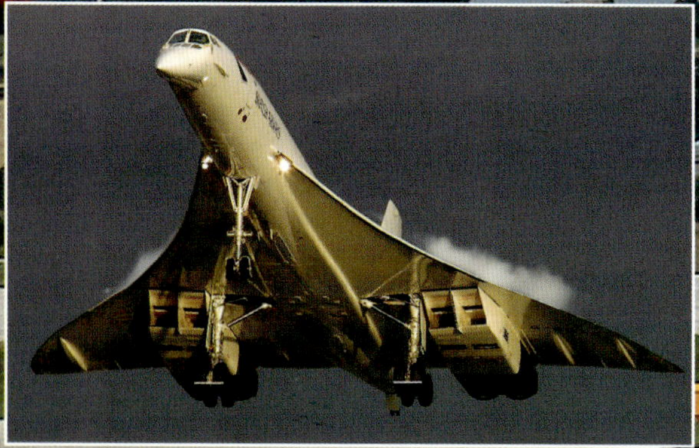

civilian passenger flights from Roundhay Park to London, the forerunner of services from Leeds Bradford International Airport, (LBA). During WWII, the AVRO Aircraft Company built 250 Blenheims, 4,500 Ansons, 695 Lancasters, 45 Yorks and 25 Lincoln bombers here. In 1986, 60,000 people watched the first Concorde arrive at LBA. Today, Jet 2 fly from LBA to many destinations in Europe and also to New York.

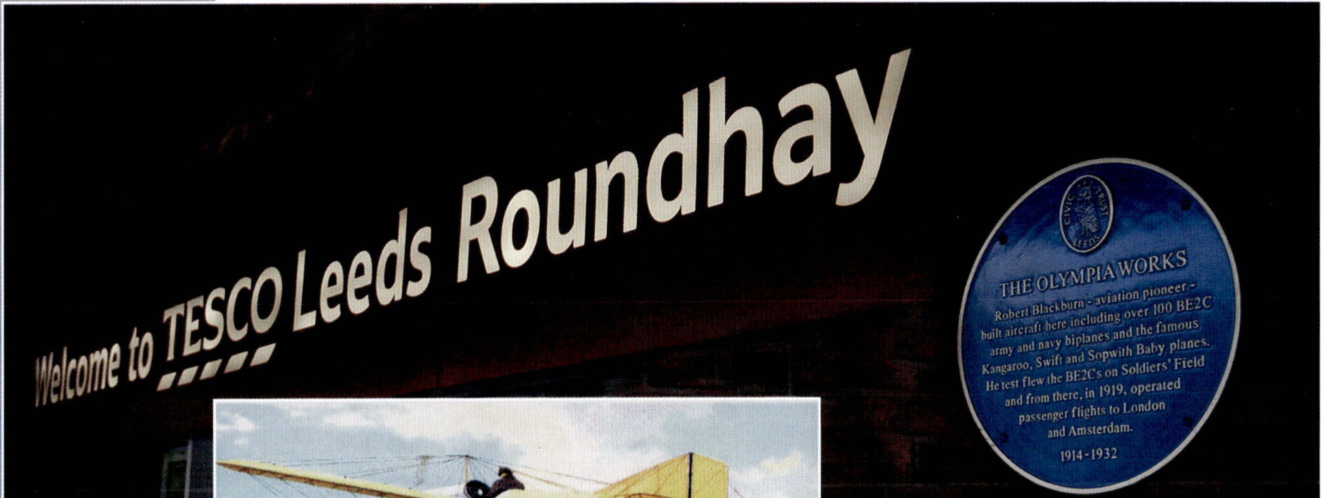


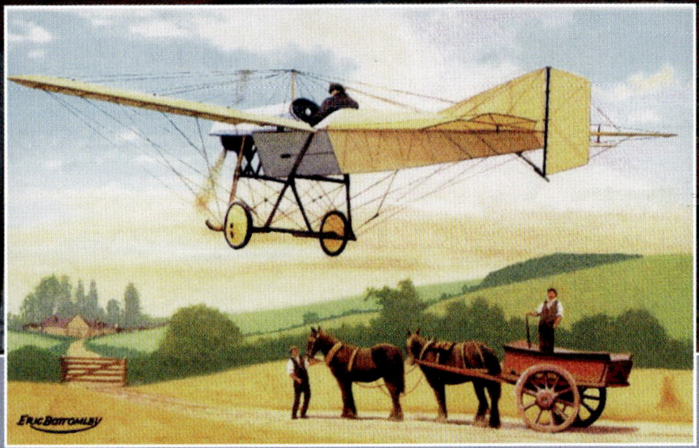


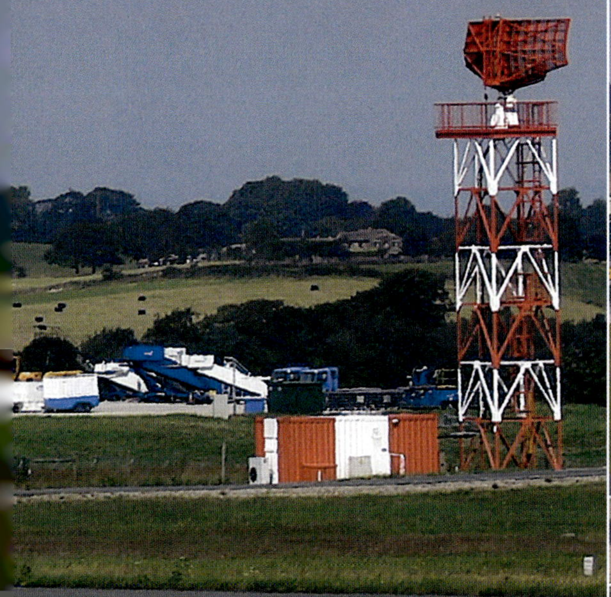

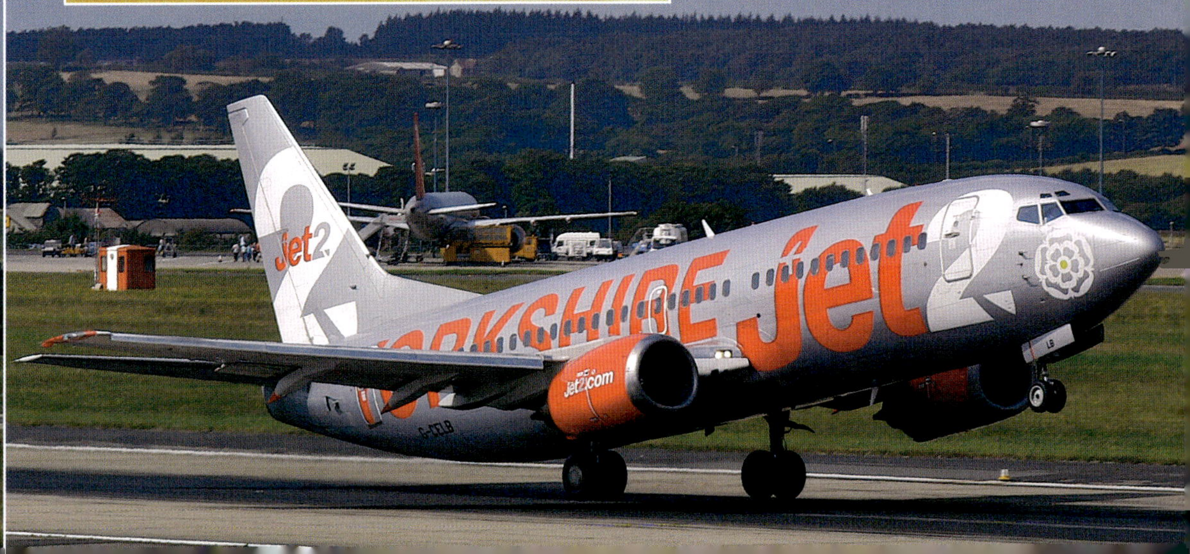

2.30 pm

The Roman Emperor Constantine looks out with imperious grace across the lawns of York Minster. While he was Caesar, the Roman Empire was ruled from Eboracum (York). After the Romans left, the Anglo-Saxon King Edwin of Northumbria made Eferwic (York) his capital. With the Vikings, York was re-named Jorvik. When King William the Conqueror took over, he first burnt the city to the ground, then re-built it with the longest city walls in England and began York Minster. During WWII, the Canadian aircrew of 6 Group had their unofficial HQ at Betty's Bar in the centre of York where the mirrors scratched by a diamond ring can still be seen downstairs.

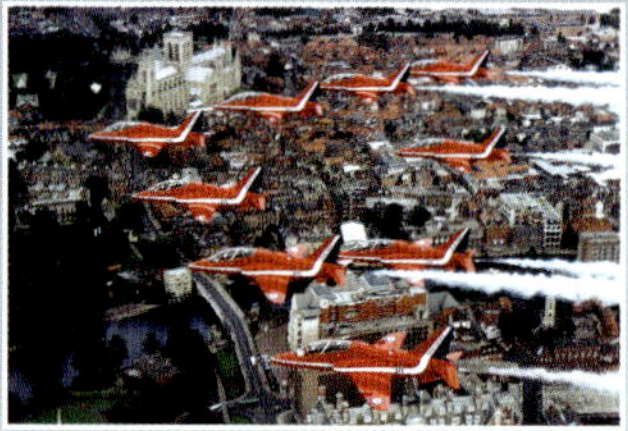

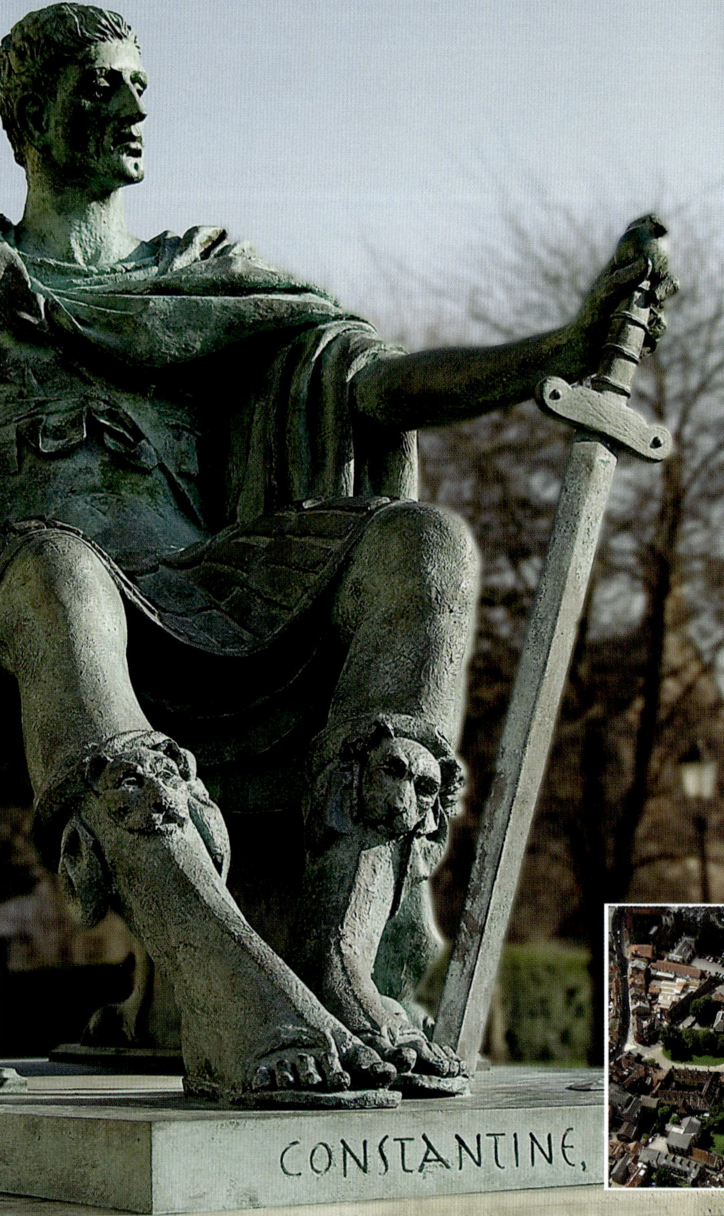


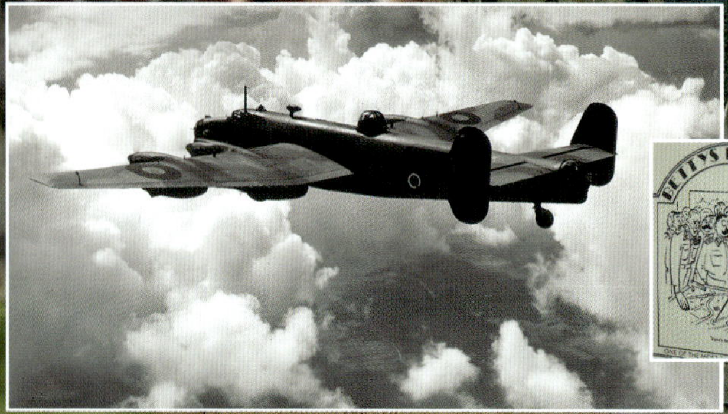

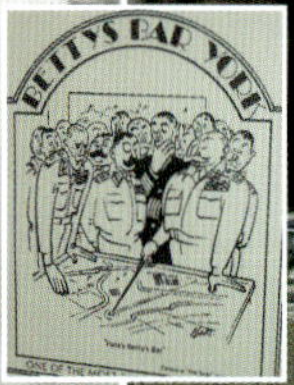

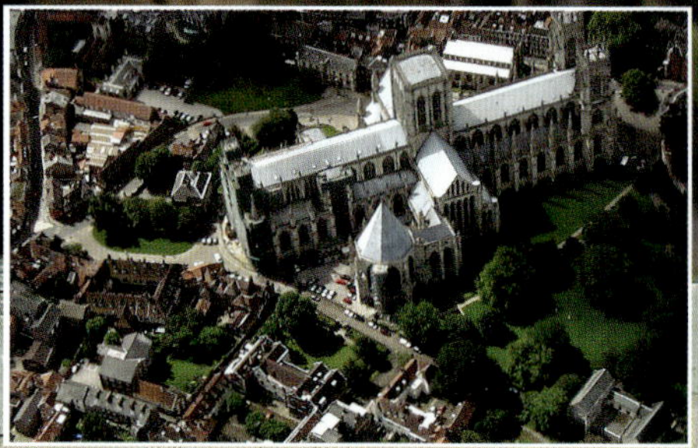

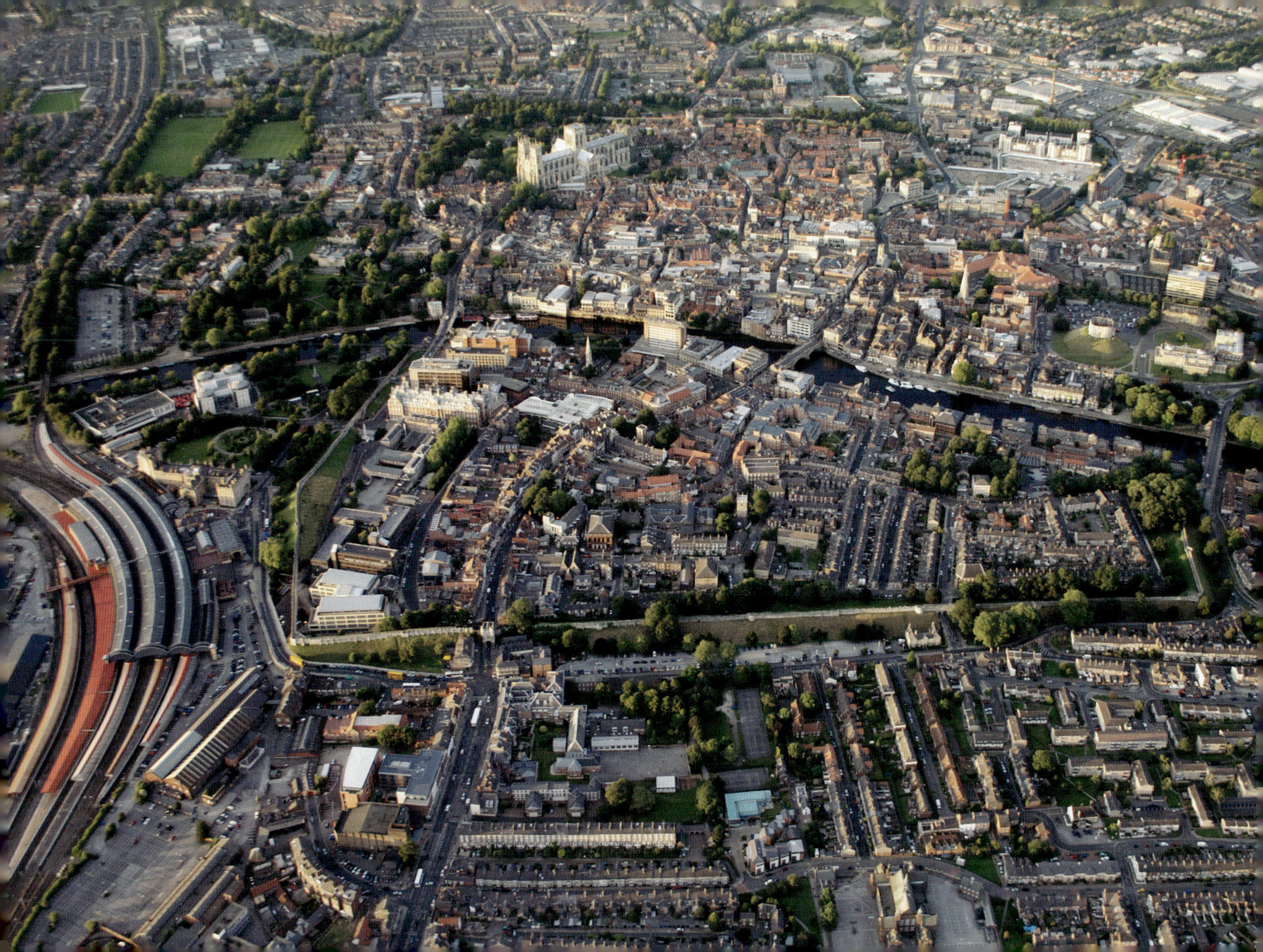

# Chapter 4

## Afternoon

## 3 pm

Beyond the gaze of the sophisticated statue of Orpheus at Harewood House is the tiny, now world famous, hamlet of Emmerdale where the Woolpack is

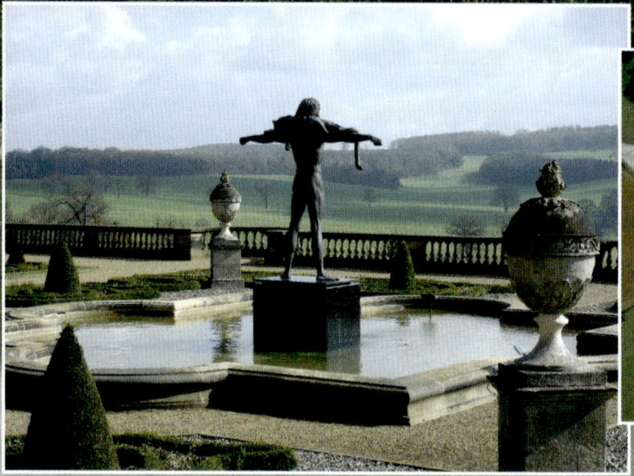

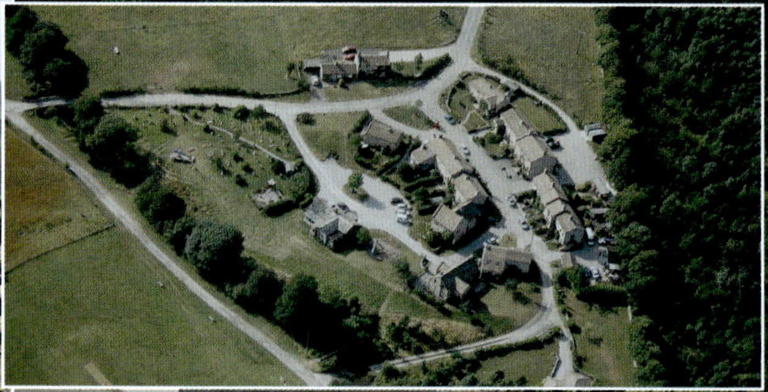

deserted and the village is empty. The reason becomes obvious across at the farm where, between the general debris and the pig sty, the funeral of Alice Dingle is taking place, one of the most moving episodes in this soap opera which has been running since 1972. On 30th December 1993 Emmerdale attracted its highest ever audience of 16 million when an aircraft crashed into Emmerdale killing Mark Hughes, Elizabeth Pollard, Archie Brooks and Leonard Kempinski. Chris Tate also lost his legs.

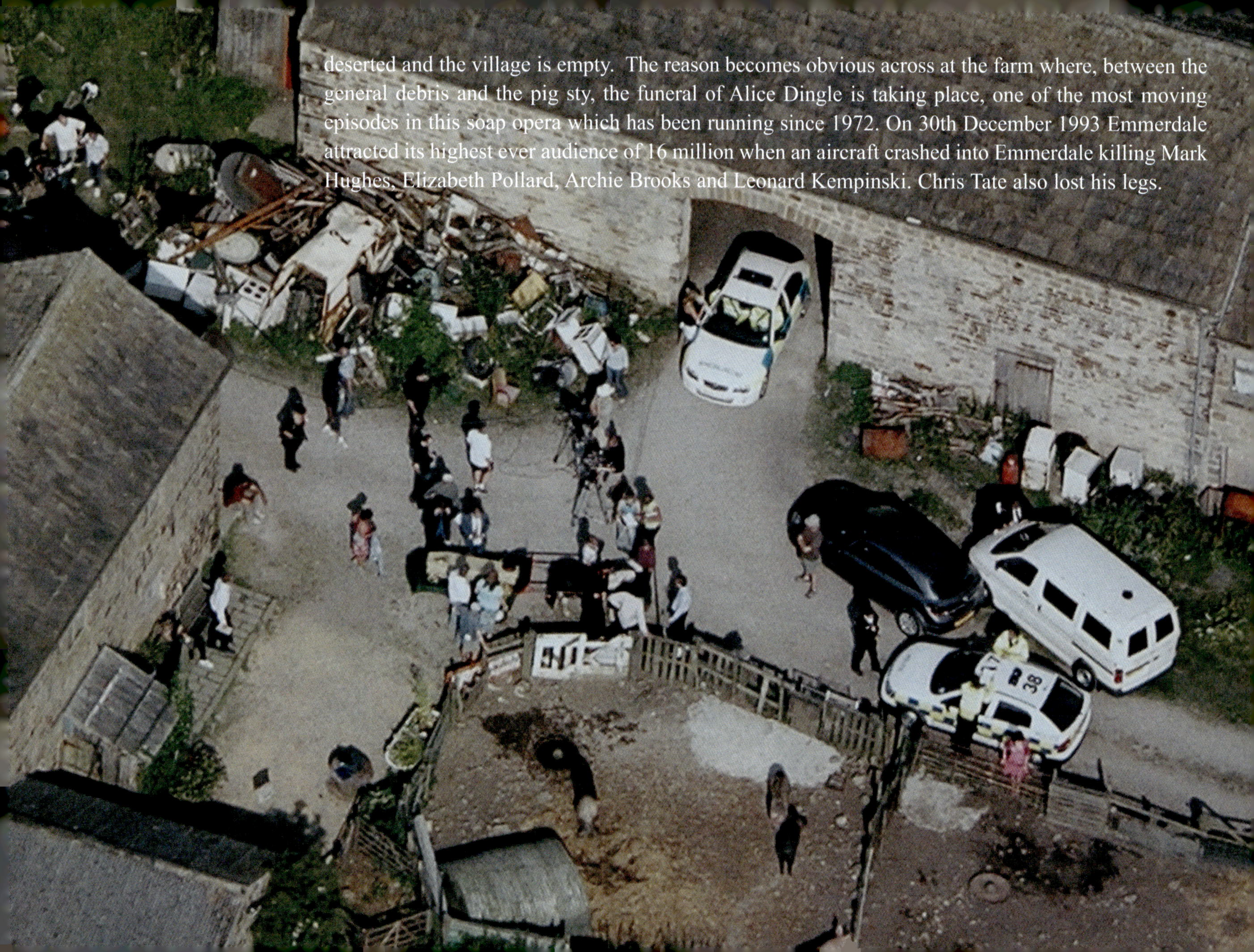

3.30 pm

Variations of the British weather. Under the dark skies, the trio of new Great Northern AS350 Air Ambulances lift and depart on a press demonstration. Should it be called, the new AS350 can carry a fallen rider at speeds of 150 mph, to be at the hospital within ten minutes flying time, comfortably within the 'Golden' hour. Above the southern edge of the Vale of York, a well dressed pilot of a Jet Provost performs a wing-over above the neat

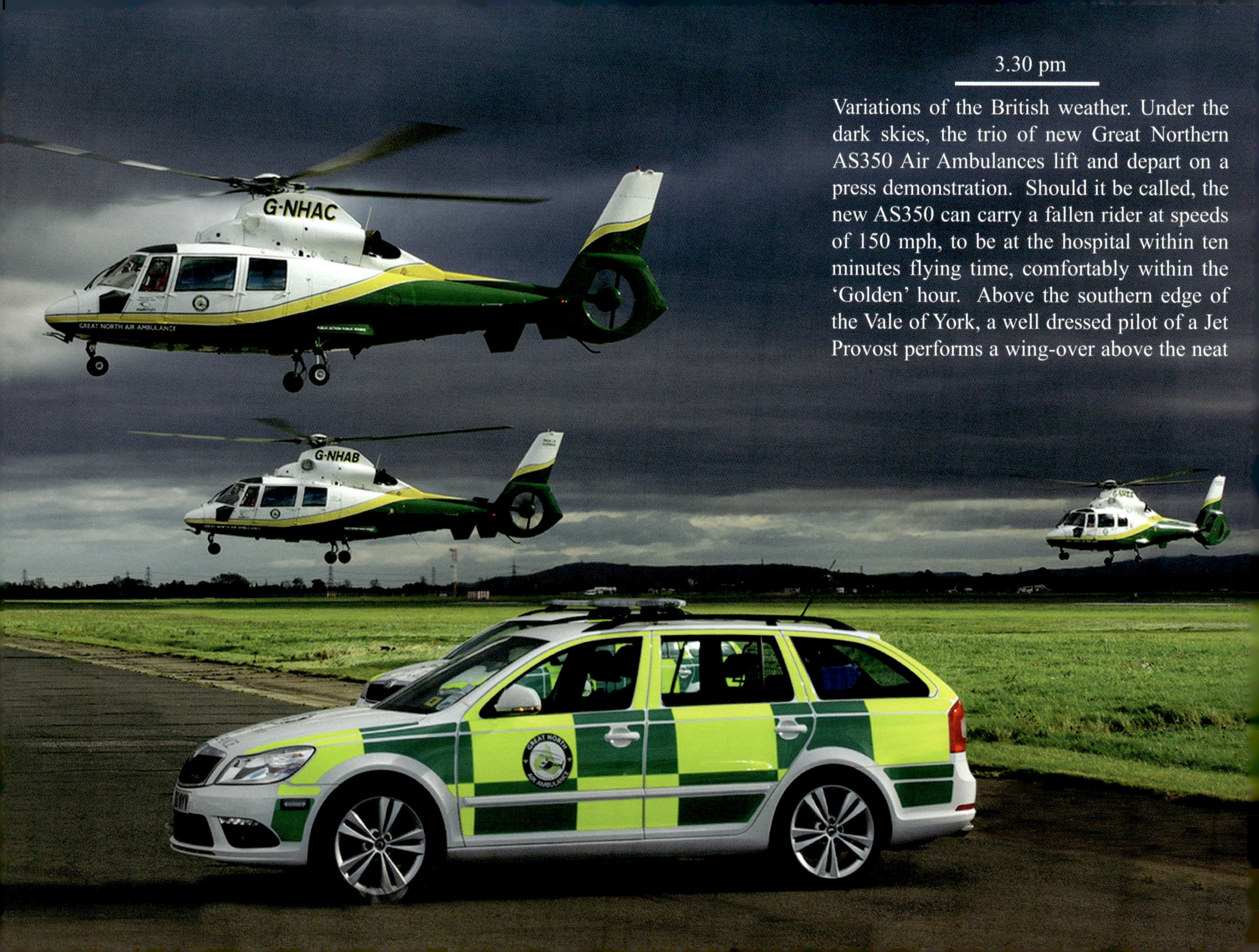

fields system. The pilot, wearing bone done and oxygen mask, is tightly strapped into his Martin Baker ejection seat, activated by pulling down the yellow and black stripped handle, to be propelled in milliseconds to safety.

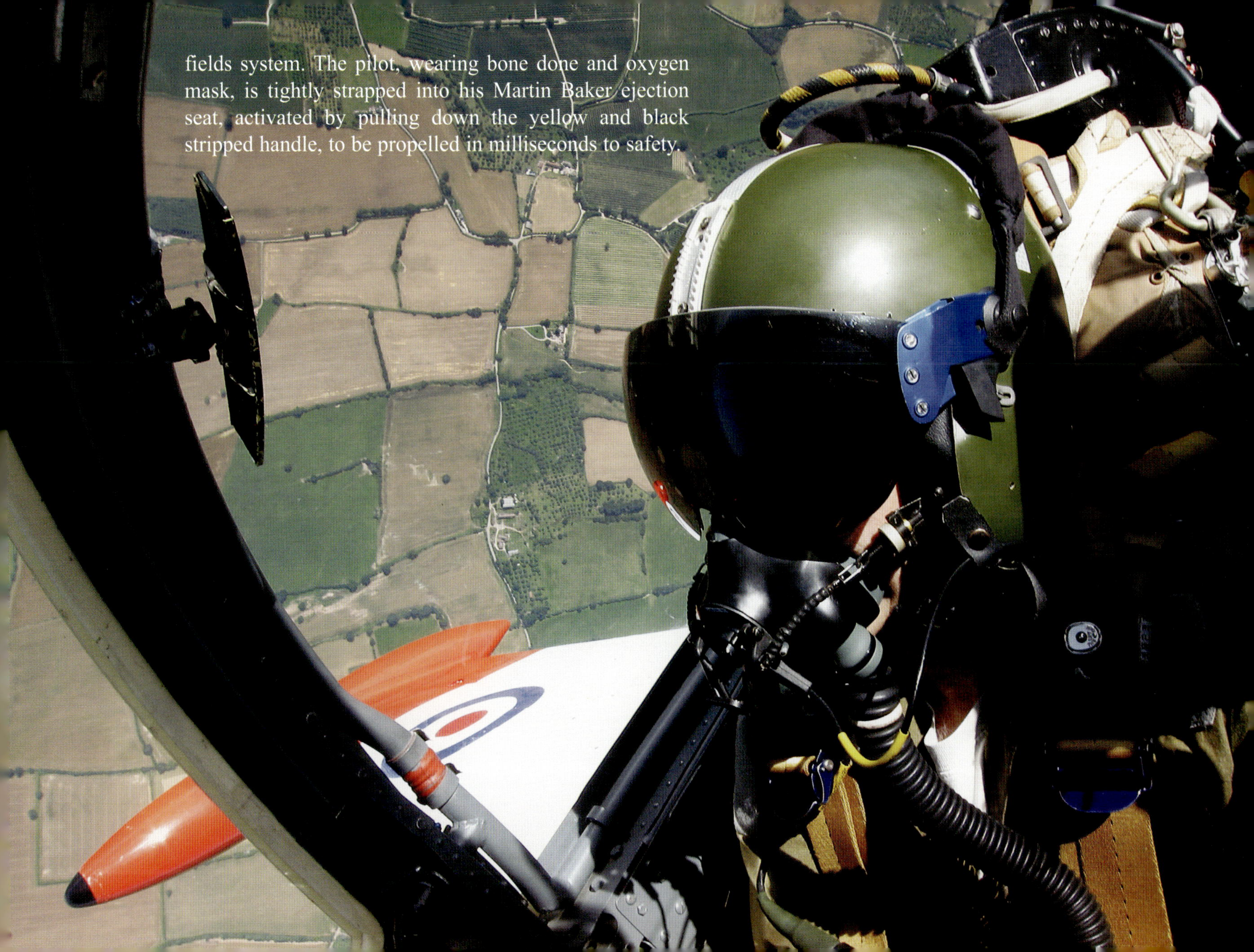

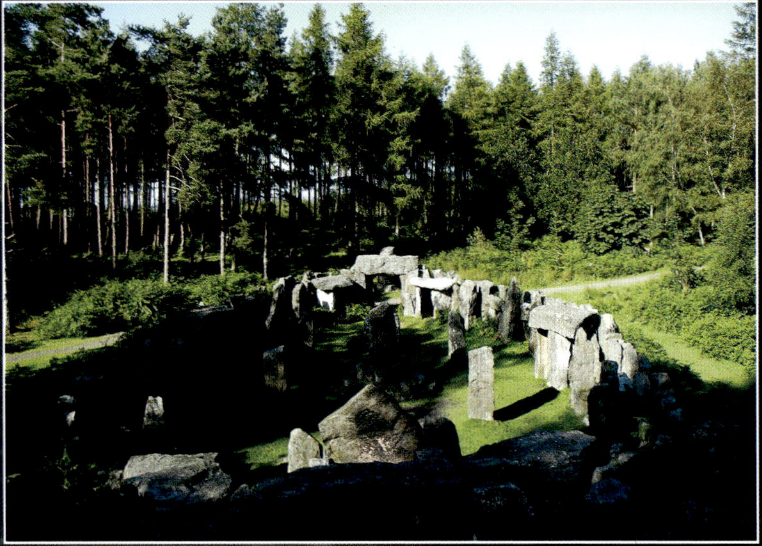

## 4 pm

Teamwork across Yorkshire shows in the final few minutes of the Huddersfield v Harrogate game where steam rises from the scrum as the shadows lengthen. One mile north of the village of Ilton, the so-called 'Druid' circle, shown left, is utterly silent disturbed only by a zephyr breeze. In the early 19th century, a team of unemployed men were paid a shilling (5p) a day by William Danby of nearby Swinton Hall to build this megalithic folly, one of many entirely bogus Stonehenge's which were inspired by fashionable fascination with the Druid culture. Opposite page, behind the village of Sutton-under-Whitestonecliffe, (which with 27 characters is the longest place name in England), is Sutton Bank. At the top of the Bank is a glider launching site and on the south-east flank is the White Horse. Inset and framing the Horse is the 'Gemini' aerobatic team flying their Jet Provost Mk IVs in mirror

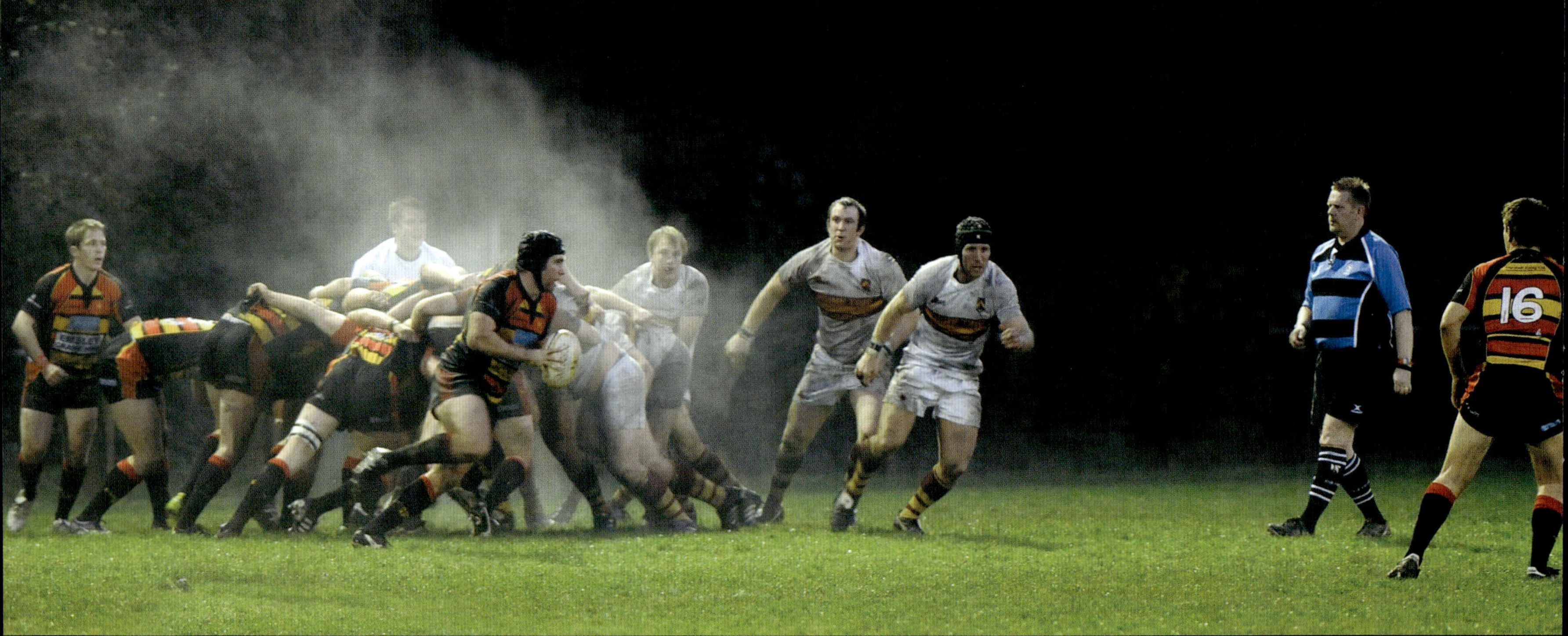

formation in 1972. The White Horse was created in 1857, some say by school master John Hodgson and his pupils but the nearby plaque states that Thomas Taylor and a team of 55 men cut out the shape then moved six tons of lime to whiten the exposed rock. In 1925, a Yorkshire Evening Post restoration fund raised sufficient money to restore the White Horse and provide for a triennial grooming.

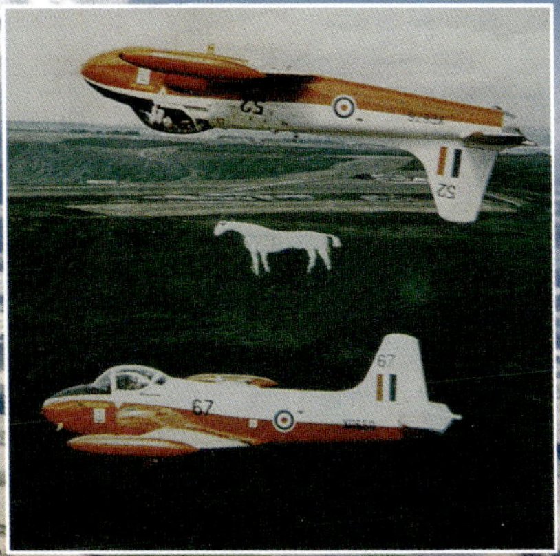

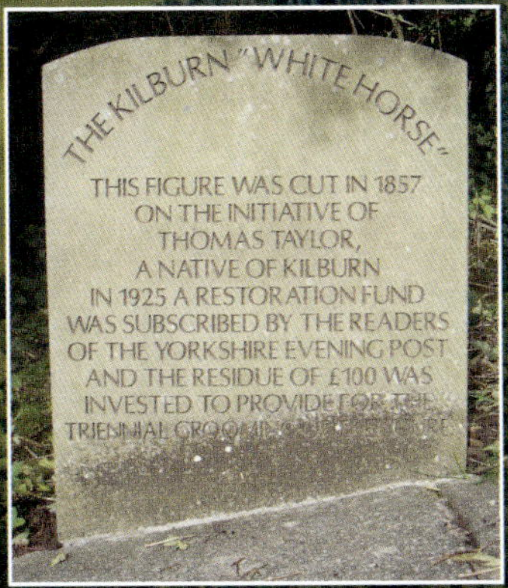

4.30 pm

*Conduit*, ridden by Frankie Dettori wins the St Leger in style. This event was devised by Anthony St Leger, an army officer who lived near Doncaster. The inaugural race was held at Cantley Common on 24th September 1776 and the first winner was an unnamed filly owned by the event's organiser, the 2nd Marquess of Rockingham. The title *St. Leger Stakes* was decided at a dinner party held in 1777 when it was suggested that it should be called the Rockingham Stakes in honour of the host. However, the Marquess proposed that it should be named after Anthony St. Leger. The event was moved to its present location, Town Moor, in 1778. The St. Leger Stakes has inspired a number of similar events around the world including the Irish St. Leger, the Deutsches St. Leger, the St. Leger Italiano and

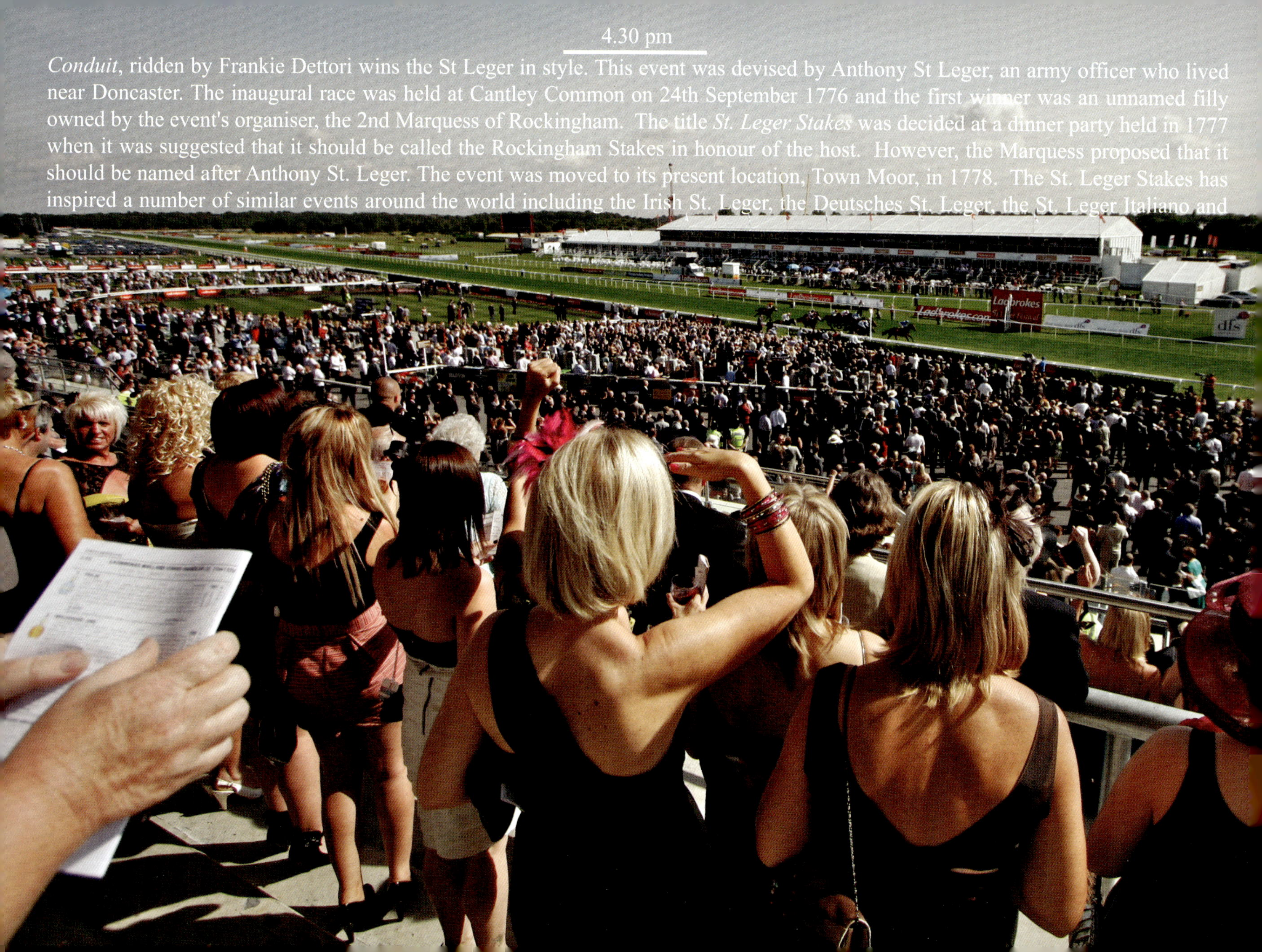

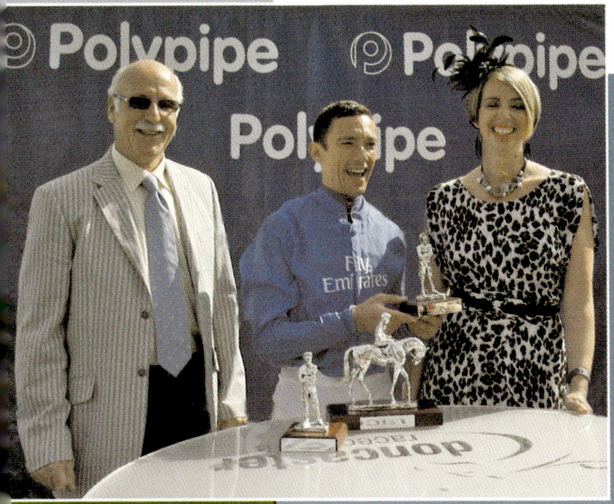


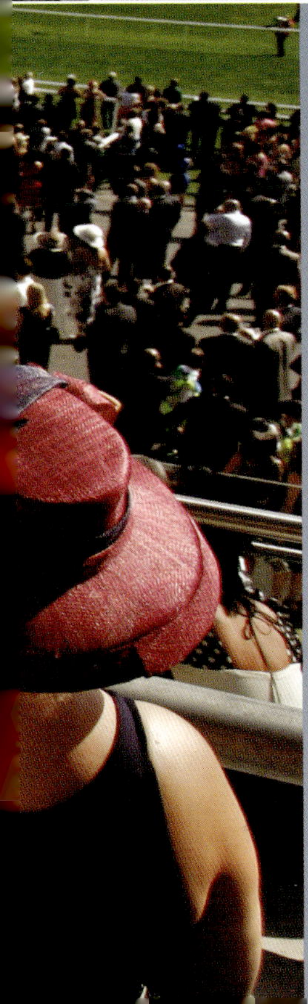

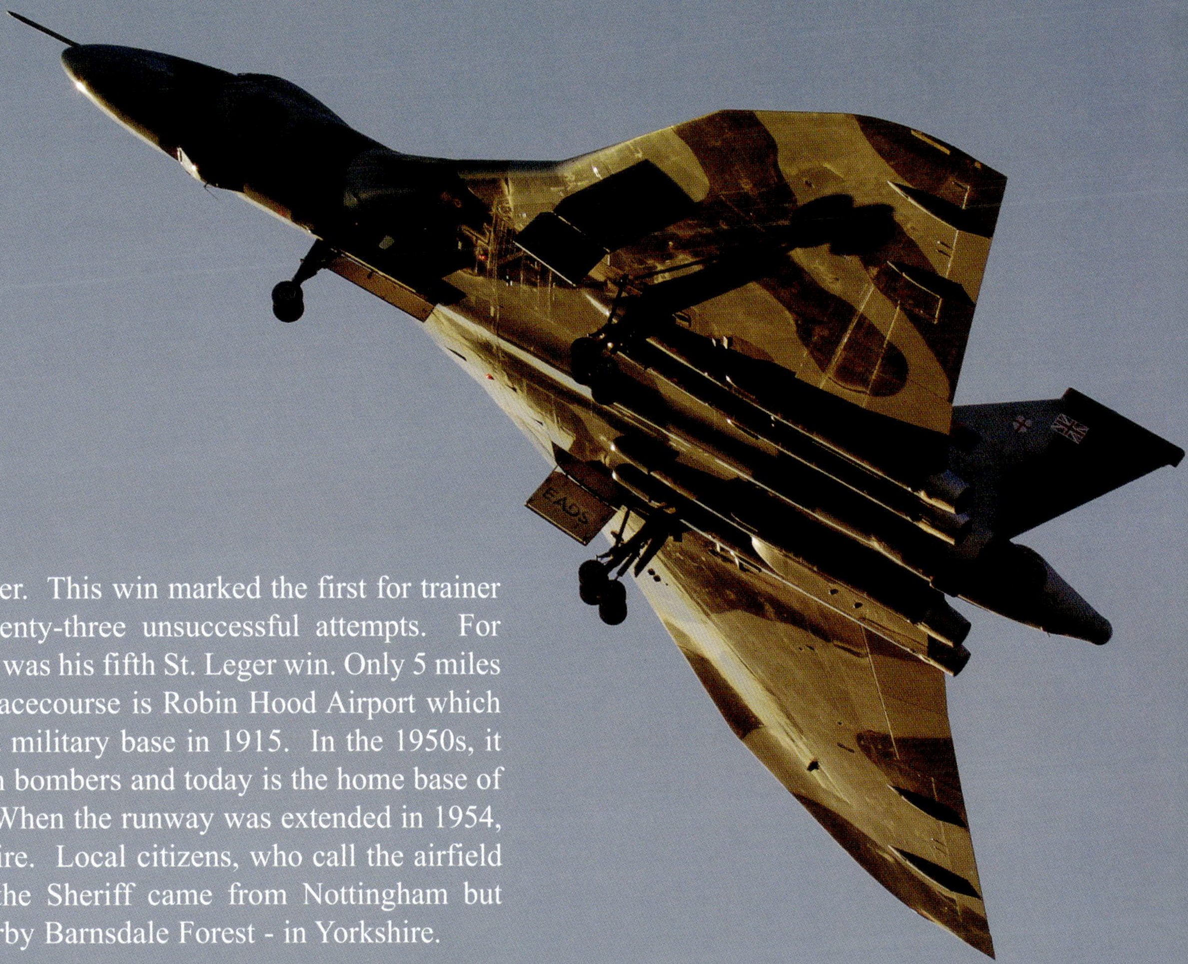


the New Zealand St. Leger. This win marked the first for trainer Michael Stoute after twenty-three unsuccessful attempts. For jockey Frankie Dettori, it was his fifth St. Leger win. Only 5 miles to the south-east of the racecourse is Robin Hood Airport which was first established as a military base in 1915. In the 1950s, it became a base for Vulcan bombers and today is the home base of the only flying Vulcan. When the runway was extended in 1954, it ran into Nottinghamshire. Local citizens, who call the airfield 'Finno', point out that the Sheriff came from Nottingham but Robin Hood lived in nearby Barnsdale Forest - in Yorkshire.

5 pm

The Wakefield chapel was built by King Edward IV in memory of his father, Richard Plantagenet know as Richard of York, father also of Richard III, who was slain near Sandal Castle in 1460 in the Battle of Wakefield. This is also the origin point of the mnemonic 'Richard of

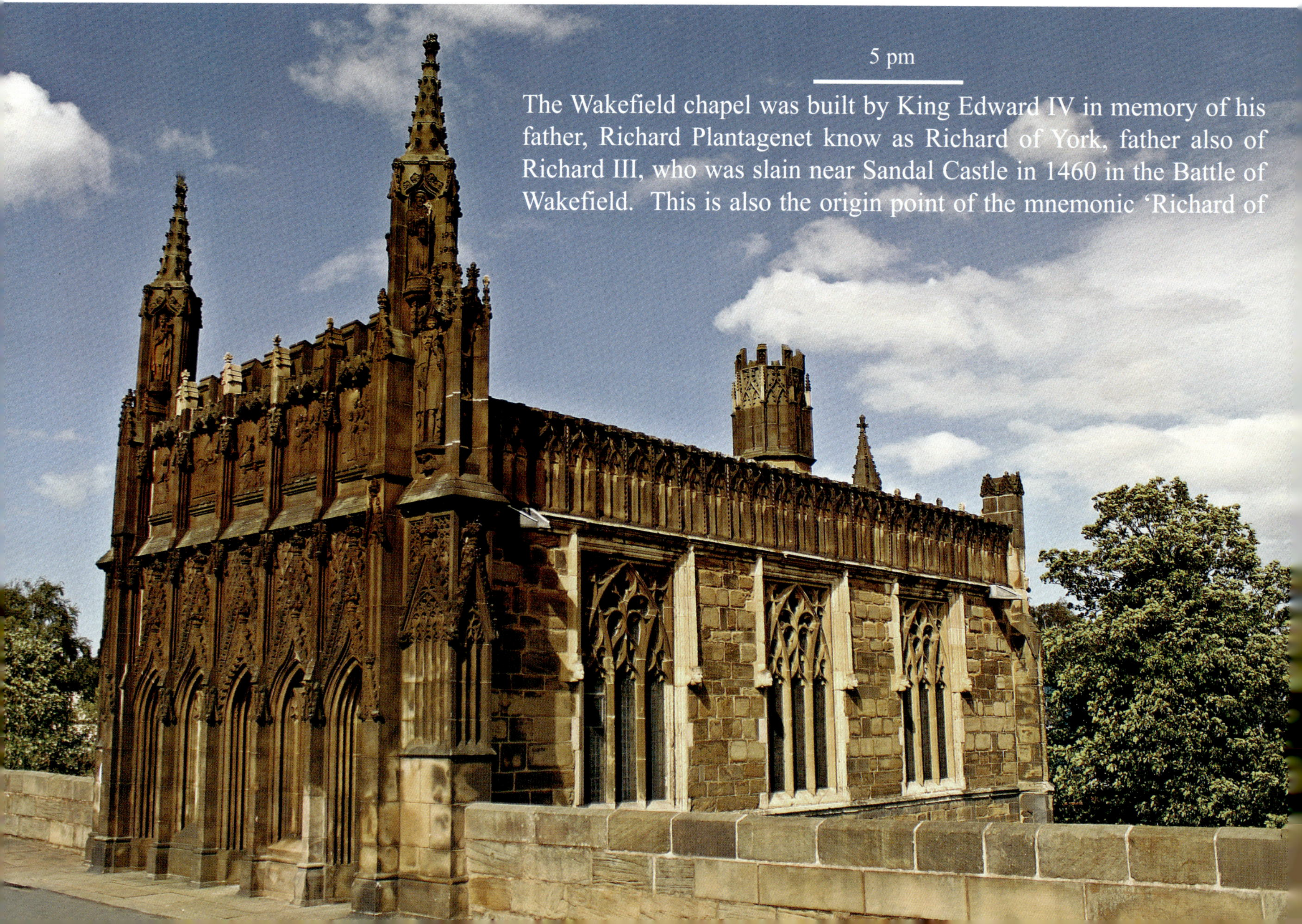

York gave battle in vain' created to remember the colours of the rainbow - red, orange, yellow, green, blue, indigo and violet. Here, an aviator approaches

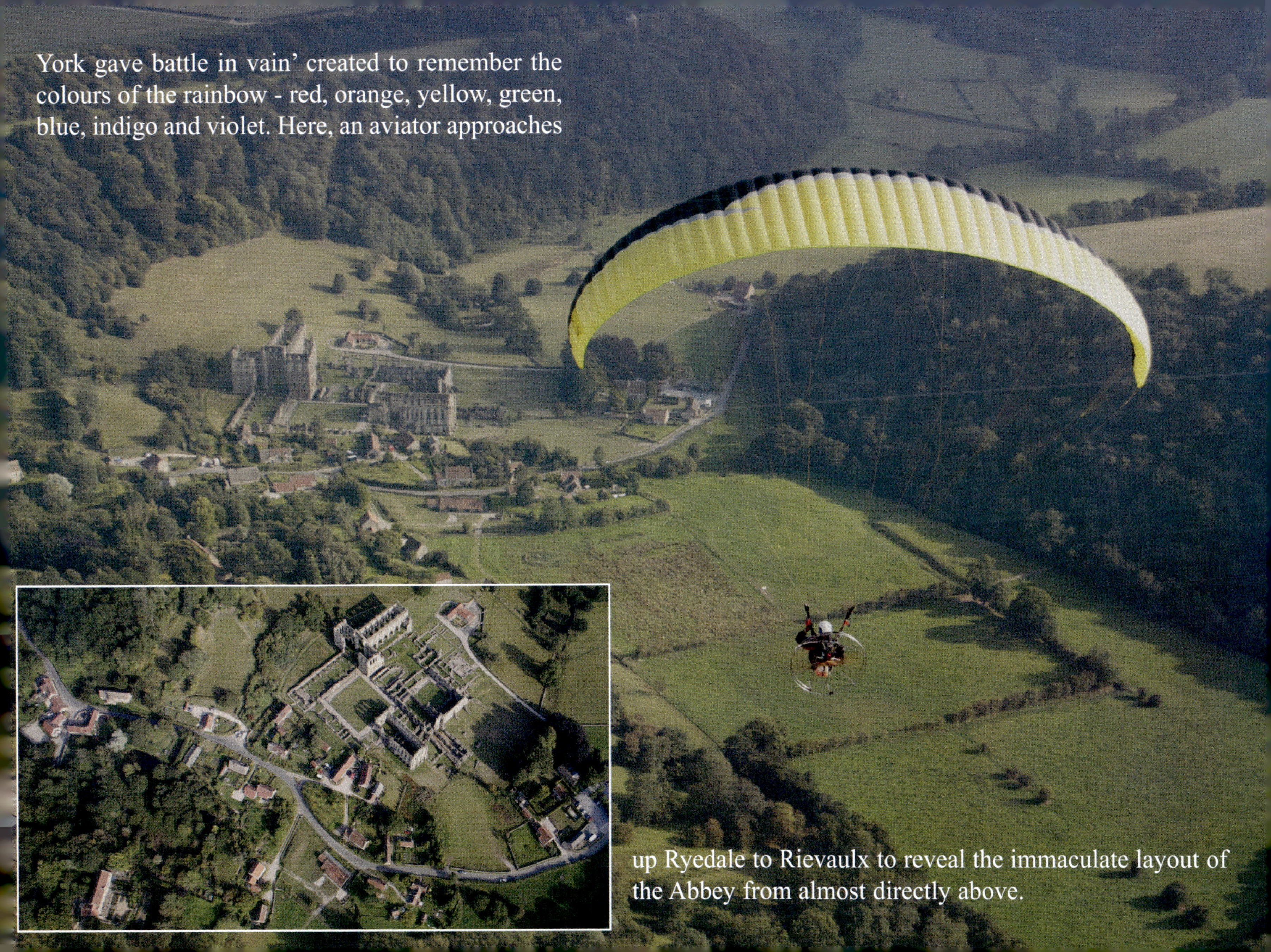

up Ryedale to Rievaulx to reveal the immaculate layout of the Abbey from almost directly above.

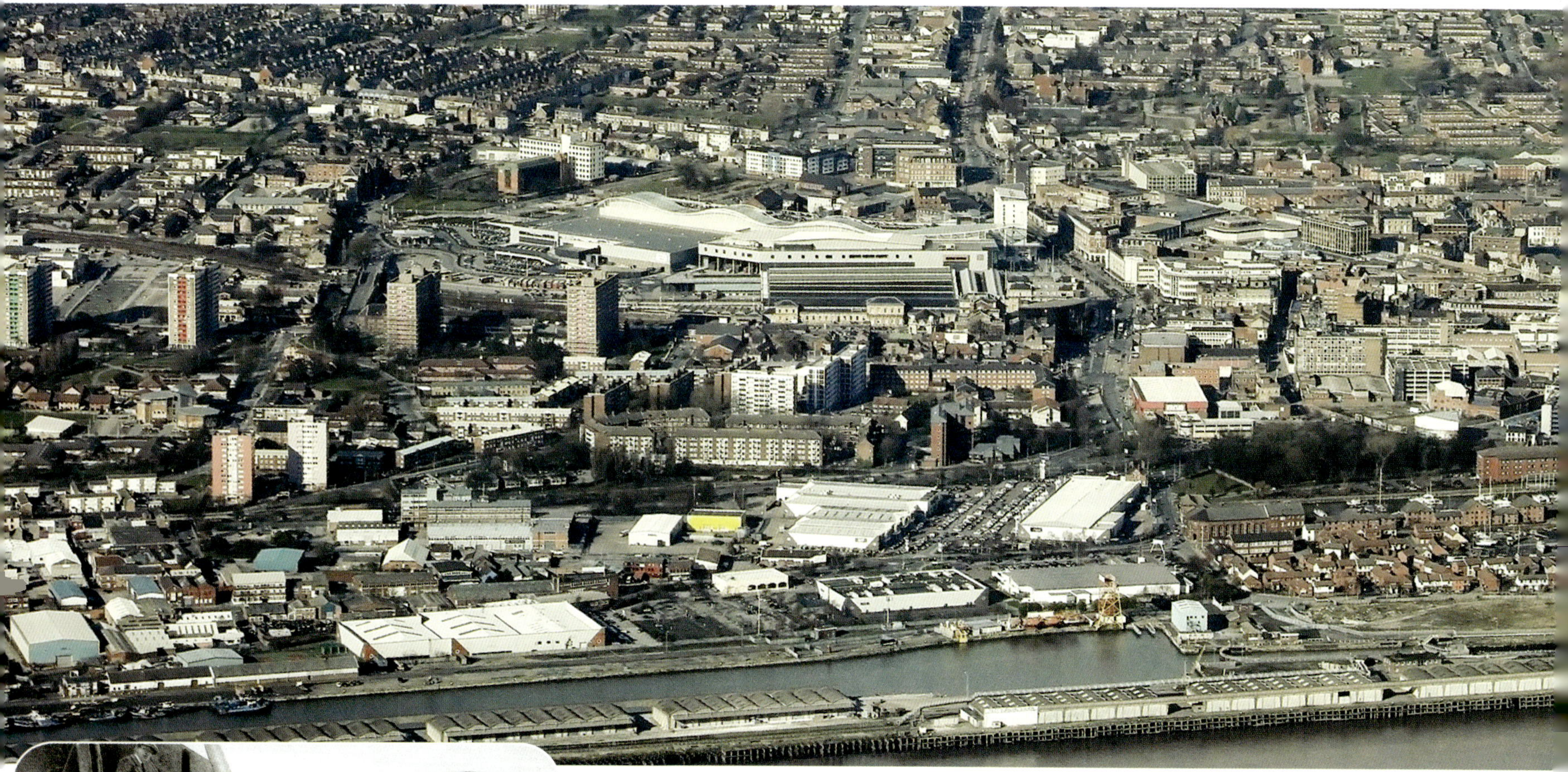

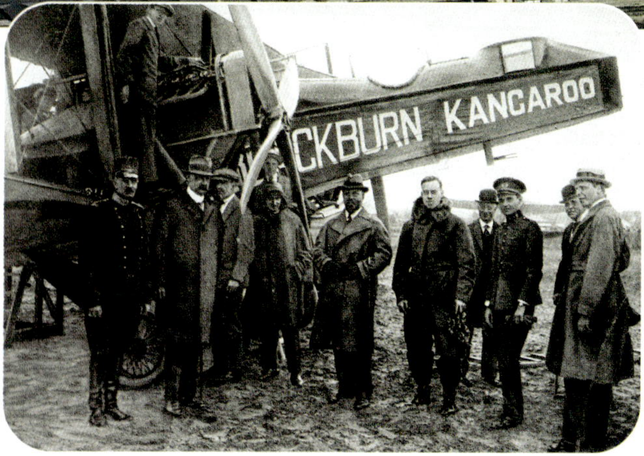


5.15 pm

Modern Hawk jet fighters are built near Hull at Brough but aviation has been part of life around Hull for many years. On 30th September 1919, the North Sea Aerial Navigation Co Ltd started a regular passenger service between Roundhay Park and Hounslow Heath - now LHR using the Blackburn aircraft shown left. Amy Johnson, born in Kingston-upon-Hull on the 1st July 1903 and with only 85 hours flying experience, departed from England on the 5th May 1930 in a single-engined de Havilland DH 60G Gipsy Moth, G-AAAH, named 'Jason'. She flew the 11,000 miles to Darwin, Australia arriving on the 24th May 1930 – the first woman to fly solo from

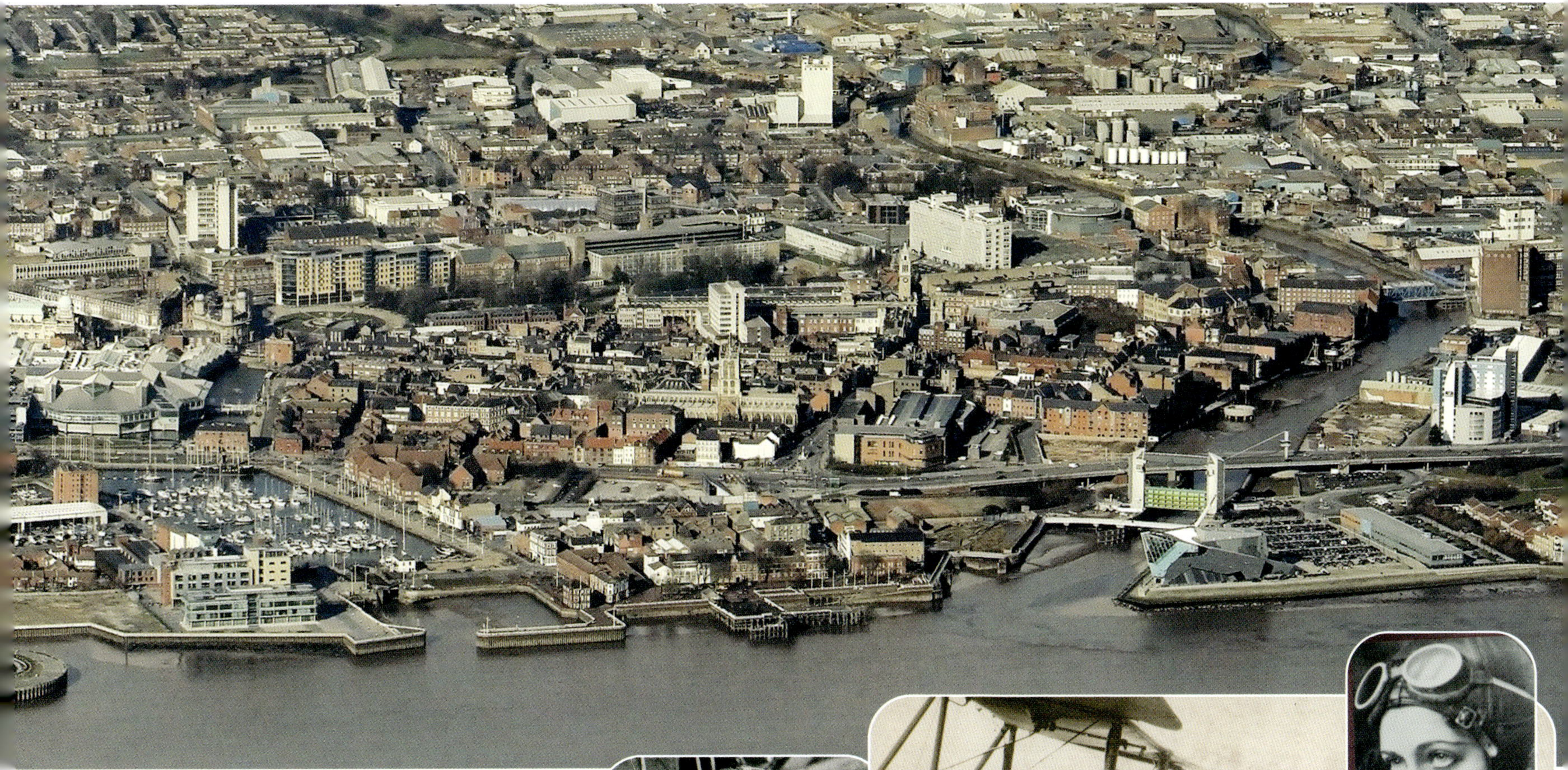

England to Australia. King George V awarded her the CBE (Commander of the British Empire) and the Daily Mail awarded Amy £10,000, a stupendous sum in 1930. During WWII, Amy flew with the Air Transport Auxiliary delivering aircraft to front-line units but disappeared while flying an Airspeed Oxford over the Thames Estuary. Her body was never found. Her aircraft, G-AAAH, is preserved in the Science Museum.

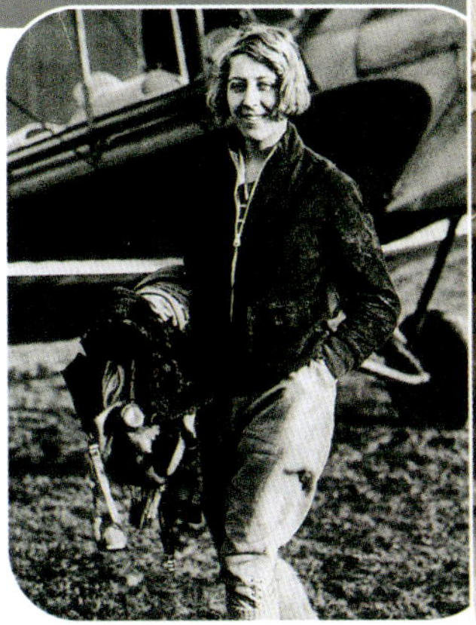

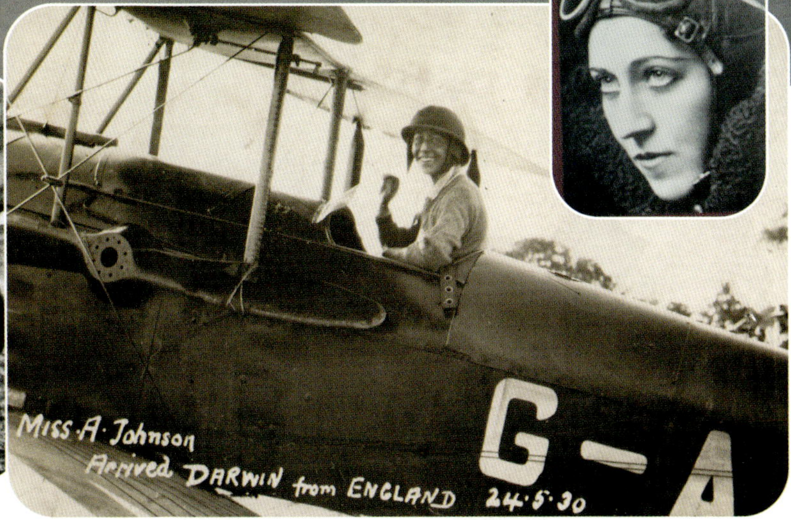

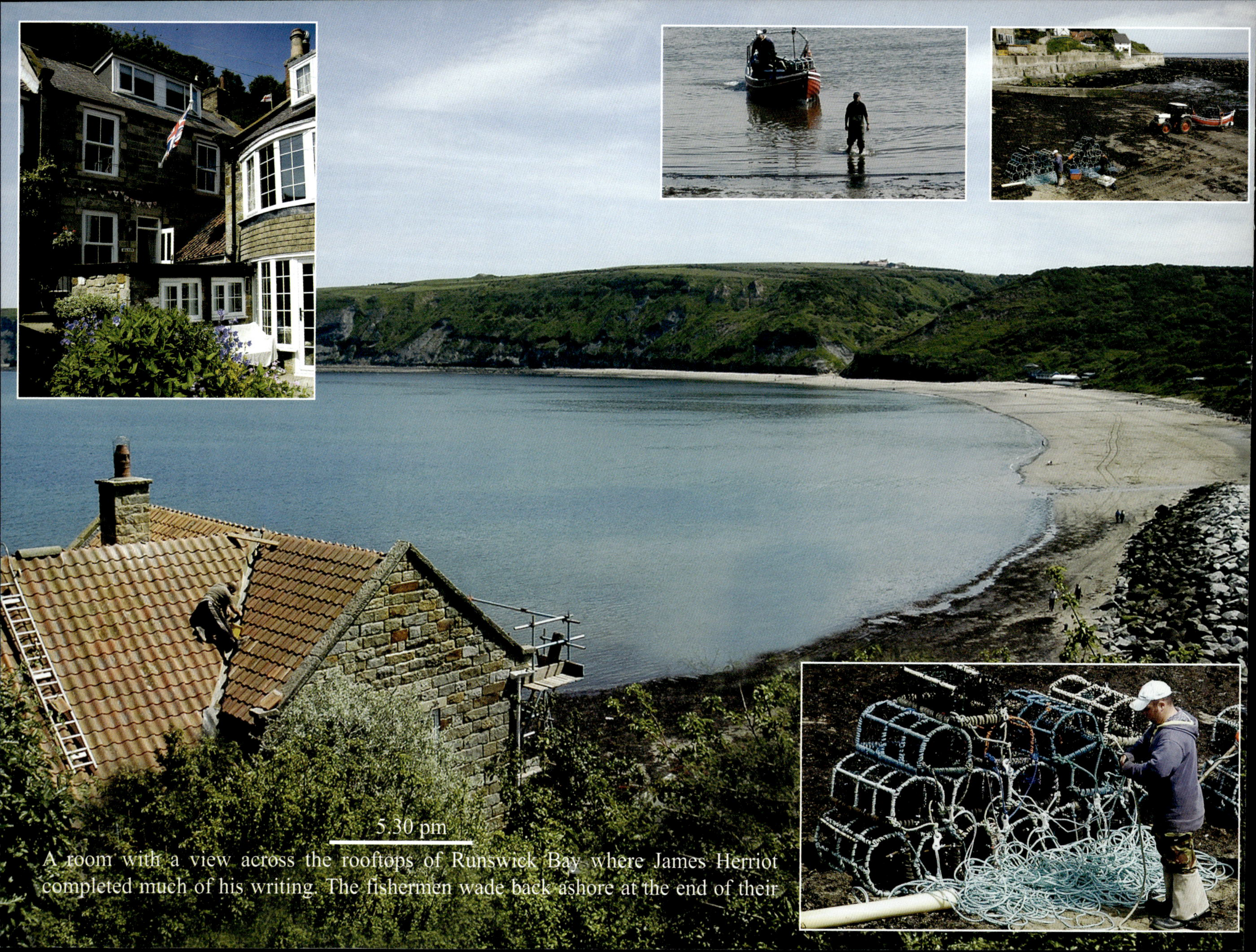

5.30 pm

A room with a view across the rooftops of Runswick Bay where James Herriot completed much of his writing. The fishermen wade back ashore at the end of their

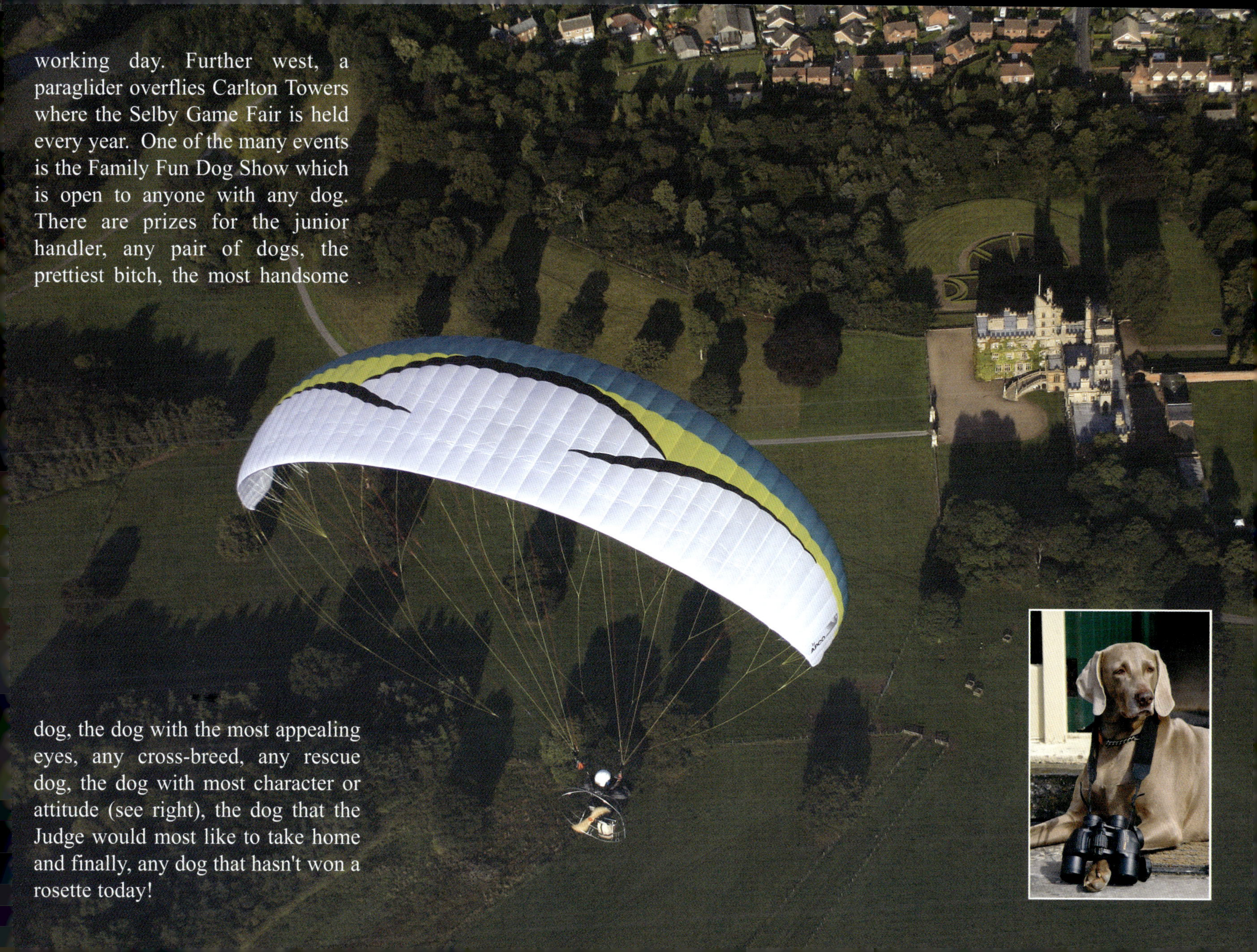

working day. Further west, a paraglider overflies Carlton Towers where the Selby Game Fair is held every year. One of the many events is the Family Fun Dog Show which is open to anyone with any dog. There are prizes for the junior handler, any pair of dogs, the prettiest bitch, the most handsome dog, the dog with the most appealing eyes, any cross-breed, any rescue dog, the dog with most character or attitude (see right), the dog that the Judge would most like to take home and finally, any dog that hasn't won a rosette today!

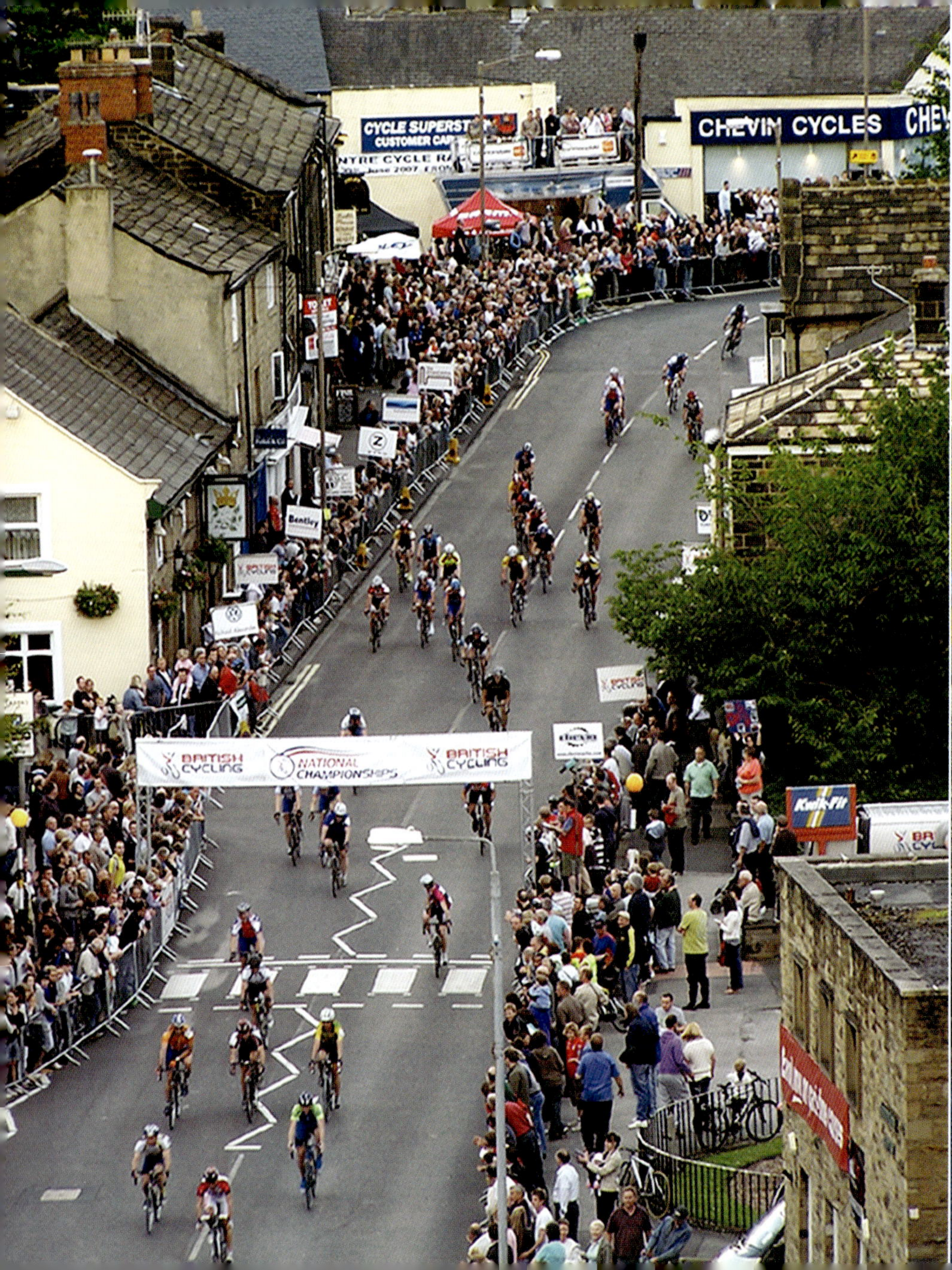


5.45 pm

The Otley cycle races get underway while, below, two boys do what boys always do. Opposite page, the film crew are on the last scene of the day, perched on a grassy ledge on Otley Chevin. The series, Helicopter Heroes, first screened by BBC1 in 2007, is now

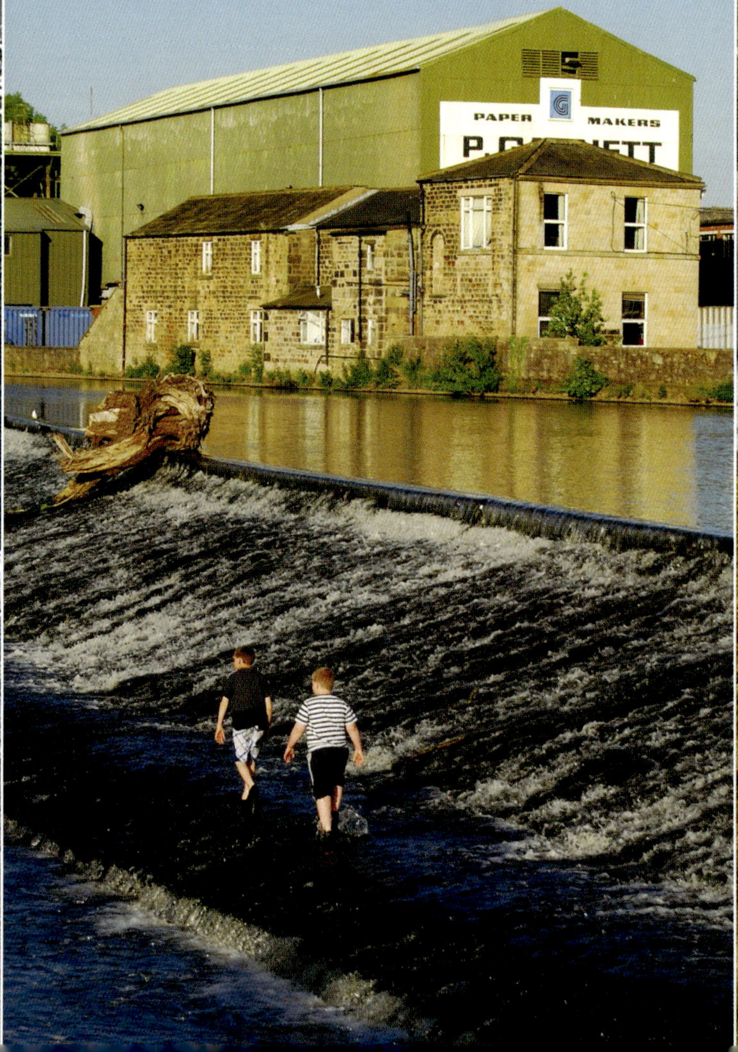

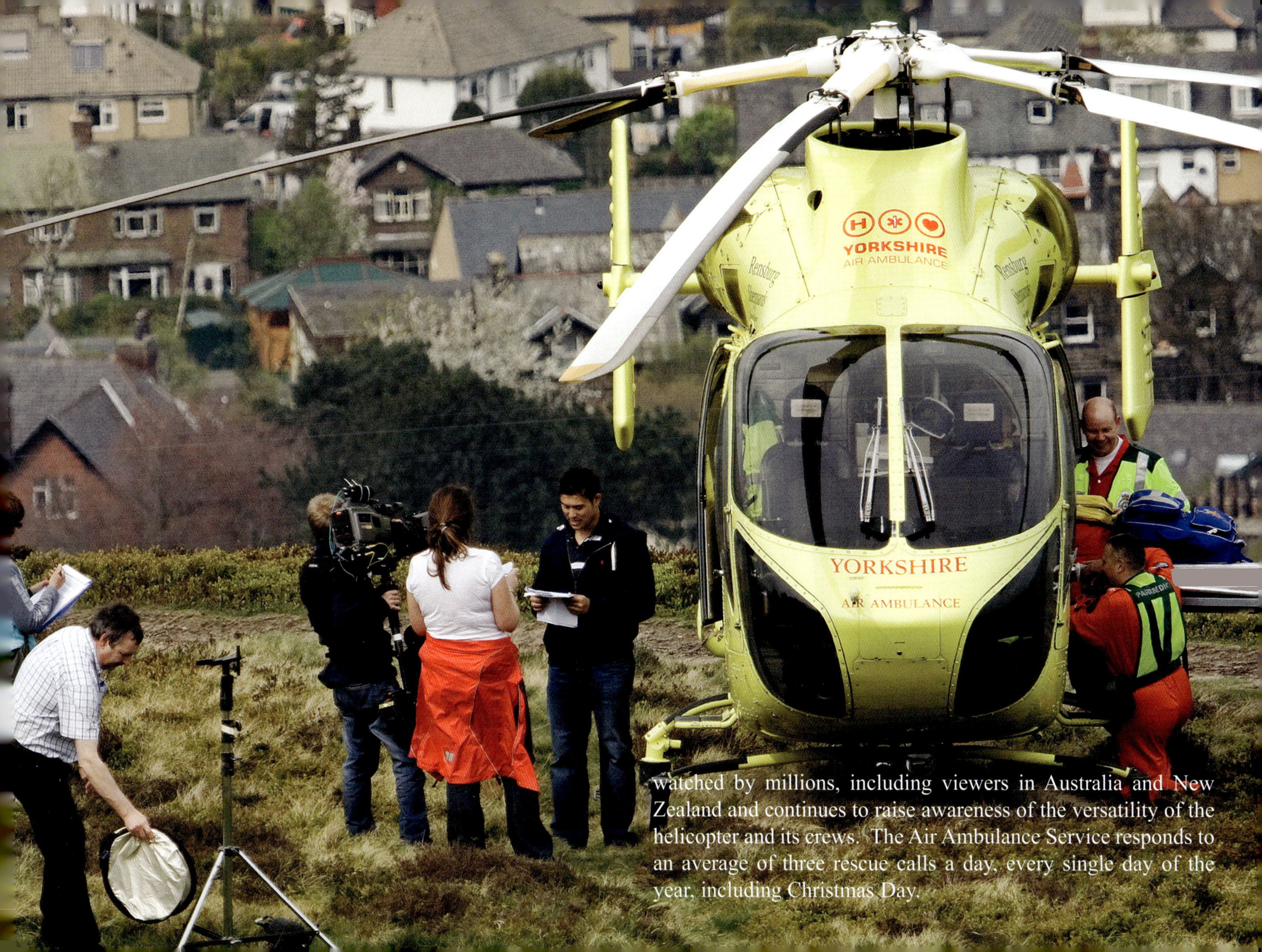


watched by millions, including viewers in Australia and New Zealand and continues to raise awareness of the versatility of the helicopter and its crews. The Air Ambulance Service responds to an average of three rescue calls a day, every single day of the year, including Christmas Day.

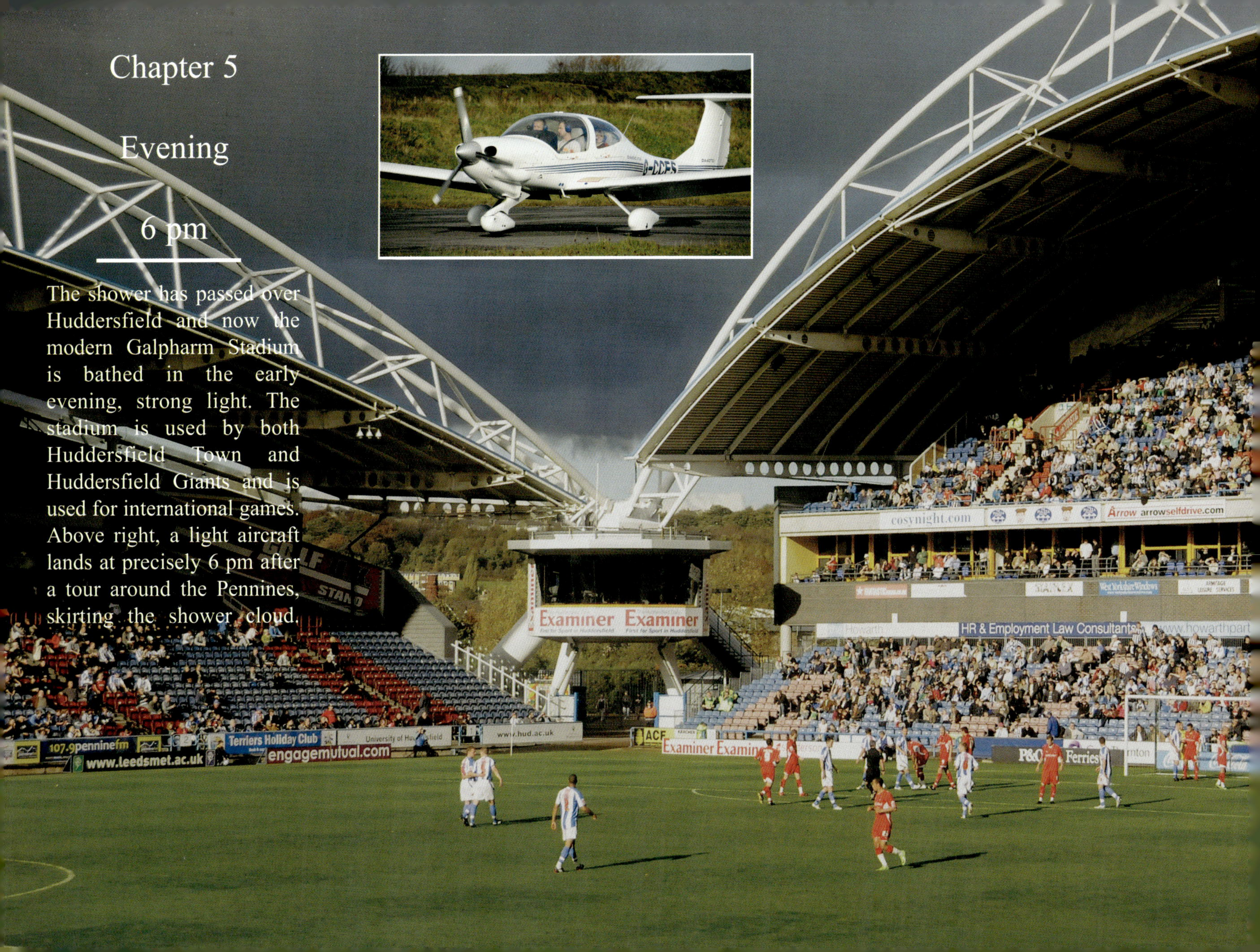


# Chapter 5

## Evening

### 6 pm

The shower has passed over Huddersfield and now the modern Galpharm Stadium is bathed in the early evening, strong light. The stadium is used by both Huddersfield Town and Huddersfield Giants and is used for international games. Above right, a light aircraft lands at precisely 6 pm after a tour around the Pennines, skirting the shower cloud.

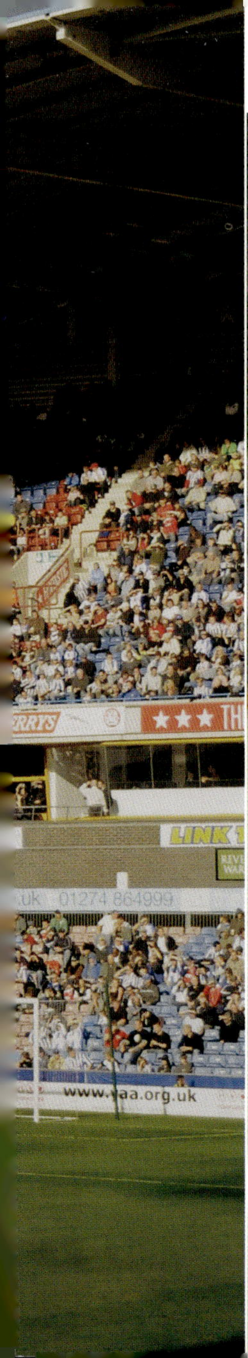

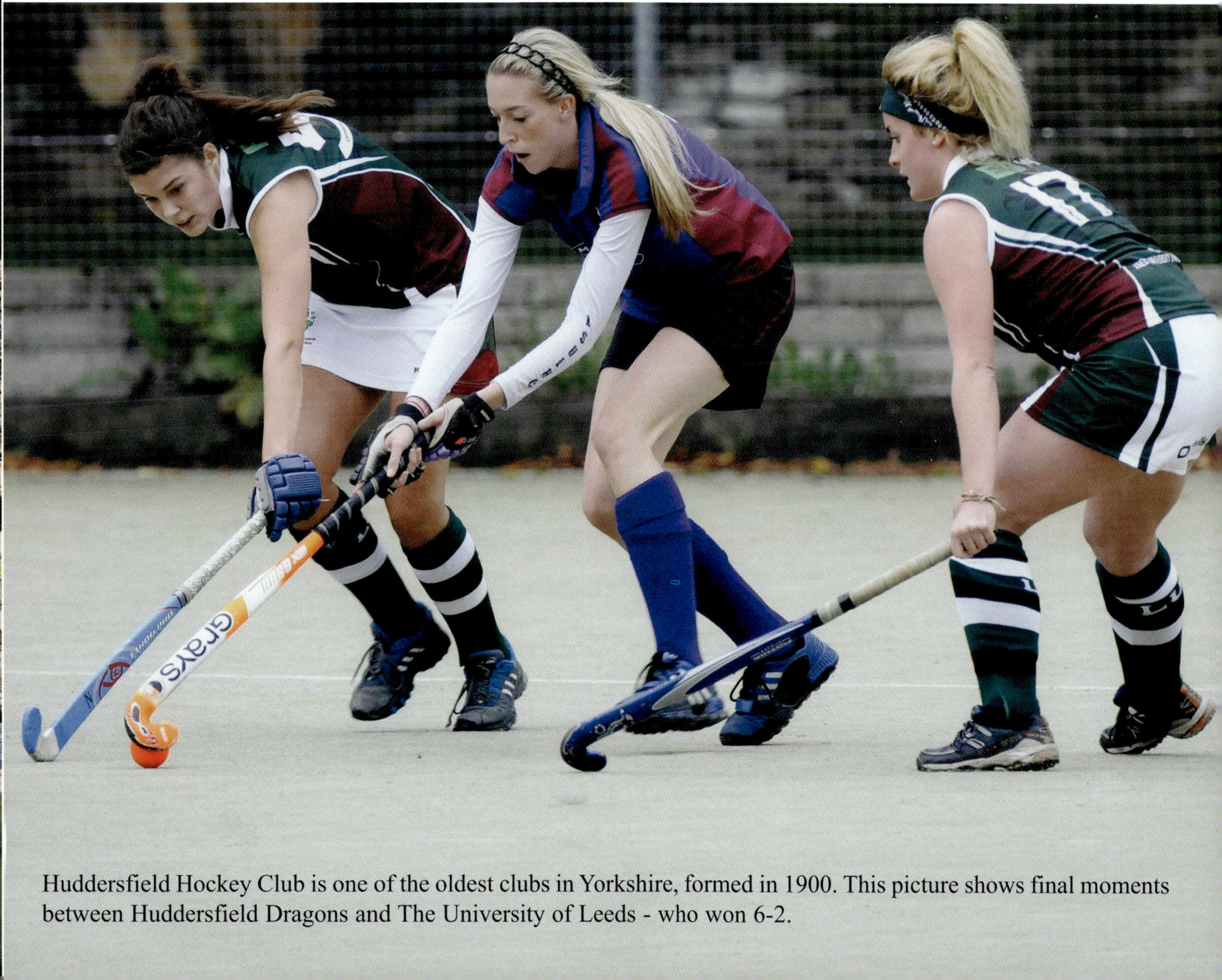


Huddersfield Hockey Club is one of the oldest clubs in Yorkshire, formed in 1900. This picture shows final moments between Huddersfield Dragons and The University of Leeds - who won 6-2.

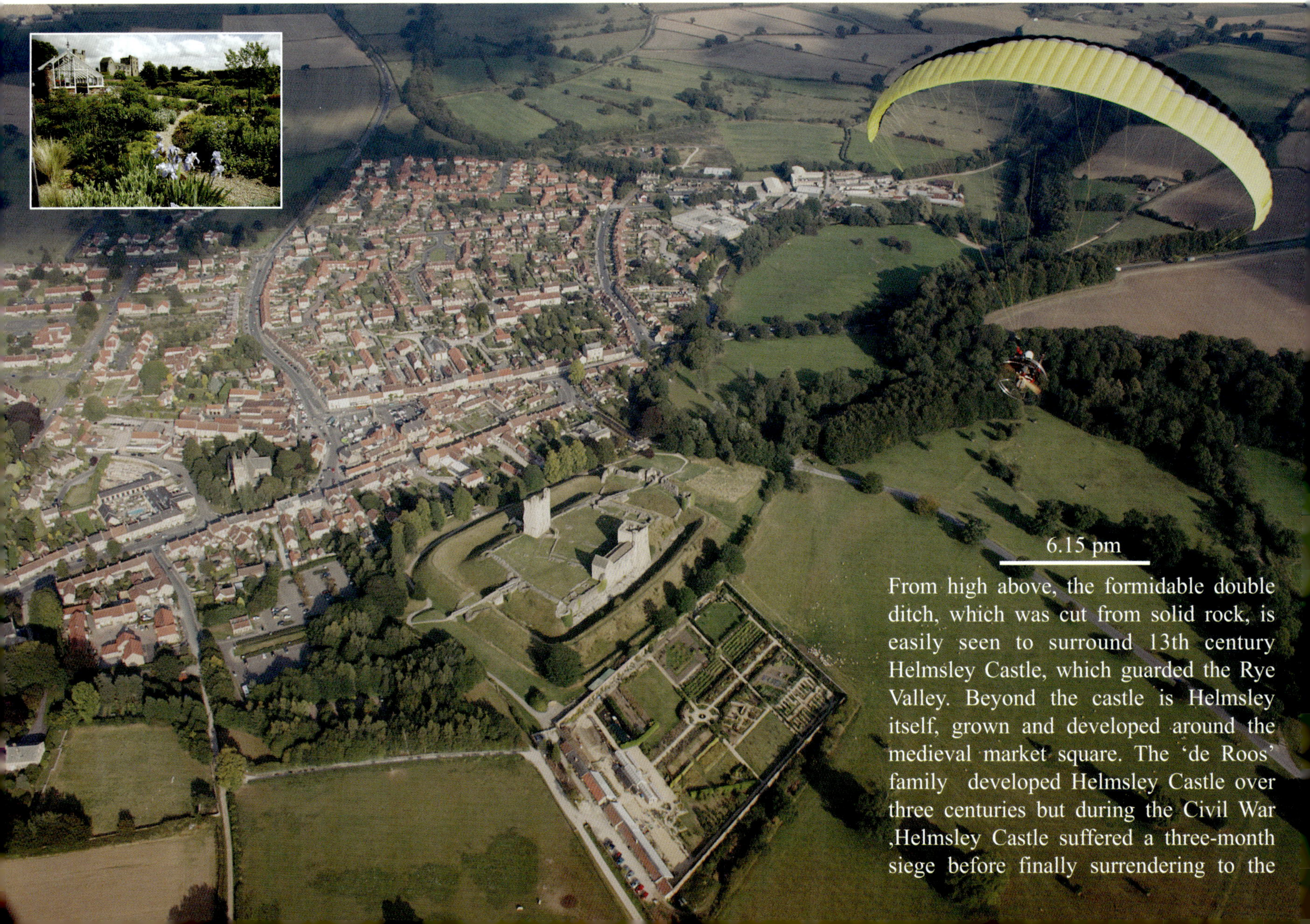

6.15 pm

From high above, the formidable double ditch, which was cut from solid rock, is easily seen to surround 13th century Helmsley Castle, which guarded the Rye Valley. Beyond the castle is Helmsley itself, grown and developed around the medieval market square. The 'de Roos' family developed Helmsley Castle over three centuries but during the Civil War ,Helmsley Castle suffered a three-month siege before finally surrendering to the

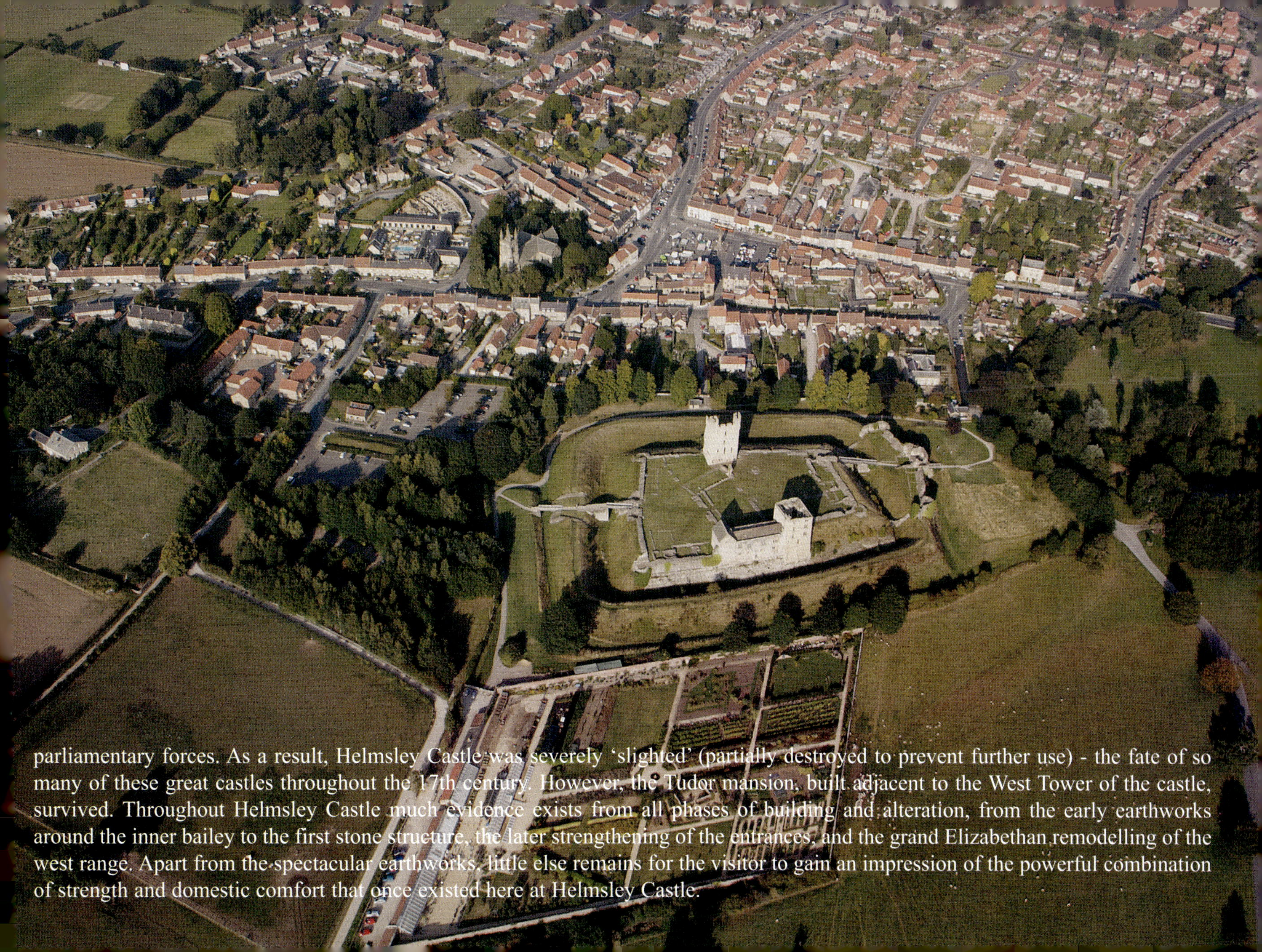

parliamentary forces. As a result, Helmsley Castle was severely 'slighted' (partially destroyed to prevent further use) - the fate of so many of these great castles throughout the 17th century. However, the Tudor mansion, built adjacent to the West Tower of the castle, survived. Throughout Helmsley Castle much evidence exists from all phases of building and alteration, from the early earthworks around the inner bailey to the first stone structure, the later strengthening of the entrances, and the grand Elizabethan remodelling of the west range. Apart from the spectacular earthworks, little else remains for the visitor to gain an impression of the powerful combination of strength and domestic comfort that once existed here at Helmsley Castle.

## 6.45 pm

Cricket is Yorkshire. British Prime Minister Harold Wilson, himself a Yorkshireman from Huddersfield, described Fred Trueman as the 'greatest living Yorkshireman'. *Fiery Fred* is regarded as one of the greatest fast bowlers in history. Opposing the English players were cricketers such as Sir Don Bradman, the only Australian cricketer to be knighted. On the 11th July 1930, in the 3rd Test at Headingley,

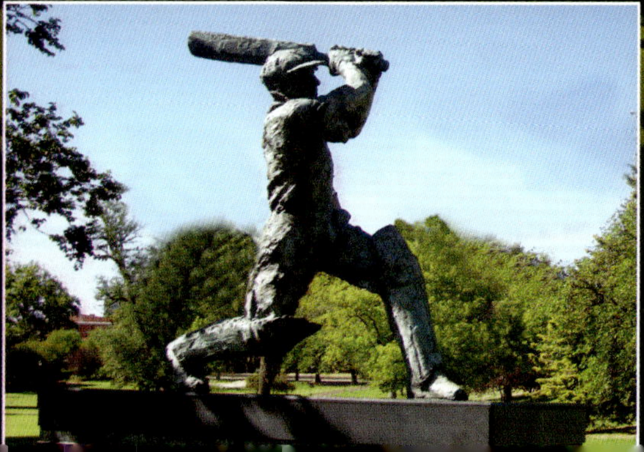

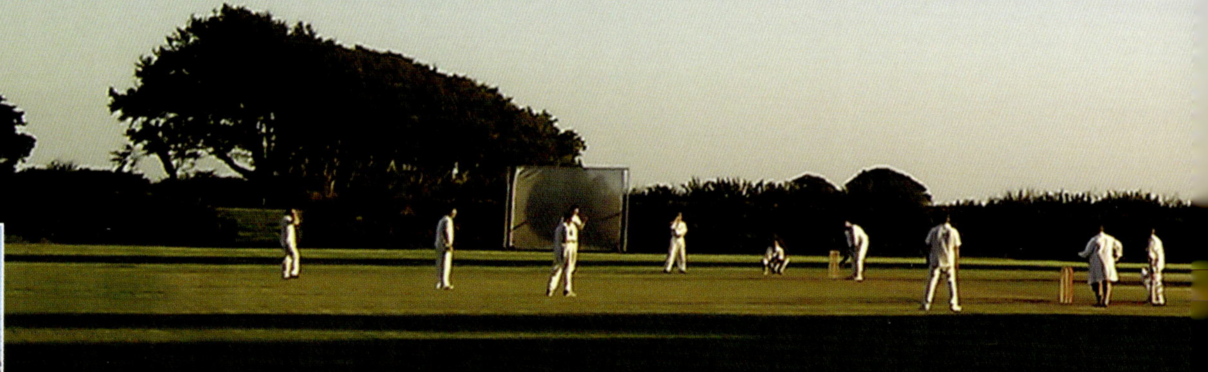

Leeds, Don Bradman scored a century before lunch, added another century between lunch and tea, before finishing the day on 309 not out. He remains the only Test player to pass 300 in one day's play. For the unaware, cricket is an English game where there are two sides, one out in the field and one in. Each man that's in the side that's in goes out, and when he's out he comes in and the next man goes in until he's out. When they are all out, the side that's out comes in and the side that's been in goes out and tries to

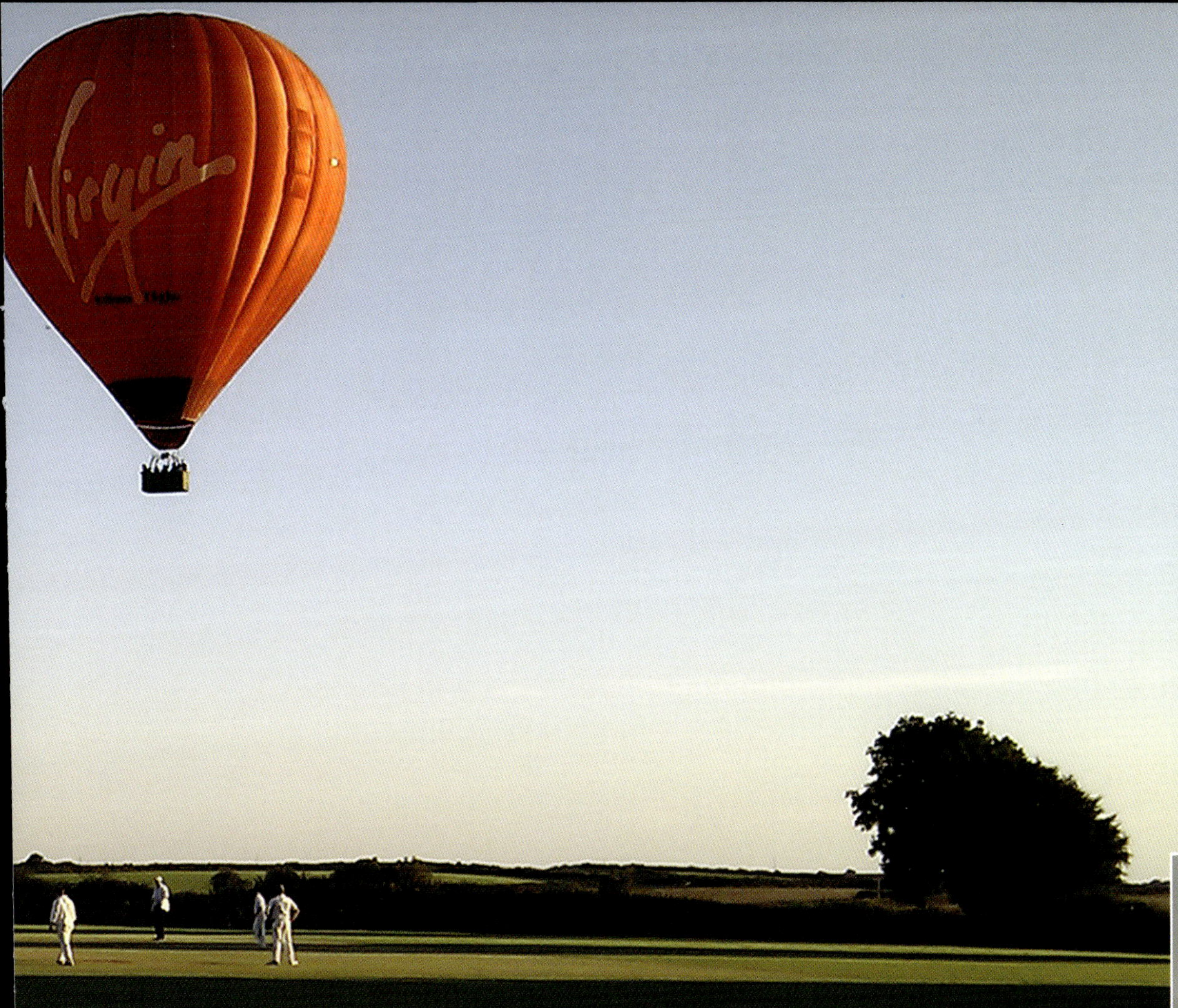


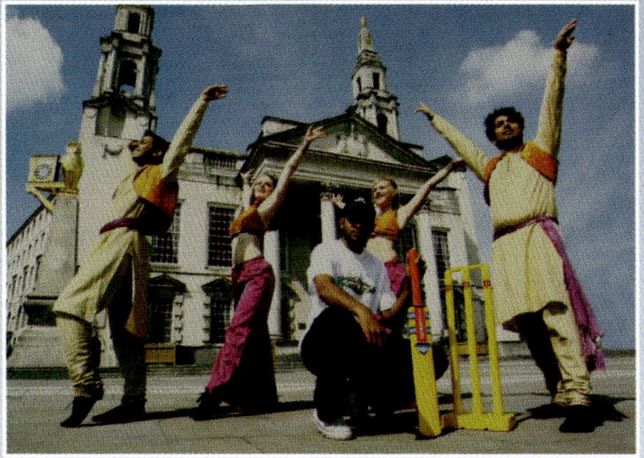

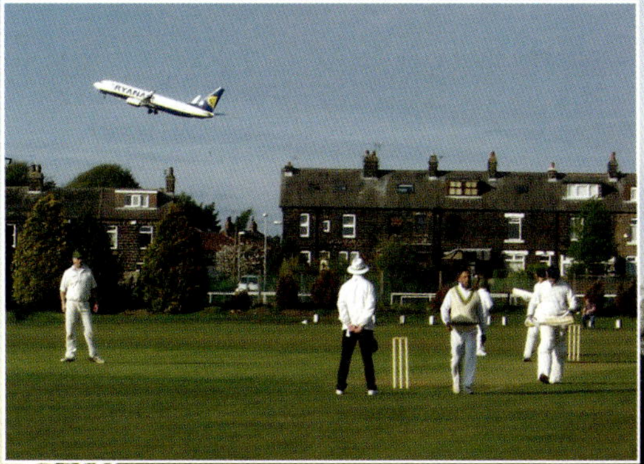

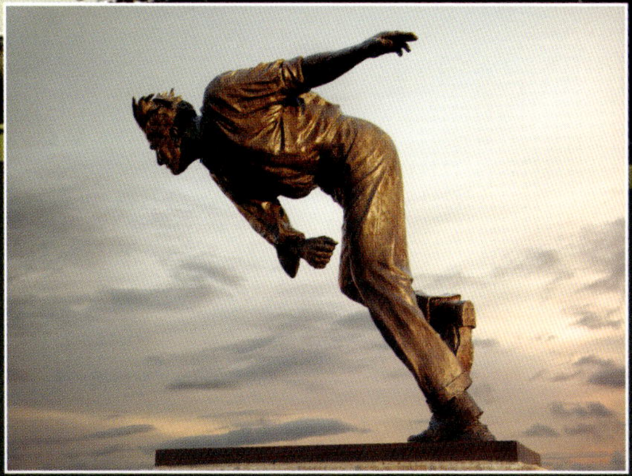

get those coming in, out. Sometimes you get men still in and not out. When a man goes out to go in, the men who are out try to get him out, and when he is out he goes in and the next man in goes out and goes in. There are two men called umpires who stay out all the time and they decide when the men who are in are out. When both sides have been in and all the men have been out, and both sides have been out twice after all the men have been in, including those who are not out, that is the end of the game.

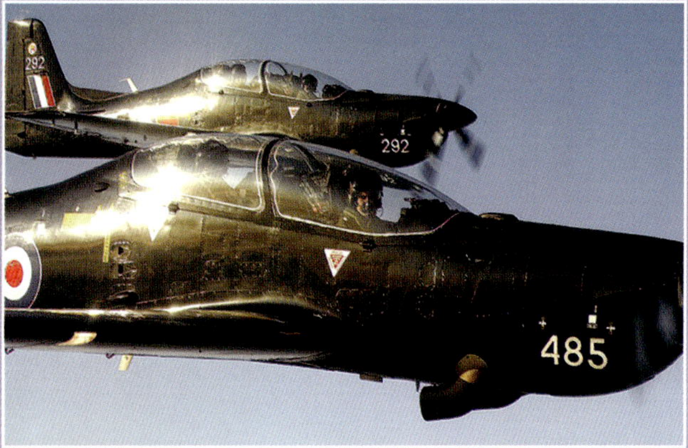


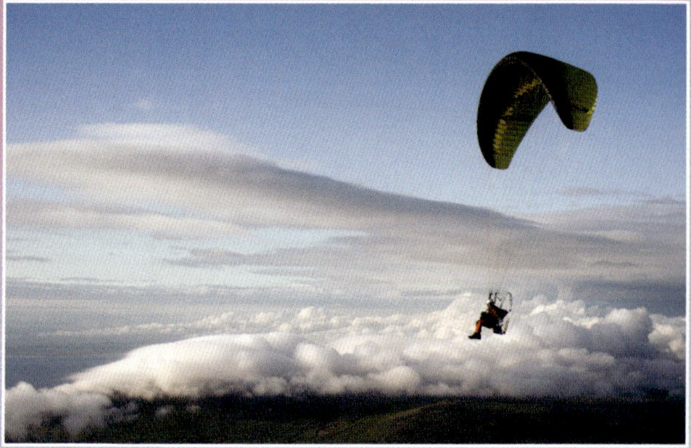

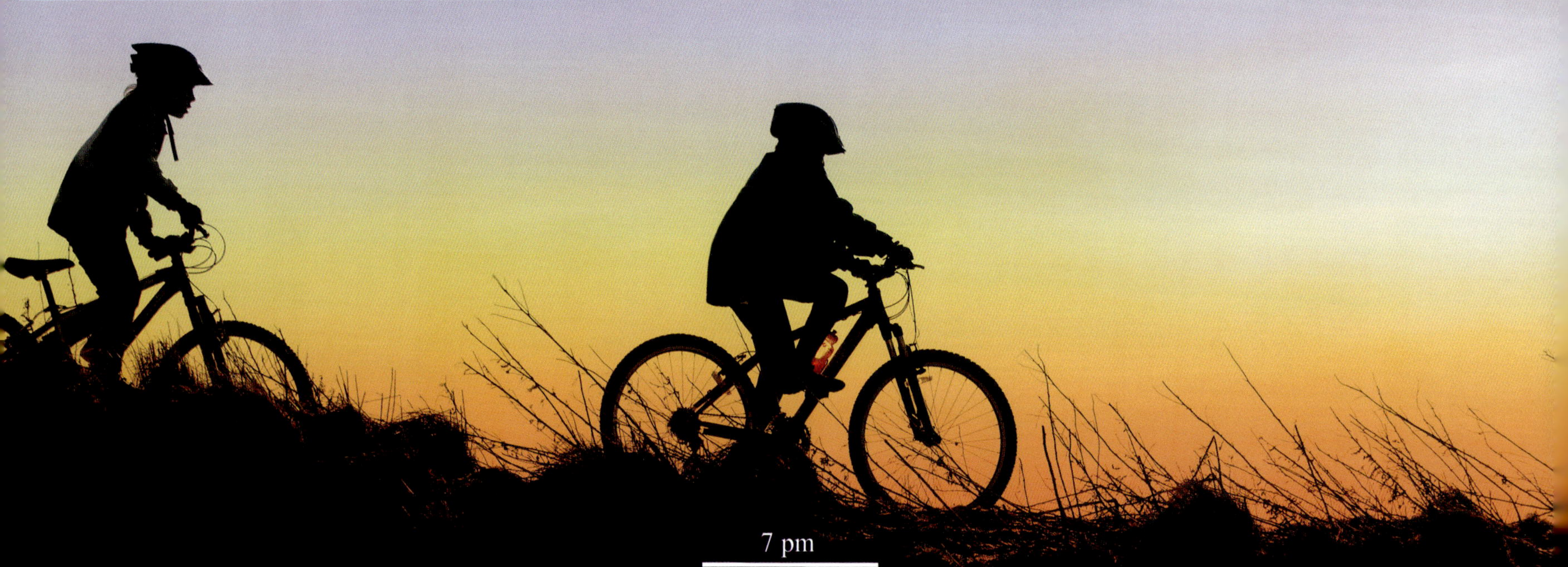

7 pm

In the early evening, a variety of helmeted figures are descending across the Howardian Hills to their final destinations - in the case of the black Tucanos, the pilot is HRH Prince William during his basic flying training at RAF Linton-on-Ouse. Opposite page, early in 1699, Charles Howard, 3rd Earl of Carlisle, resolved to build himself a fabulous new home in Yorkshire. His friend, the playwright Sir John Vanbrugh, was chosen as the architect and in 1700, building work began. The result is one of Yorkshire's finest historic house and estate, home to the Howard family for over 300 years. Here is a magnificent 18th-century residence set within 1,000 acres of

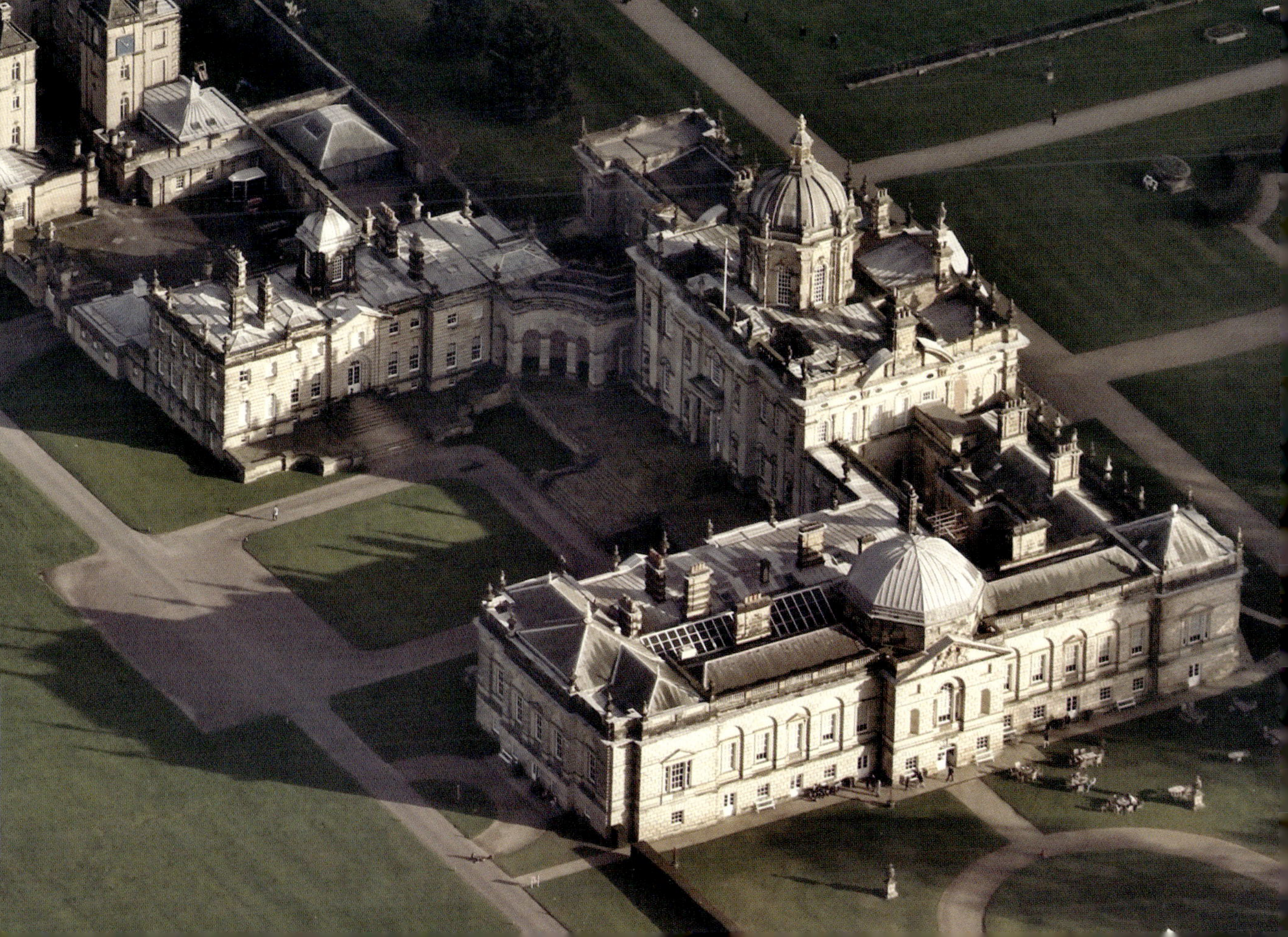

breathtaking landscape in the Howardian Hills, an Area of Outstanding Natural Beauty. Castle Howard has formed the backdrop to many classic films including *Lady L*, directed by Peter Ustinov and starring David Niven, Sophia Loren and Paul Newman was made in 1965; *The Spy With a Cold Nose,* a spoof cold war spy thriller starring Lawrence Harvey with Castle Howard masquerading as the Kremlin in Moscow was made in 1966 but it was *Brideshead Revisited,* Granada TV's 1981 production of Evelyn Waugh's novel, starring Anthony Andrews, Jeremy Irons and Diana Quick, which has achieved mythic status as one of the great costume dramas of all time.

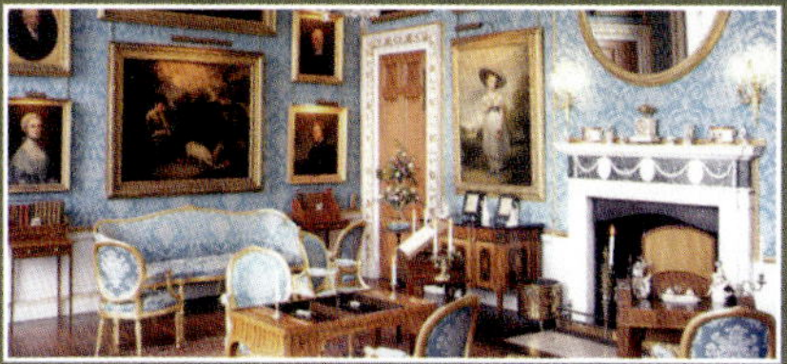

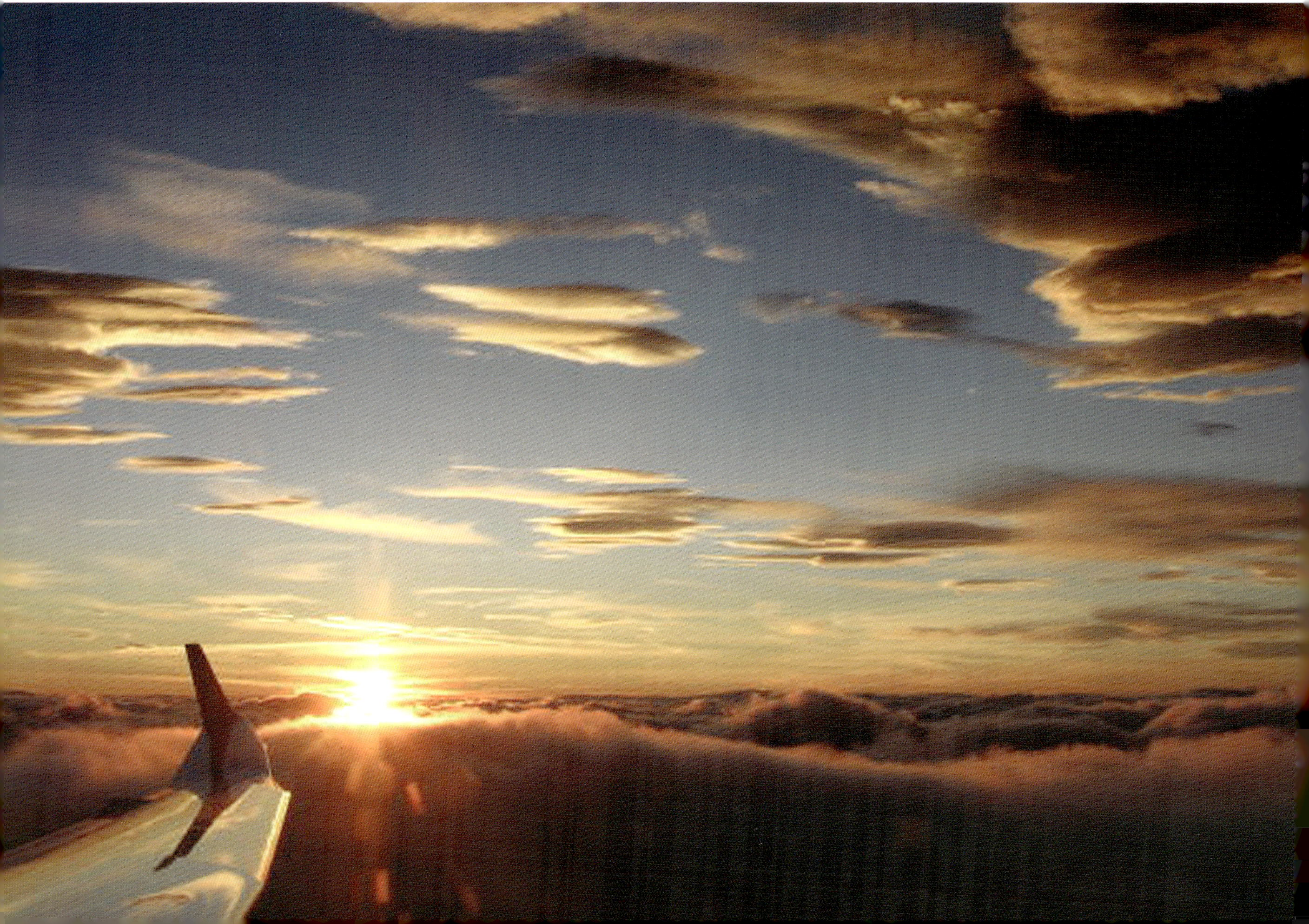

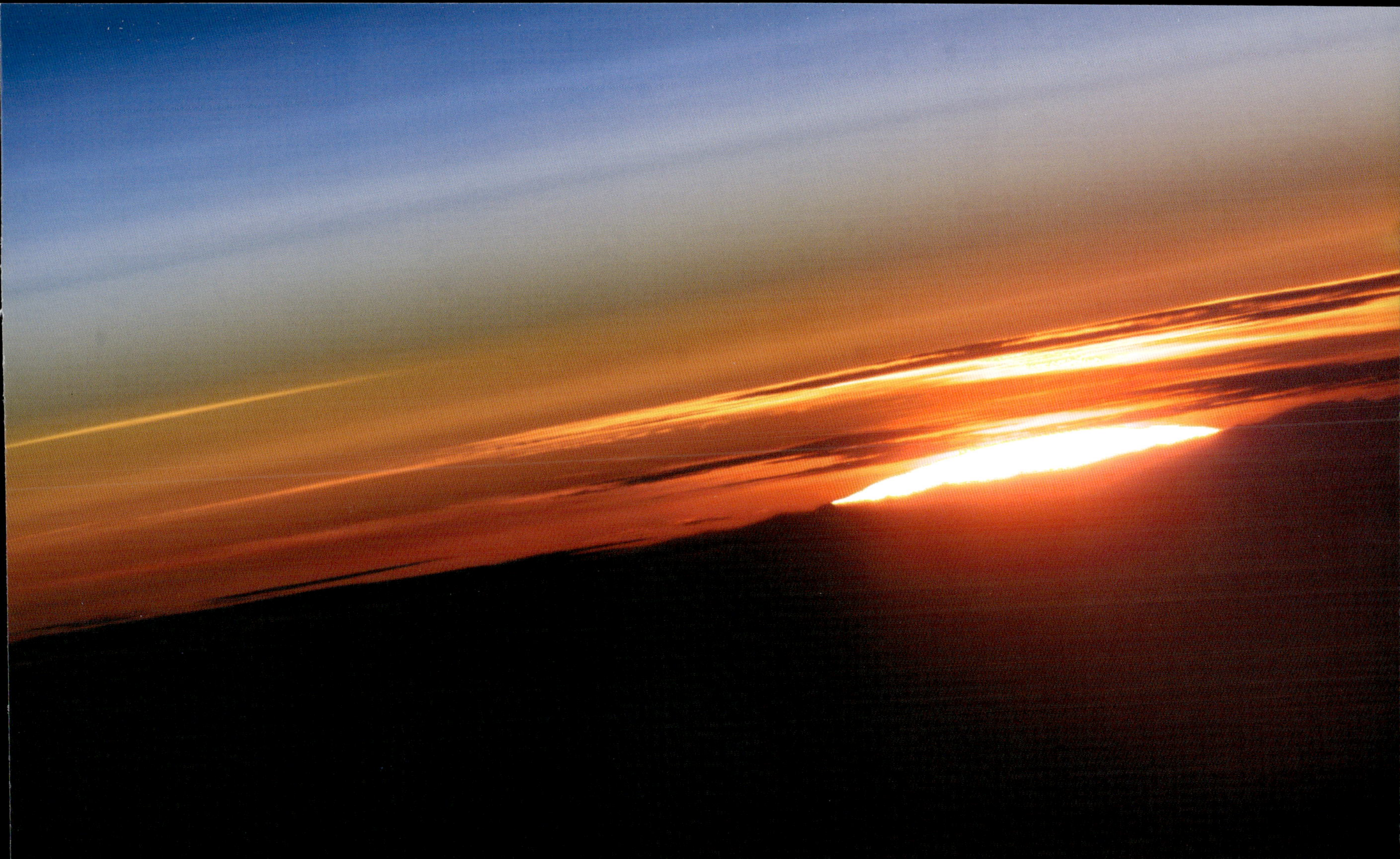

7.15 pm

Early evening - still time for earthbound mortals to have one last tug launch from Sutton Bank to see a magnificent sunset above the clouds over a high performance wingtip.

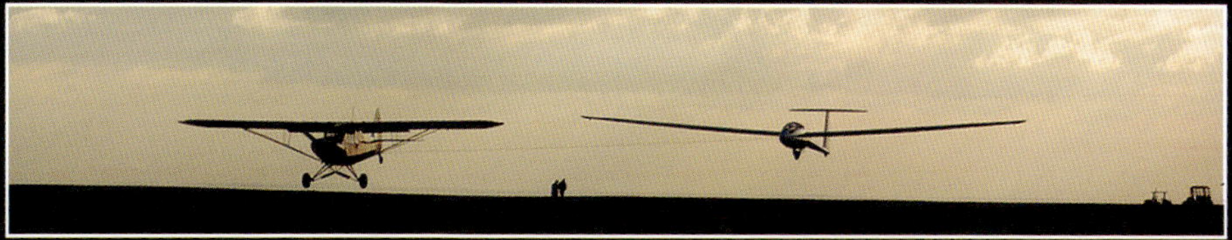

## 7.30 pm

Towards the end of our day, it seems appropriate to end almost where 'Aeronautics' first began at the sunset against the sea cliffs at Bempton and a backlit tree above a sloping dale. For it was here that Cayley observed the numerous sea birds, floating on the up draughts that flow whenever the wind is easterly. Cayley could study the birds, quite close at hand, and observe the curvature of their wings. From such observations, he deduced the classic forces in balance - Lift, Weight, Thrust and Drag. Little wonder that he is know as the '*Father of Aeronautics*'. From such beginnings, only 200 hundred years ago, on the 18th May 1991, Britain and Yorkshire's first astronaut, 27-year-old, Miss Helen Sharman from Sheffield, blasted into orbit on board a Soviet Soyuz TM-12 space capsule which made a textbook launch from the Baikonur cosmodrome in the Soviet Republic of Kazakhstan. With Helen were fellow cosmonauts Anatoly Artebartsky and Sergei Krikalyov. Her parents and sister watched from a viewing stand one kilometre away and saw their daughter smile and wave to the on-board camera. She carried a photograph of the

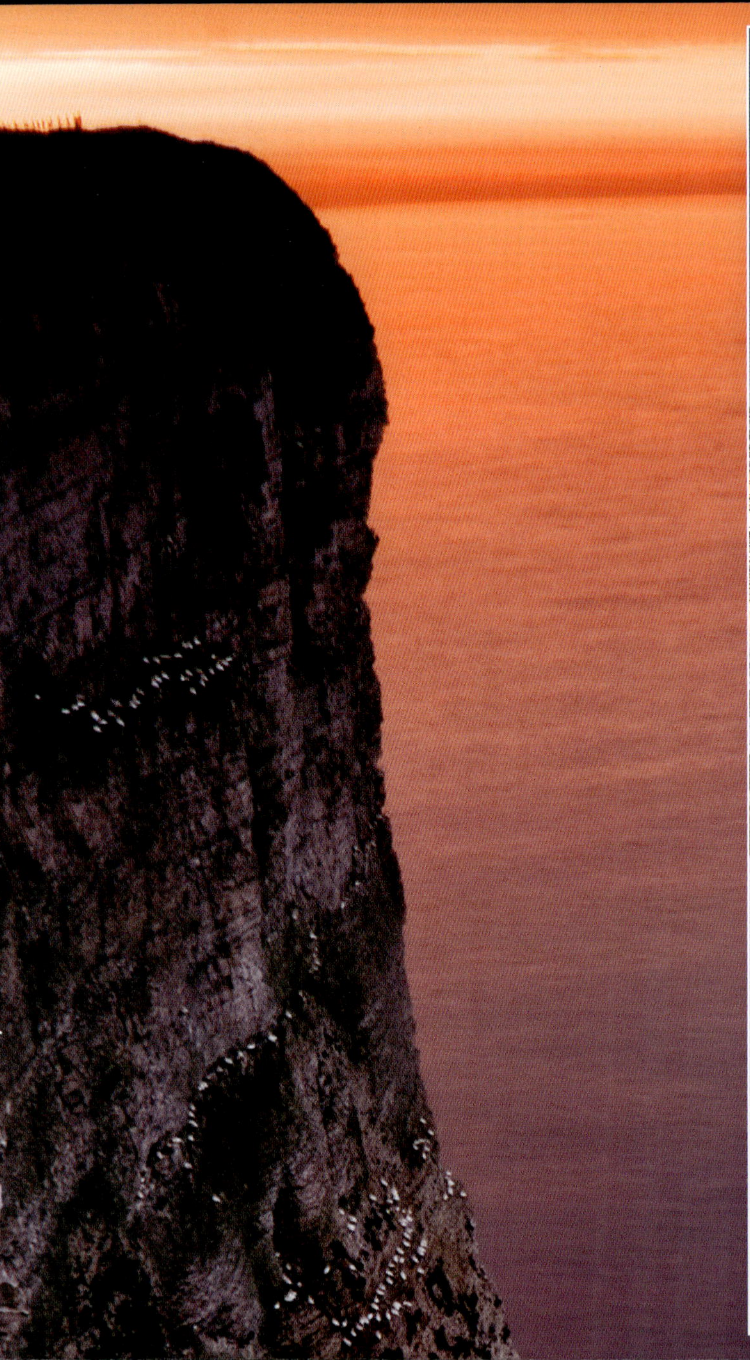

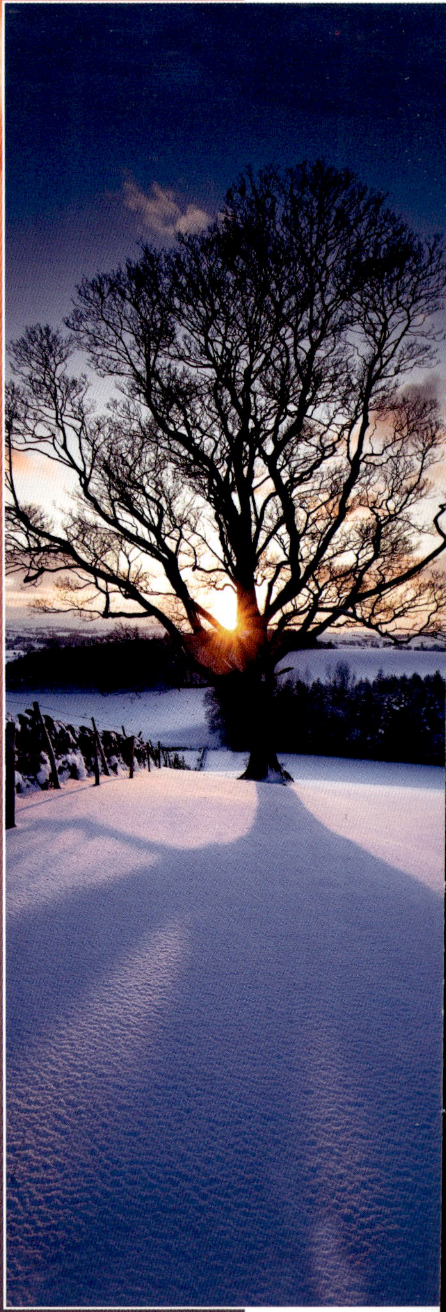

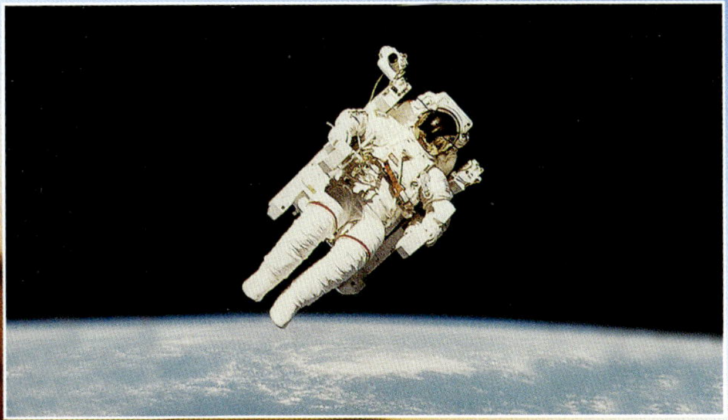

Queen, a butterfly brooch from her father and a 'space passport' in case her spacecraft is forced to land outside the Soviet Union. Miss Sharman won her place in space in 1989 after answering an advertisement she heard on the radio – '*Astronaut wanted. No experience necessary.*' She was eventually selected from over 13,000 applicants to be the British member of the Russian scientific space mission, Project Juno. After 18 months training in Star City, 30km north-east of Moscow (she now speaks fluent Russian), she spent eight days in space doing medical and agricultural experiments. She took photos of the British Isles but did not do a space walk unlike the US astronaut above. Seven days later, Helen came back to Earth in the Soyuz capsule with Commander Musa Manarov who held the record for the longest time in space at 541 days. Helen was awarded the OBE in 1993. The Mir space station was decommissioned and burnt up on re-entry into Earth's atmosphere on 23rd March 2001.

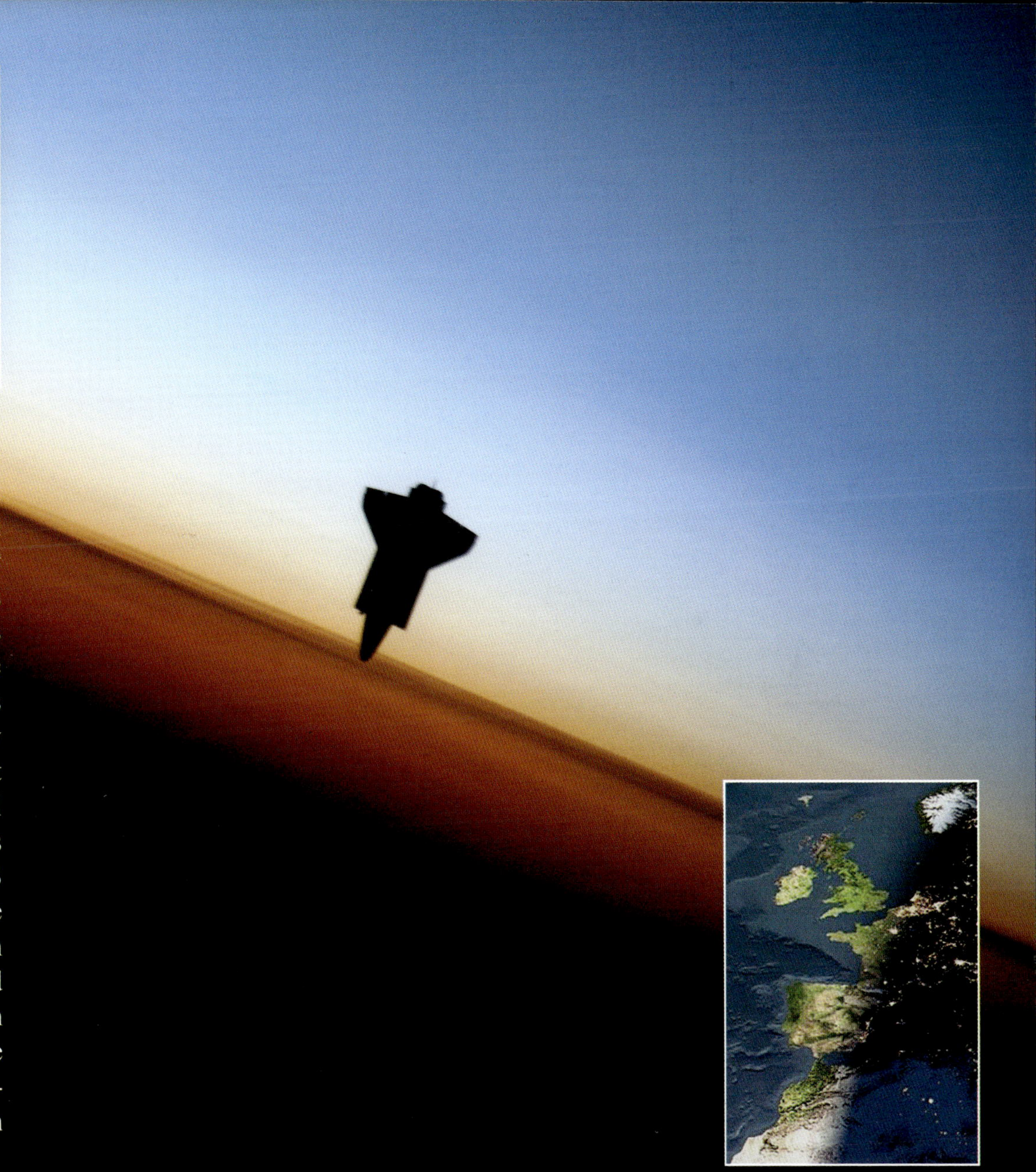

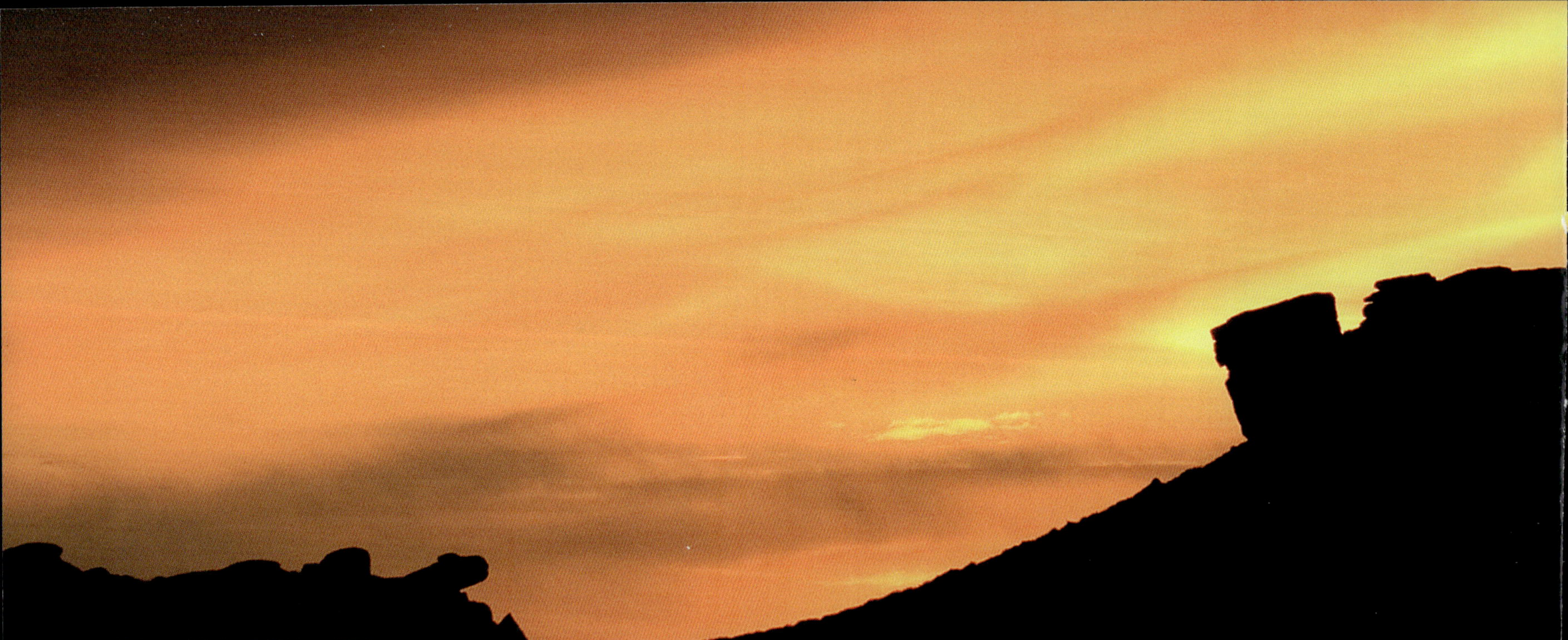

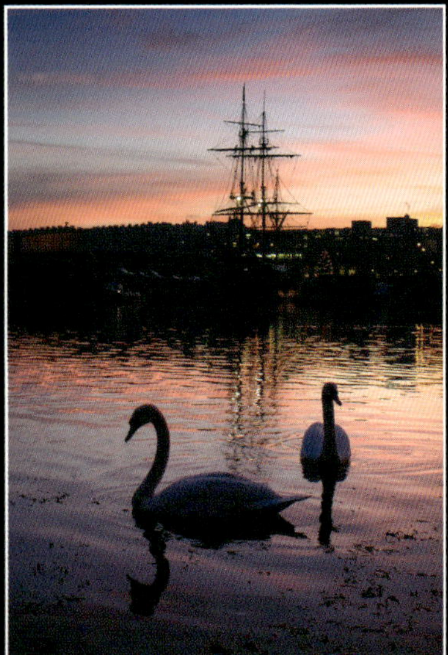

7.45 pm

Four climbers and one sheep are silhouetted against the sunset on Cubar Edge while swans, shown left, are pictured against the silhouette of HMS Endevour in Whitby harbour. Whitby is linked to Anchorage by Captain James Cook, one of the greatest surveyors, sailors, and explorers of all time. Cook's third voyage (1776-1779) resulted in the navigation of coastal Alaska. Today identical statues of Cook stand in Whitby and in Anchorage to commemorate his nautical

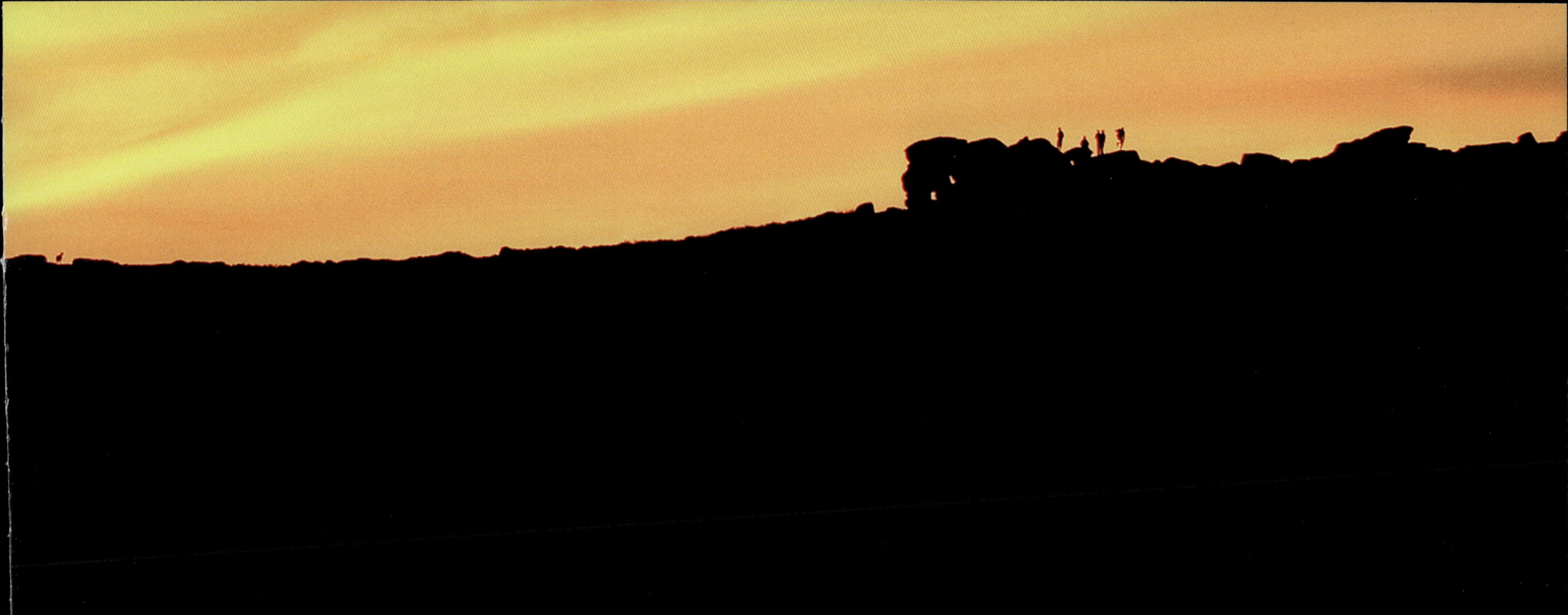

accomplishments. The Captain Cook Memorial Museum, in Whitby, occupies the 17th Century house where Cook lodged and trained as a sailor prior to his epic voyages of exploration. Whitby and Anchorage became sister cities in 1978. In direct contrast to Whitby, spires in Leeds are silhouetted against the Parkinson Building and the Clothworkers Centenary Concert Hall.

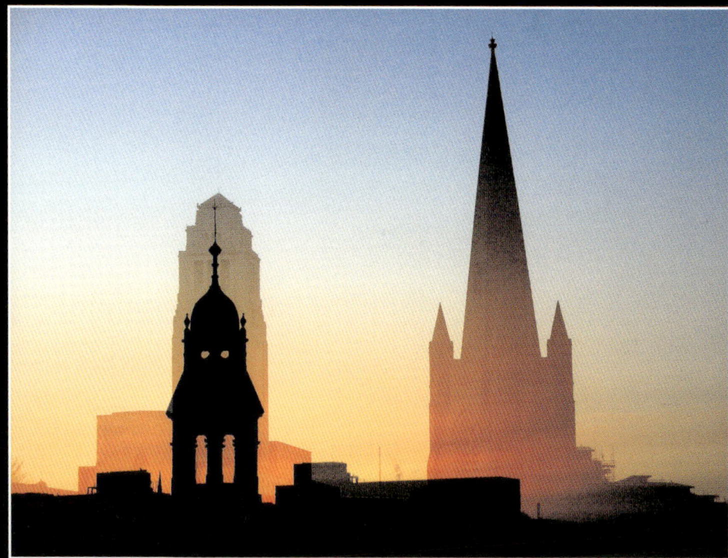

8.0 pm

The full moon rises behind the Emley Moor TV mast and the still waters of the River Nidd reflect a mirror image of the railway bridge across Knaresborough. The two carriage-ways of the M62 connecting Hull to Manchester via Morley divides around Stotts Hall farm - there is a well-known urban legend that the motorway planners had to build it around the farm because the owner refused to sell their land - in reality this was done due to the geology of the area. The dam in the right foreground is Booth Wood Reservoir and the sparkling light is the location of the Turnpike Inn. This Inn originally opened in 1822 as The Derby Inn and it has had a chequered history. Now it has been fully restored and being two minutes from junction 22 of the M62 - the highest motorway point in England at 1,221 feet (372 m) and equidistant between Manchester and Leeds, makes it an

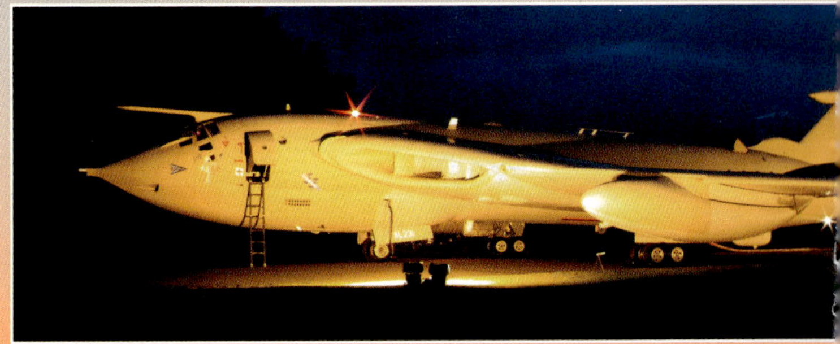

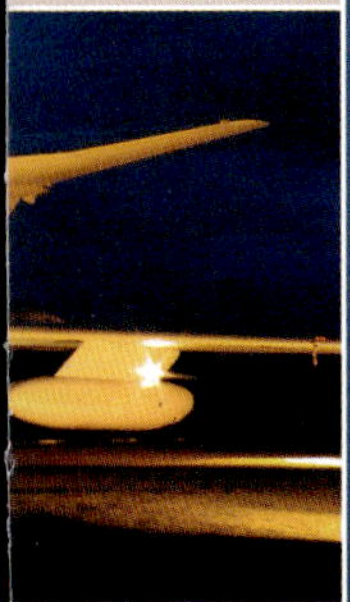

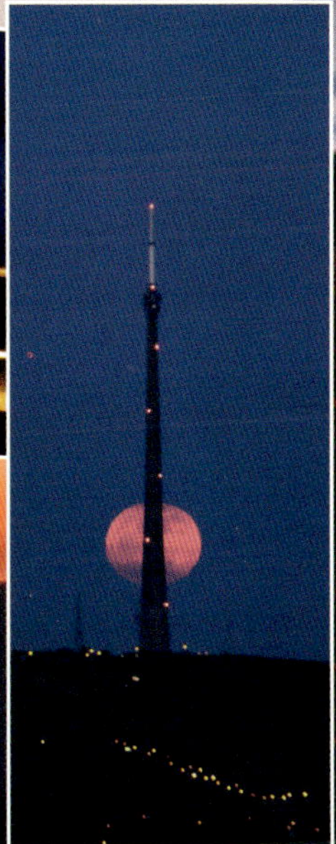

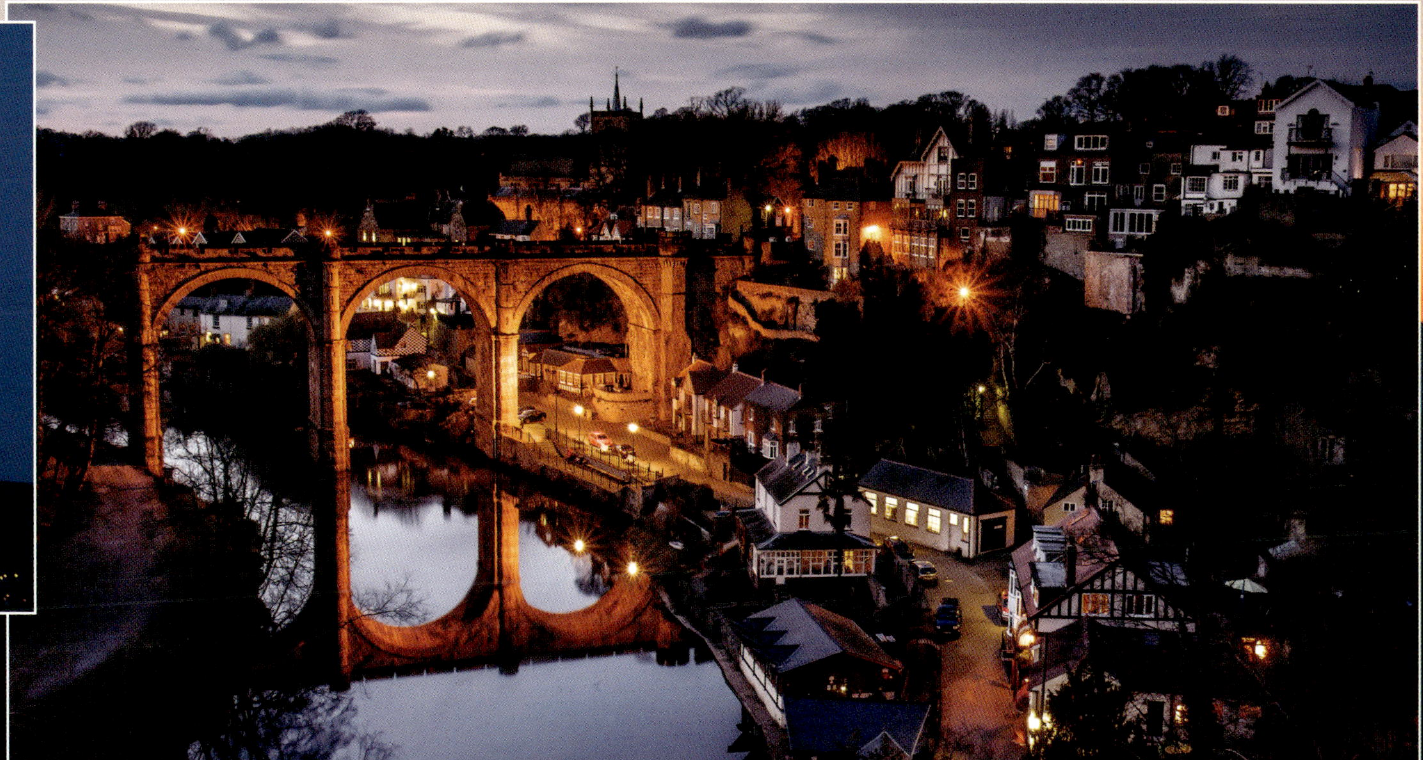

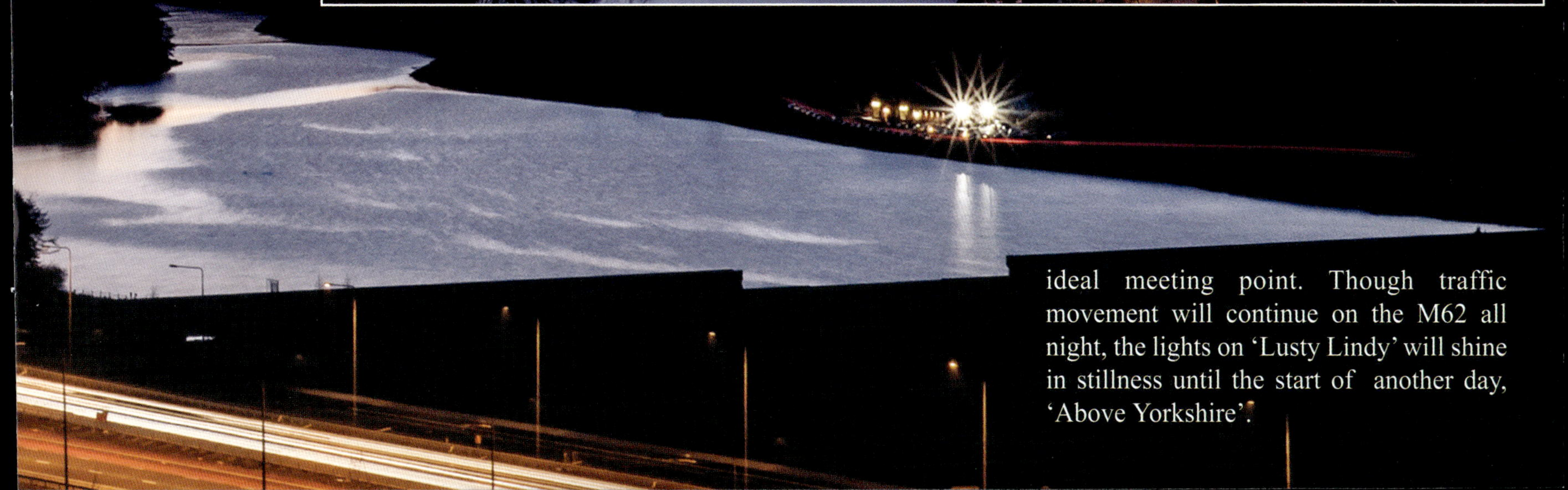

ideal meeting point. Though traffic movement will continue on the M62 all night, the lights on 'Lusty Lindy' will shine in stillness until the start of another day, 'Above Yorkshire'.

Many, many people contributed to the success of this project; first, our thanks to Alan Titchmarsh - a Yorkshireman if ever there was one, who kindly wrote the foreword, his wife Alison and Caroline and Neil Mitchell; Geoff O'Connor, Imperial War Museum (P29, 42, 43, 57, 68, 69) - the RAF photographs are British Crown copyright reproduced by permission of the Controller of Her Britannic Majesty's Stationary Office; The Mayor of Anchorage (P91); the BBC (P41); Touchstone Pictures (P55); Leeds Archive Office (P27, 28); NASA (P86 & 87); Betty's Bar in York (P60); Ian Wormald of the Sir George Cayley Museum and Sir Richard Branson, Charamine Clarke and Lucy Atabey of Virgin; Mr Howard & Rachel Underwood of Castle Howard (P85); thanks also to Tony Cunnane, Red Arrows and Gordon Bartley, Andrew White and Nigel Penistone of British Aerospace (P56); Wikipedia; British Pathe; Abby McClymont of the Yorkshire Air Ambulance; Mick Frost from DLRAA for proofreading; Jim Entwhistle from Great Northern Air Ambulance; Paul G. Allen, Jennifer Bragg & John Dibbs of the Flying Heritage Collection (P27 & 43); Michael Rhodes & the Ernest Fawbert Collection (P36); Museum of Whitby (P24 & 25); thanks to the Warner Bros PR Dept (P34); Air Team Images (P2, 6 & 14). It was a pleasure to meet and fly with the following aviators; Paul Haxby and his daughter Amelia (P1, 19, 21, 30, 37, 45, 49, 61, 65, 70, 75, 80, 81, 84), a great paramotor instructor and photographer - see his webpage www.axbsport.com; Miles at Aerographics (P62 & 63); Richie Toon, Ken Arkley, Richard Cole & Mike Smith (P14, P60), all of the Yorkshire Gliding Association; Maurice Lees, founder member of the Sherburn Flying Club; with especial thanks to Mike Stevenson (P17, 28, 29). We enjoyed the company of fellow photographers and artists; the late David Atkinson (Back cover, P27, 28, 38, 42, 46, & 73); Thomas Ackroyd (P76); Dan Arkle (P90); John Ash (P20); James H. Baker (P93); Neil Bates (P54, 55); Ronnie & Margaret Barraclough (P42); Brian Baines (P72); Richard Benson (P68 & 69) - see his amazing website www.danum-photos.co.uk; Emma Bohan (P91); Andy Beach (P69) who is also an Air Ambulance Volunteer; John Booth (P25 & 61); Gordon & Margaret Bunney (P11 & 95); Ron Curtis in Blackpool (P20); Mick Carver (P34); Keith Camsell (P39) - see his amazing Flikr site, cigarpix; Andrew Clayton (P25); Lee Collings (P27); Richard Cole (P87); Tim Cullen (P45 inset); Brian Davies (P84); Anne Duffield & Mark Grossick (P36); Levon Dymond - see flikr.com/photos/noveli77 (P45); Hugh Dodson (P46); Mark Edwards (P21); Suzanne Freestone (P82); Fergal Goodman (P31); Steve Glover (P82); John Grossick (P37); Sean Gibson (P32); Alan Green P30); Allan Harris (P67); Craig Hannah (P39); Mark Heath (P33 & 62); Jonathan Hodd (P47); Tony Hutton (P83); R Jordan (P28); Viv Kendon (P62); Anthony Lockett (P26); Catherine Lutton (P86); Laura@The Beauty Sanctum (P37); Brand-new-Yorkshireman, Vaidotas Miseikis (P93) see www.vmphotography.net; Malcolm Mee (P93); special thanks to Ray & Elizabeth Morris who climbed the extra mile to help (P23, 38, 40, 41, 50, 51, 55, 57, 67, 68, 78 & 85) - see his website www.????.co.uk; Mark Morton (P47); The Master of low flying aircraft photography, Tony McGill (Cover) - see more of his really great photographs on www.flikr.com; Jamie Moss (P94); Robert Nowell (P29 & 51); Chris Ogilvie (P58 & 59); Edward Osmotherley (P55); David Packham (P27); Mark Postlethwaite (P26); Glen Poole (P71); John Potter (P52); Tony Roberts (P20); Scott Robertson (P84); Pollys Dad (P20); Laura of Richmond (P37); Paul Richards (P14); Stephan Rowe (P82); Erik Runis (P82); Sam Saunders (P76); Geoff Soden (P52); Stuart Sunley (P36); Les Thompson

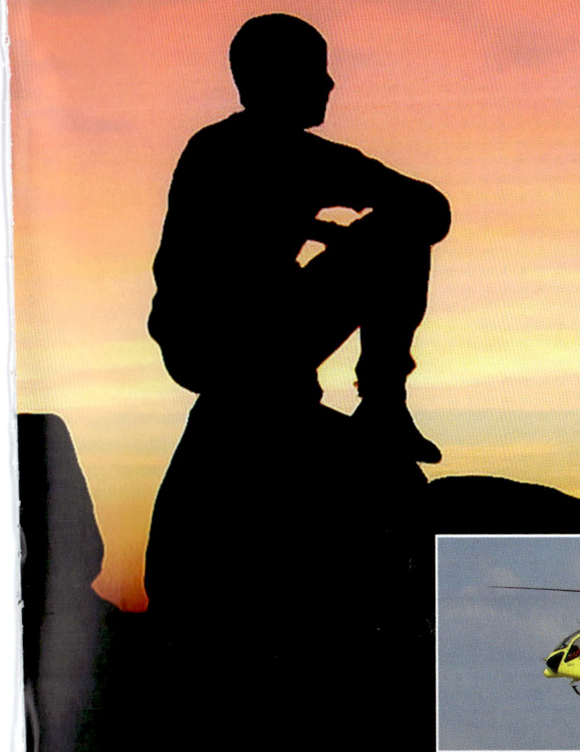

(P35); Jason Theaker (P88) see www.jasontheaker.com; Lauren Tucker (P21); Janine Turner (P18); Alan Vaughan (P16); Terry Walsh (P31); Tony Welham (P65); Ian Wilkinson (P46); Spencer Wilmot (P58); Andrew Wright (P8/9) and Adrian Wynn (P52 & 53). Thanks too to all my family; Christine my wife; Marc & Patrick; Kerri, Robert, William & Max; Robert; Simone, Cyrus, Isa and Layla; Nicholas and my youngest son, William. In turn, it is my pleasure to support the Yorkshire Air Ambulance, the Great Northern Air Ambulance Service and the Children's Air Ambulance. All UK Air Ambulances rely solely on donations from the public. And finally, this book is dedicated to my father & mother, Bill & Maud, pictured below, who educated me then let me go round the world.

John J. Nowell *BA (Hons) FRGS LRPS*,
Born in Morley.

Location Index:



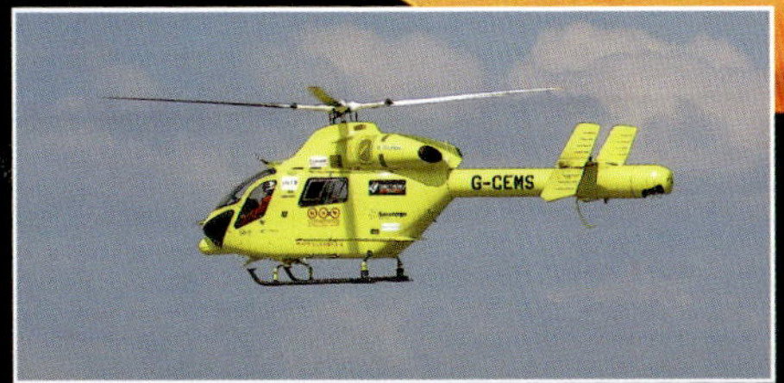


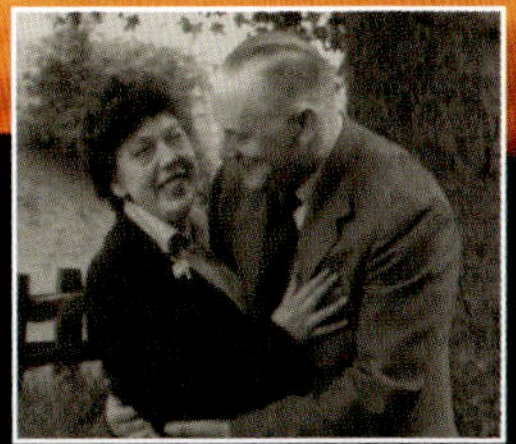

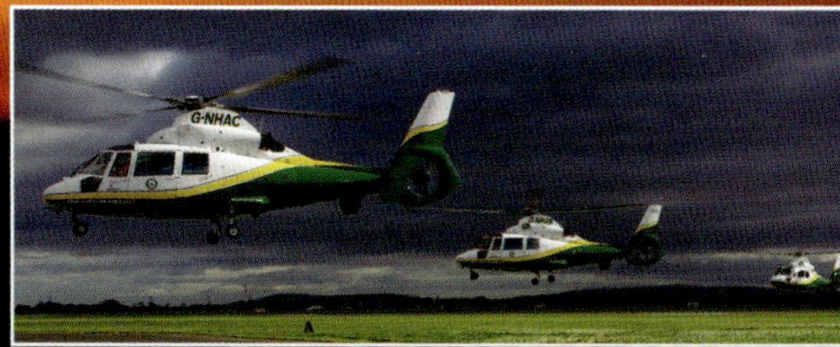

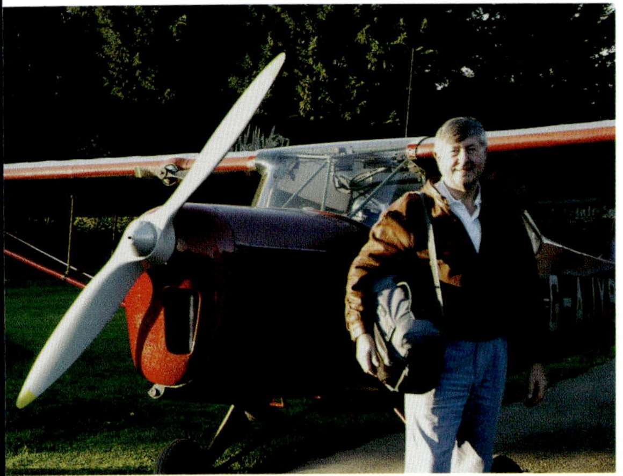

John Nowell met Christine in Changi, Singapore where she introduced him to photography. John had completed his first solo in a glider over Lincolnshire at the age of 16. Christine Nowell was born in Skegness, the daughter of a RAF Air Gunner and grew up in Wainfleet within sight of the bombing range. John joined the Royal Air Force and flew with 206, 205 and 230 Squadrons, some of the old flying boat squadrons and it was the records of their early exploration flights that formed the basis of his 'Now & Then' series of books. His first book, '*A Day Above Oman*' has been re-printed 14 times and his discovery of a collection of 5,000-year-old, perfectly preserved tombs in Oman made the front page of The Times and led to a Fellowship of the Royal Geographic Society. Christine's first book was '*Now & Then - Abu Dhabi*' and they both produced '*Now & Then - Rutland*'. John & Chris have six children; Marc, Kerri, Robert, Simone, Nicholas and William, three sons-in-law; Robert, Cyrus & Patrick; and four grandchildren; William, Isa, Max and Layla. John's first novel, written for a bet, was '*7 Lives*' and this book, '*A Day Above Yorkshire*', is his 18th photographic book. He and Christine are now working on '*A Day Above Malta*', '*A Day Above The Costa Brava*' and '*A Day Above The Lake District*'.

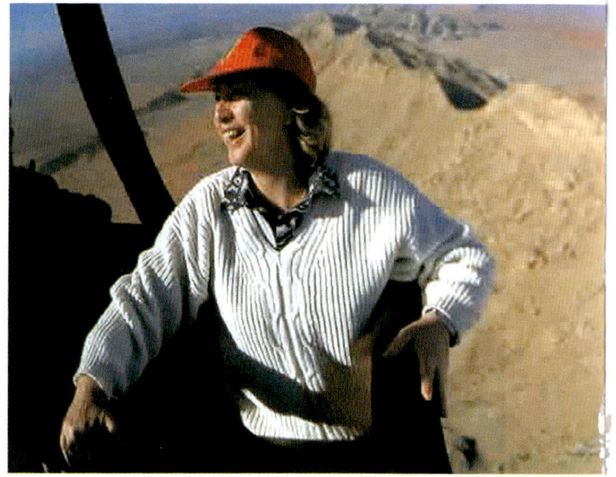

Below are some of the other books in the series - follow us at twitter.com\zodiacbooks or visit www.zodiacpublishing.co.uk

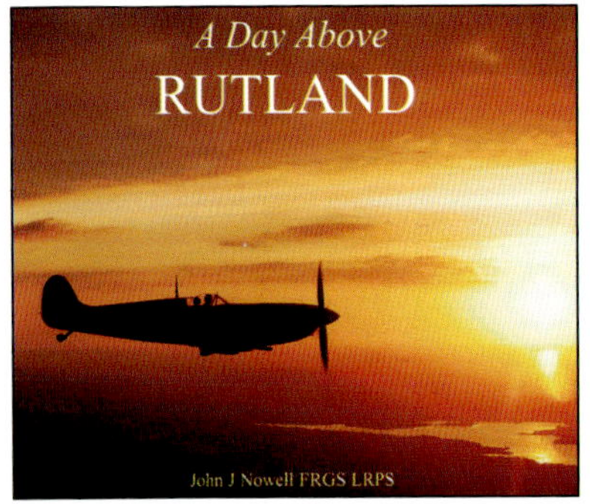


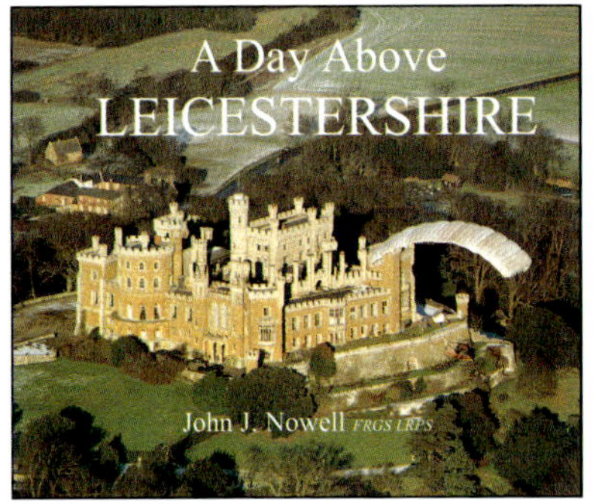


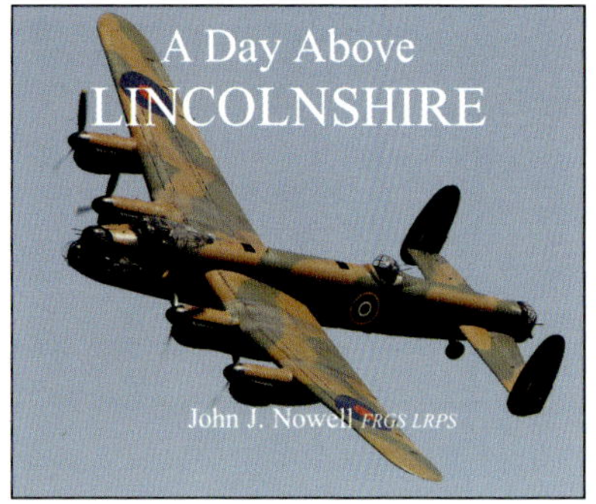


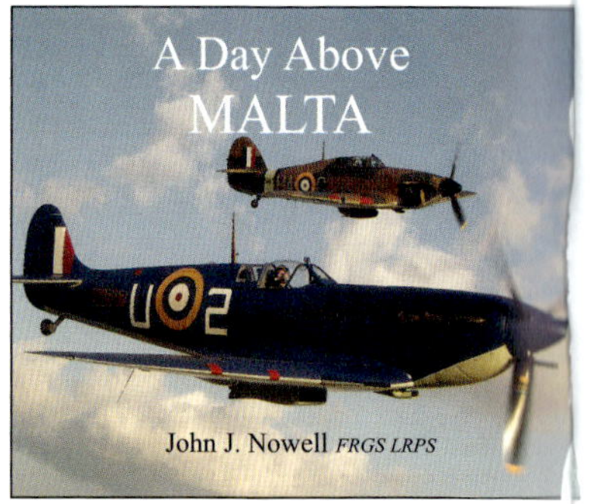

(P35); Jason Theaker (P88) see www.jasontheaker.com; Lauren Tucker (P21); Janine Turner (P18); Alan Vaughan (P16); Terry Walsh (P31); Tony Welham (P65); Ian Wilkinson (P46); Spencer Wilmot (P58); Andrew Wright (P8/9) and Adrian Wynn (P52 & 53). Thanks too to all my family; Christine my wife; Marc & Patrick; Kerri, Robert, William & Max; Robert; Simone, Cyrus, Isa and Layla; Nicholas and my youngest son, William. In turn, it is my pleasure to support the Yorkshire Air Ambulance, the Great Northern Air Ambulance Service and the Children's Air Ambulance. All UK Air Ambulances rely solely on donations from the public. And finally, this book is dedicated to my father & mother, Bill & Maud, pictured below, who educated me then let me go round the world.

John J. Nowell *BA (Hons) FRGS LRPS*,
Born in Morley.

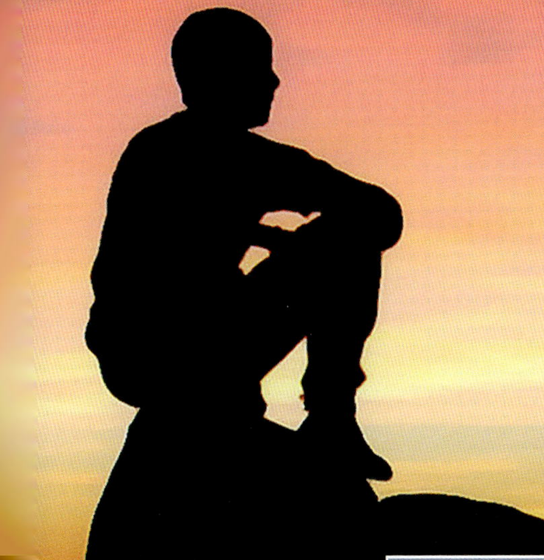

Location Index:



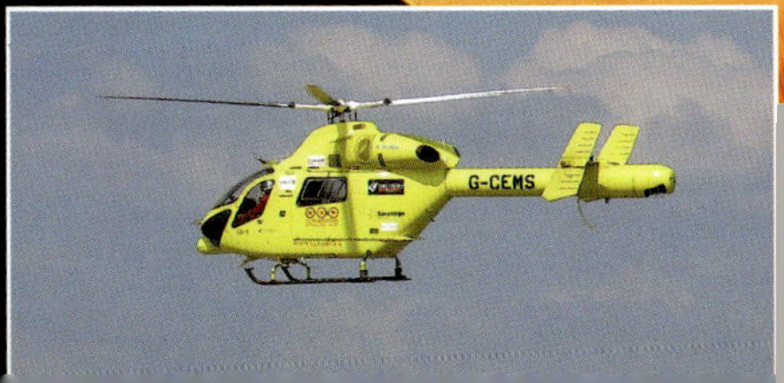


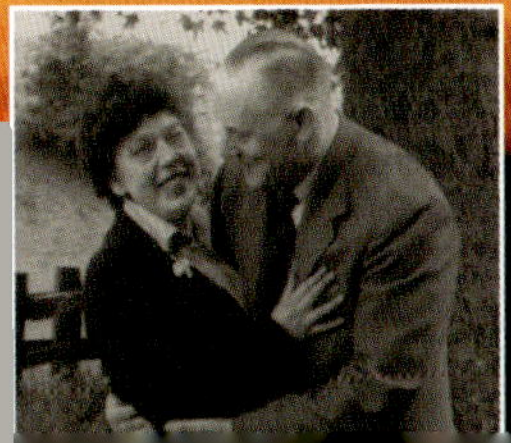

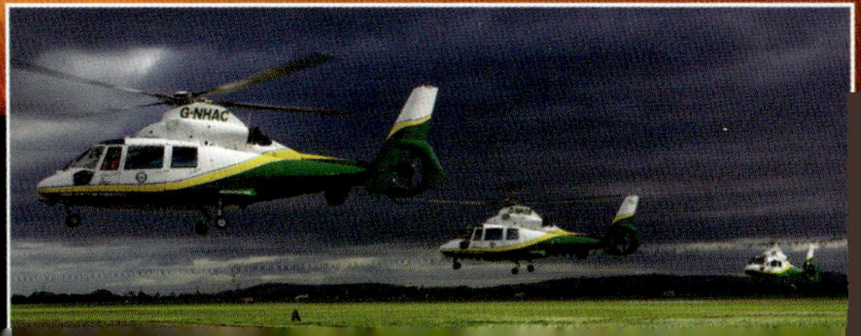

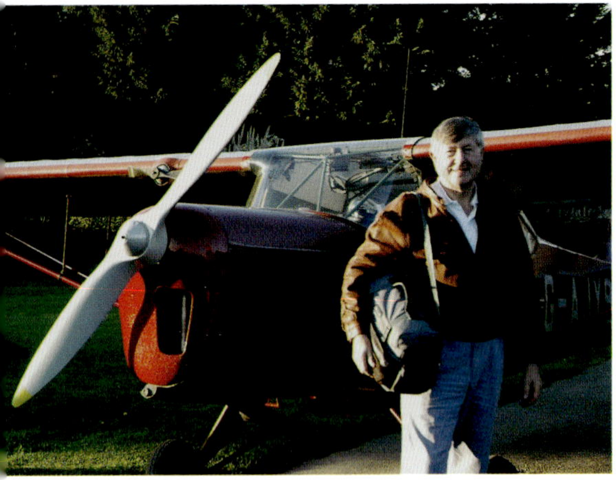

John Nowell met Christine in Changi, Singapore where she introduced him to photography. John had completed his first solo in a glider over Lincolnshire at the age of 16. Christine Nowell was born in Skegness, the daughter of a RAF Air Gunner and grew up in Wainfleet within sight of the bombing range. John joined the Royal Air Force and flew with 206, 205 and 230 Squadrons, some of the old flying boat squadrons and it was the records of their early exploration flights that formed the basis of his 'Now & Then' series of books. His first book, '*A Day Above Oman*' has been re-printed 14 times and his discovery of a collection of 5,000-year-old, perfectly preserve tombs in Oman made the front page of The Times and led to a Fellowship of the Royal Geographic Society. Christine's first book w '*Now & Then - Abu Dhabi*' and they both produced '*Now & Then - Rutland*'. John & Chris have six children; Marc, Kerri, Rober Simone, Nicholas and William, three sons-in-law; Robert, Cyrus & Patrick; and four grandchildren; William, Isa, Max and Layla. John first novel, written for a bet, was '*7 Lives*' and this book, '*A Day Above Yorkshire*', is his 18th photographic book. He and Christine a now working on '*A Day Above Malta*', '*A Day Above The Costa Brava*' and '*A Day Above The Lake District*'.

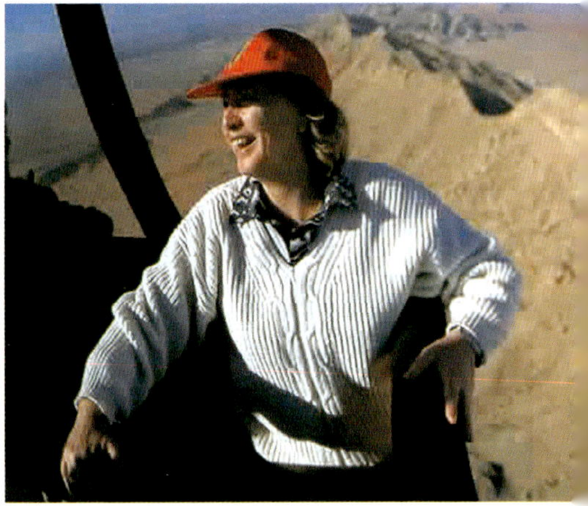

Below are some of the other books in the series - follow us at twitter.com\zodiacbooks or visit www.zodiacpublishing.co.uk

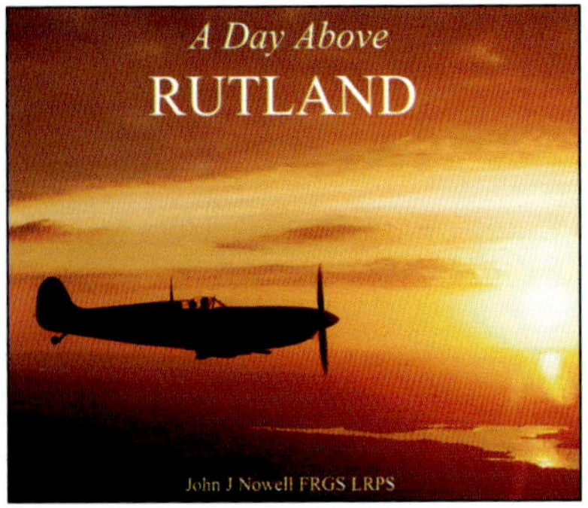


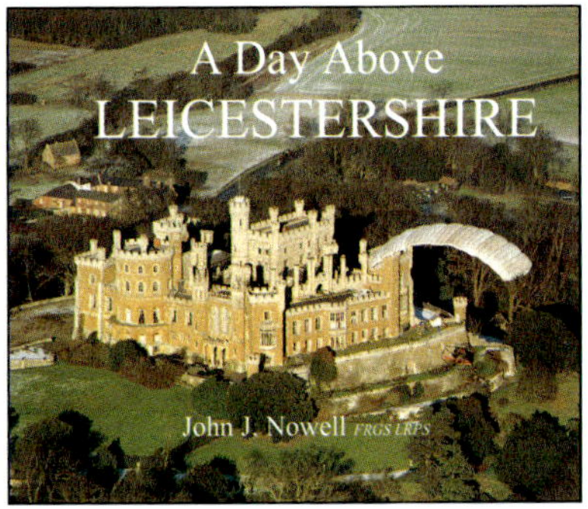


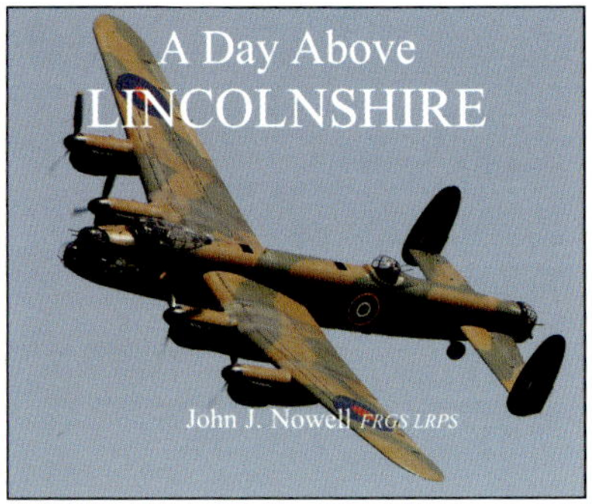


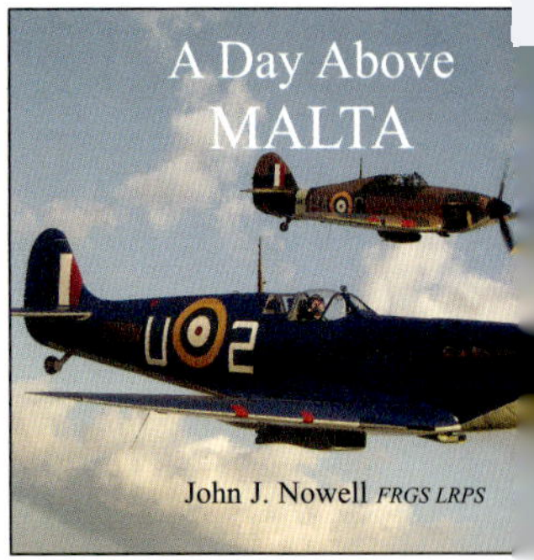